A Blast from the Past

by ANDREW PATERSON

To A Blantyre Lassie
with best wishes,
Andrew Paterson.

The author has identified his right under the Copyright, Designs and Patents Act, 1988, to be recognised as the author of this work.

Printed by Airdrie Print Services

Graphic design by John R. Young, Stonehouse

Published by Andrew McAnulty Paterson

ISBN 0-9550000-0-9

Dedication

I dedicate this book to the memory of my grandfather, Andra McAnulty, whose inspiration has remained within me throughout my life, and also to my immediate family and the many other descendants of Andra, both at home and abroad, who have waited so patiently for its completion.

Acknowledgements

It would not have been possible to collate and compile the contents of this book without the help of so many people; first and foremost amongst these being David Young and Pearl Murphy who work in the Reference Department of Hamilton Library. Their patience and advice throughout my research has been invaluable.

I would also like to thank George Archibald, a hard working 'volunteer' at the Scottish Mining Museum, who gave me great encouragement in the early days and Marjorie Clarke, of Christian Aid, who took the time and trouble to proof read my initial efforts. My grateful thanks also to Irene Grether, Annie and Jean Burns, Bridget Hendry, Jim Cornfield, Guthrie Hutton, Wilma Bolton, Bill Riley (www.billpitwork.net), Jim Rouse (www.mcpitz.com) and Dave Reid (fifeminingheritage.org.uk) for their collective assistance.

Help given by various people at the National Library of Scotland, The Mitchell Library, Blantyre Library, Dunfermline Carnegie Library, The Scottish Mining Museum and the Blantyre Miners' Welfare is also greatly appreciated.

Special thanks are due also to Jim Leonard and the other members of the Lanarkshire Family History Society for their encouragement and support.

Finally, I would like to thank graphic designer John Young who, when asked, immediately volunteered to design the covers of the book and lay out the text and photographs. John's transformation of my typed efforts and photographs into the finished article have, without doubt, greatly enhanced its presentation and enjoyment and I am deeply indebted to him. His wife Helen makes a lovely cup of coffee too!

Foreword

Andra McAnulty spent his whole life campaigning for better working/living conditions for the less well of members of society. He was born into a Lanarkshire mining family in 1860 and started his own working life down the pit when he was only ten years of age. When he was sixteen, he and his two brothers were involved in an underground explosion in Dixon's Pit in High Blantyre, which killed one of his brothers and inflicted serious injuries on himself. Seven weeks later, while he was still recovering from his injuries, a massive explosion in the same pit killed 215 miners, one of whom was his father. A few years before his death, Andra told the author (his grandson) the true, gruesome story of The Blantyre Pit Disaster, its effect on the village and the flawed Public Inquiry which followed.

These events were the catalysts which inspired Andra to devote the rest of his life to improving the lot of, not only his fellow miners, but also their wives and families as well. This involved taking on the rich and callous coal-owners in particular and The Establishment in general, which he did to great effect. Despite his lack of a formal education, he eventually became the first President of The Lanarkshire Miners Union, Chairman of Blantyre Parish Council and Chairman of Blantyre School Board. He was a founder member of the first Scottish Independent Labour Party led by Keir Hardie and was, in fact, also one of his election agents when Keir first offered himself for election as an M.P.

Andra lived with the author's family in the latter years of his life until his death in November, 1949 at the age of eighty-eight. During this time, he spent many hours describing not only The Disaster to the author but also painted a mental picture of the harsh living conditions endured by mining families of his era as they struggled to survive. He himself had twelve children (one of whom was the author's mother) and, as well as an insight into their working and social activities, the individual, tragic incidents which cost the lives of each of Andra's five sons in adulthood are revealed in great detail.

Copyright: *Andrew McAnulty Paterson 2004*

Contents

The Old War Horse

Last of the old leaders - thus was my grandfather Andrew McAnulty described in the now-defunct *Blantyre Gazette*, on the day that he unfurled the National Coal Board flag at Dixon's Colliery in High Blantyre, Lanarkshire. The *"old war horse"*, as the paper went on to depict him, was then 86 and *"still going strong."*

In his address to the large crowd which had assembled on the 6th. January, 1947 to witness this historic occasion, he told them that he had been in the mining industry since he was ten years old. He also told them that he had been associated with great pitmen's champions like Keir Hardie, Bob Smillie and William Small senior in the early days of the Lanarkshire Mineworkers Union (he himself was the first president of the union from 1920 - 1924). He said he was proud of this fact and that he had lived long enough to see the great aim of these men and himself - the nationalisation of the mines - realised.

Andrew McAnulty

When I came across this newspaper article during my family history research, I realised that there must be a lot more information about his activities hidden away in newspapers and books which were printed during his lifetime. After resolving to seek this information out, I was soon to discover that finding it was no simple task.

Had Andra, as he was known to all and sundry, lived and worked in the present era, his pioneering work on behalf of the miners and other facets of his career and achievements in local government would no doubt have been catalogued by modern technological methods. This would have been relatively easy to research but, although the newspapers of the late eighteen hundreds and the early nineteen hundreds did report on many of his activities, it has been a time consuming (but worthwhile) task tracing and in many instances, deciphering the various articles containing these references to him. Anyone who has trawled through old newspapers and/or microfilms will appreciate what I mean and in this respect I owe a lot to the very helpful and patient staff in the history department at Hamilton Library, for their assistance in this part of my research.

Fortunately, in addition to the information that I gleaned from these media sources, the fact that he lived with my family for several years before his death in my mid teens, afforded me many opportunities to hear at first hand his own account of many of the things that had happened in his lifetime. The greatest, by far, of these opportunities came about when a schoolteacher at St John's Grammar School, Hamilton, to whom I shall be eternally grateful, encouraged myself and several others to participate, by means of interviewing the eldest living members of our respective families about their lives and times, in a project entitled, 'The Most Unforgettable Character I've Ever Met.' When I approached my 'Papa' about this, he was, as with most other things in his life, extremely enthusiastic about the concept and said that he would help me in any way he could.

This was nothing new to him because he, of course, had been interviewed on many occasions in his lifetime by journalists and by serious writers and historians alike, as they wrote their articles and histories of the lives and times of the Scottish miners and the great personal sacrifices that people like himself and others had made in their attempts to improve the working and living conditions of their fellow miners.

I'm sure that neither of us realised that the events in his life, both personal and otherwise, that he and I were to discuss over a period of time would make such a deep and lasting impression on me. I certainly never realised that the copious notes I made of our discussions, which I have zealously guarded to this day, would be so beneficial in helping me to write my humble account of *his* life in the Scottish mining community.

Author (age 14)

Andra and I had had a great affinity since the day that my family arrived on his doorstep at 55 Victoria Street, Blantyre, Lanarkshire, having, literally, been bombed out of London during the German 'blitz' of 1941. My father, who had been the victim of a gas attack at Paschendale during the First World War and who was therefore unfit for active service in the second, had been working as an engineer in Ford's, Dagenham factory which was a prime target for the German bombers during the 'blitz.' Weeks of the family living/sleeping in an Anderson Air Raid Shelter in the back garden of our home had finally persuaded my father to say: *'Enough is enough'* and bring myself, mother, brother and sister back home to seek refuge in my grandfather's home in Scotland. At eight years of age I was the youngest member of the family.

Being by then in his eighty first year and having previously lived on his own, Andra welcomed us enthusiastically into his home and both he and the family soon settled to enjoy the mutual benefits of this arrangement. His immediate benefit was, of course, that he had one of his daughters to look after him in his declining years. Ours was the mere fact that, not only were we given the opportunity to enjoy time with this impressive man, we were able to resume a more normal way of life after the hazardous time we had endured in London since the beginning of the war.

Main Street, High Blantyre

We hadn't been long there when my mother (as mothers do), fortuitously took me through to his room at the rear of the house and bade me demonstrate my scholastic skills to my Papa by means of reading out loud to him. To this end, she had chosen a poem that he had sent in to the local newspaper (the *Blantyre Gazette*) that week for publication. The paper had just been delivered to the house for him and, when I had finished reading his poem, he intimated that he would like me to stay and read the rest of the paper to him. I didn't immediately understand why but they both explained to me that he was blind in one eye (due to an accident in the pit when he was a miner) and that the sight in his other eye was pretty poor. Although he was still an avid reader of books it took considerable effort on his part to manouvre the columns of a newspaper into his 'line of sight' and he apparently had been having great difficulty in reading the *Gazette*.

I must have done reasonably well on this first occasion because thereafter it became my weekly 'duty'on a Friday to go and read this paper to him and, on some other days, a daily paper also. Not content with that and despite my tender years, he also used these occasions to seek my opinion of and discuss some of the articles that I read to him. This not only gave me a great opportunity to see how his mind worked but also ensured that I took more than a passing interest in events that were happening both locally and beyond. My mother always said that, that, no doubt, was his intention from the outset!

Despite the intervening years I can still vividly remember how, on each of these occasions and on the subsequent ones involving my school project, he would settle himself comfortably in his wing-backed leather chair at the side of his coal fire and bid me sit on a little wooden chair opposite. This seat was directly underneath a large portrait of the Scottish poet Robert Burns which had pride of place on his wall. The following ritual would then ensue. First he would produce a little clay pipe with an extremely short stem and a small tobacco pouch. The latter contained up to an ounce of 'thick-black' tobacco which had been purchased from a local shop in High Blantyre owned by a Mr. Harrison. (Harrison's was the only shop where Andra would countenance buying his tobacco from, because he knew that Mr. Harrison would carefully cut the tobacco from a rope-like coil of fresh tobacco and weigh it before wrapping it in newspaper for his customers). Andra would then cut a small piece of the tobacco and knead it with the fingers of his right hand in the palm of his left hand until he was satisfied with the texture, before pushing it into the bowl of the pipe. After a few sucks at the pipe to ensure that the tobacco was correctly packed, a flame from the fire was then transferred to the tobacco via a piece of rolled up newspaper and, when he was assured that it was well ignited, a pipe lid was attached to the pipe and he was ready to talk.

Looking Towards High Blantyre Cross

On one such occasion, seeing the proximity of the flame to his face due to the shortness of the stem, I asked him why he didn't get a new pipe with a longer stem. He explained to me that he did require to renew his clay pipe quite often because they broke so easily but the first thing that he did with a new pipe, like most miners, was to break off the narrow end of the stem to enable him to get a better 'draw' on the tobacco. Being a non-smoker (still) and never having had the pleasure(?) of puffing on a clay pipe I was, thank goodness, in no position to question that. I had a big enough problem coping with the smoke from his pipe which wafted around me as we spoke. We shared a good laugh one day when I produced my gas mask which I had brought with me from London but, unfortunately, I wasn't able to use it and talk at the same time!

Having settled, he was very patient with me as I laboriously made notes of our discussions. Like everyone else who talked to him I was impressed by the indomitable spirit and zest for life which he still displayed despite being in his eighties. By any standards, then or now, some of his recollections of his early days were extremely harrowing to say the least. Thinking that for this reason they would not be suitable, I hesitated to present the first draft to my teacher but my fears proved to be groundless. When she saw the outcome of our initial discussions she, being a lot older and wiser than me and realising what an extraordinary life he had led, encouraged me to expand somewhat on the original concept to such an extent that I learned much more about his life and times than I would normally have done. What was even more important however was the fact that I was encouraged to keep a record of our conversations which I still have. This has been invaluable in trying to tell his story.

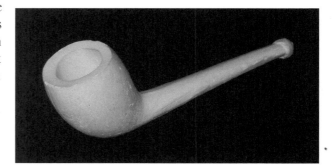

Clay Pipe

From Potatoes to Pits

Andra explained to me that his father Peter was born in County Down in Ireland. In 1845 at the age of 22 Peter, like millions of his fellow-countrymen, was a victim of the Irish Potato Famine, which had been indirectly caused by a combination of the agricultural policies of a corrupt government and absentee, British landlords. The large estates of these landlords were run by agents, many of whom were villainous to say the least, and these were under extreme pressure to maximise income from the many, like Peter's family, who rented small plots of land of 5 acres or less from the absentee landlords.

Because of the intense pressure placed upon them to raise sufficient funds to pay ever increasing rents, the people who worked these plots of land were driven to changing their previous agricultural policies. Fields which would normally have been used to grow a variety of crops were now used solely for growing potatoes. The reason for this was simply that a farmer could grow triple the amount of potatoes as grain on the same plot of land. When one considers that a single acre of potatoes could support a family for a year, it is easy to understand why, gradually, the people's diet consisted largely of potatoes. When one further considers that, as a result of this policy, about half of the population of Ireland came to depend on potatoes for subsistence, it is easy to see that this was a disaster waiting to happen.

Happen it did in the summer of 1895 and the results were devastating. It began when, what has been described by historians as a *'blight of unusual character'* borne on the wind, swept across Ireland and devastated the potato crop. The immediate result of this was that fields the length and breadth of the land were covered in *'black rot'*. Thereafter, a few days after the potatoes were harvested, they began to turn into a slimy, decaying, *'mass of rottenness'*. Those who ate these rotting potatoes quickly succumbed to cholera and typhus and entire communities were literally wiped out. Official figures indicate that, over the next ten years, 750,000 Irish people died as a result of this disaster.

Observers at the time described the epidemic as *'famine fever'* and reported that cholera, typhus, dysentery, scurvy, and infestations of lice, spread rapidly through the countryside. They also reported seeing children crying with pain and looking *'like skeletons, their features sharpened with hunger and their limbs wasted.'*

To add to their woes, hundreds of thousands were evicted from their homes by the landlords because they couldn't pay their rent, causing many of them to either seek refuge in crowded, disease-infested workhouses or, as Peter did, decide to emigrate to another land to attempt to make a new life for themselves. Approximately another 2 million Irish people made the same decision so that, eventually, the Irish population was vastly reduced.

Having made this decision, Peter had to chose either Great Britain, Canada or the United States of America. Having heard rumours that the vessels which made the long journey across the Atlantic Sea were nicknamed 'coffin ships' due to the many deaths on board during the voyage, fate decreed that he chose the shorter trip to Scotland. He later told Andra that, although he had previously only ever worked on farms in Ireland, the prospect of a regular weekly wage after years of deprivation, albeit working in a coal mine, had also influenced his decision.

Little did Peter realise when he made this decision, that the coal owners had encouraged their migration to Scotland because they knew that, in their desperation for work, the Irish people would accept even lower wages than the Scots and that, initially at least, there would be a lot of ill feeling between the two groups which would help the owners to play one off against the other. For this reason his wages in the mines would not only be poor but would also be irregular and at the whims of the coal owners who, in their own way, were every bit as greedy as their Irish counterparts. Neither did he realise that a coal mine would eventually become his grave!

Fortune and Misfortune

Andra told me that Peter was first employed in mines in the Lanark/Carluke area and it was while he was living and working in Lanark a few years later, that he met and eventually married my great grandmother Catherine in St. Mary's Church, Lanark on 8th January, 1850. She was born in County Tyrone, Ireland and had arrived in Scotland with her family in similar circumstances to himself.

Being before 1855, when official records commenced, there is no official record of this marriage and a trip to the church in Lanark failed to unearth anything in their sparse records of the time. I was however fortunate to subsequently find the date and venue on one of their children's birth certificates, which was registered after 1855. After the marriage, the 1851 census for Lanark reveals that they set up home in a typical miners' home in a tenement type building at Cross Keys Close, 17 High Street, Lanark. This building, surprisingly, still stands to this day and is still occupied, no doubt having had a renovation or two since those early days!

Thereafter in the ensuing years, Peter, like all miners, was forced to move around from pit to pit and home to home as working and family circumstances dictated. Extracts from several family birth certificates/ death certificates reveal that, while so doing between 1850 and 1860, Peter and Catherine had five children, only three of whom, Joseph, Agnes and Mary survived. During this period they moved first to Whitburn in West Lothian and thereafter at irregular intervals to Cambusnethan, Crofthead and Craigneuk which are all in Wishaw, Lanarkshire. It was while they were living at Watson's Rows in the small colliers' village of Craigneuk, (then known by the locals as Rumbling Sykes) that Andra as he was to become known to all and sundry, was born on the 24th November, 1860.

The Cross, Lanark

Three months after Andra's birth his father Peter obtained employment at No. 1 Pit of the Thornlie Colliery, which was owned by John Leggat & Sons, Wishaw. As a consequence the family moved to one of the houses owned by their employers at 186 Main Street, Wishaw and they remained at this location for two years before moving to another of the company's tenement houses (larger) at number 10 Brown Street, which was just off Caledonian Road in Wishaw. Brown Street no longer exists due to redevelopment of the area and the tenement houses in the vicinity of 186 Main Street have been replaced by modern terraced houses.

While they were living at Brown Street another two children, William and Bridget were born , so Peter now had a wife and six children to support from his meagre wages. Life was hard but it became a lot worse in October, 1865 when the first of what was to prove to be a series of calamities befell the family.

As his father Peter related it to Andra when he was a bit older, his mother Catherine, after seeing his father off to work in the early hours of the morning, had later followed her usual morning routine of taking Andra to his school along with three of her next door neighbour's children. In return her neighbour looked after

William who was now three years old and Bridget who was only nine months old. On the way back, as she walked along the Caledonian Road towards home she saw one of her elderly neighbours, who was a surface worker at the pit where Peter worked, coming out of the close (entrance) to her home and hurrying towards her. Accidents were an almost daily occurrence in the pits and noting the grim look on his face as he approached her, she feared the worst. Peter had told Andra that, before her neighbour could speak, she had asked him, *"Is Peter killed?"* *"No Cathie"* he had replied, *"but I'm afraid he's badly burned."*

As his father graphically explained it later to Andra, he and two work mates, brothers Tam and Jimmy Brownlie, had been working together at the coal face. Tam and himself were lying on their sides howking (digging) the coal and Jimmy was shovelling it away behind them. Suddenly and without any warning, there was a deafening blast of exploding gas which emanated from the next section along from them and which was being worked by several other colliers. Instantly Tam, Jimmy and himself were engulfed by a sheet of flame, the blast of which knocked Jimmy from his feet and passed on and over all three of them in a split second. Tam and himself who were at ground level and whose heads and

Caledonian Road, Wishaw

shoulders had, fortunately, been partially shielded under the coal face, had been badly burned along the exposed back of their legs and lower backs and Jimmy, amazingly, had escaped with 'only' a broken shoulder. Peter told Andra that, bad though their burns were, he considered that they would have been a lot worse if their thick working clothes hadn't been soaking wet. Despite this, such was the intensity of the heat, only the singed shreds of their trousers remained. Of those work-mates who had been unfortunate enough to be in the immediate vicinity of the blast, two had been killed outright and several others severely burned.

The troubles of Peter and the other injured men weren't yet over however. First they had to endure a long and painful wait as they lay in complete darkness waiting to be rescued, all the while unable to move because of their serious injuries. Peter's abiding memory of this was the stoic manner in which the injured miners behaved during this terrible ordeal as they called out to comfort each other in the darkness, realising as they did that the two who didn't answer were probably dead. Eventually they could detect noises which indicated that attempts were being made to reach them. Peter said that this had helped to stiffen their resolve but one can only imagine the suffering they endured during the several hours it took their rescuers to clear away sufficient debris to allow them to reach the scene of the accident.

Once there the rescue party, which included a local doctor, laid them out on makeshift stretchers, some after having splints attached to broken limbs and commenced to take them to the surface one by one. Peter told Andra that this was a tortuous journey, lying as he was face down on the stretcher as his work-mates stumbled their way over the rubble as they weaved their way through the narrow tunnels that led to the bottom of the pit shaft. His relief when he eventually reached the surface can only be imagined.

Today, Peter and the other victims of the accident would probably thereafter have been looked after by paramedics as they were conveyed by ambulance to the casualty department of the nearest hospital for treatment but things were a lot different in those days. The only small local hospital at nearby Dimsdale had never been intended to be used for industrial casualties nor indeed was it equipped for this purpose.

12

To have received hospital treatment therefore these unfortunate men would have had to make a painful and agonising journey by train to Glasgow Royal Infirmary, which was about thirty miles distant. The doctor therefore followed the usual procedure in these circumstances and had them returned to their own homes for treatment. This was effected by placing them on handcarts before trundling them along the makeshift, pot holed roads to their respective places of abode. Peter told Andra that he remembered it as a very painful journey. What an understatement that was.

Although Peter had said little to Andra about the further pain he suffered in the ensuing weeks, it must be assumed that his recovery was an extremely painful one, lying as he was in that small badly ventilated and overcrowded house. It must have been a daunting experience also for his wife Catherine (my great grandmother) as she endeavoured to care for him in these vastly unsuitable circumstances.

To compound their problems, because of course Peter was unable to work for a considerable time, Andra said his father had to apply for 'poor relief.' Relying on the amazing accuracy of Andra's memory recall, I was able all these years later to use the scant details he had given me regarding dates etc to unearth at the Mitchell Library, Glasgow, a copy of the inspector's report which he had completed when he called at their home to verify and assess his injuries. The Inspector's summing up of these in his report, that Peter was 'wholly burnt', tells its own story.

Subsequent to this visit by the inspector on the 17th. of October, 1865 Peter was, according to the report, awarded 6/- per week (30p) to support his wife and himself and his six children. At the time of the accident Peter had been earning 4/6d (23p) per day so just what criteria the Inspector based his award on is anybody's guess.

The immorality of either figure is even more transparent when one considers that, at this time, while miners in the Wishaw area were being paid approximately 9d (4p) for digging out each ton of coal (in extremely difficult and dangerous conditions) A. G Simpson, owner of the Coltness Estate, was being paid royalties of 1/- (5p) for each ton extracted from the mines. This because the mine workings were underneath his land!

Further examination of the report revealed that the claim had been lodged on Peter's behalf on the 16th. of October and although the inspector had interviewed him the next day, the payment wasn't subsequently authorised to commence until the 6th. of November. Bearing in mind that, in addition to the normal housekeeping expenditure, money was also required to pay for doctor's visits, medicines, bandages etc. How the family were supposed to survive during this period is anyone's guess. Was this yet another example of how unfairly the miners and other working people were treated?

The report also noted that Peter had claimed and received relief six years previously in Whitburn, Midlothian and four years previously in Cambusnethan. Both claims, like the current one, were made after receiving injuries underground and are further indications of how he and the other miners literally risked life and limb each time they went to work. The fact that they were not culpable in any way for their accidents meant little because the mine owners accepted no responsibility whatsoever for their plight. Everyone knew that most of the accidents were caused by the owners attitude towards maximum production. This had to be achieved no matter what and the owners cared little if safety measures were ignored to make this possible. They knew that there was no chance of repercussions because the laws of the land at that time afforded no protection to the workers. Instead, they were forced on each and every occasion to seek the minimal and totally inadequate compensation available under the degrading 'poor relief' system.

Had the 6/- (30p) which was awarded to the family been the full extent of their income during Peter's incapacity they would have been in dire straits indeed. Andra said that his father had been wholesome in his praise for the total support given to themselves and the other victims of the incident by their immediate neighbours and work colleagues. Peter told him that he had been eternally grateful to these people, both for the unsolicited financial support given in the form of weekly cash donations which had been raised by means of pit head collections and for the small gifts of food which were handed in to them on a regular basis. All this from people who had little or nothing themselves but who, in typical miners' fashion, recognised that such was the dangerous environment they worked in every day and where accidents were a common occurrence, that the disaster could just as easily have 'knocked at their door' on this occasion or might still at some future date.

Andra's words to me were echoed in an article from the local Wishaw Press of that period which I discovered. This stated that:

> *'hardly a week passed without it reporting one or more serious accidents in the Wishaw pits. Reported incidents were those which involved maiming and death, whereas the vast toll of injuries, ranging from bruising to debility and eventual death from diseases contracted from pit work, were not officially recognised by employers or authorities.'*

Peter, although badly scarred, eventually was able to resume working. Not long thereafter the family removed to 1 Steele Street, Wishaw, which was one street further up Caledonian Road towards Wishaw Cross. Steel Street still exists but the tenement building which encompassed No. 1 was knocked down several years ago and the piece of land has now been utilised as a public car park.

When I visited this locale recently and stood on the exact spot where my family had lived one hundred and forty years ago, I was transported backwards in my mind for a few brief seconds and felt a lot closer to all of them as a consequence. As I gazed up and down the street however, it was extremely difficult to compare the factuality of my immediate surroundings with the harsh realities of the same area when these close members of my immediate family lived here, as described to me so vividly by Andra on many occasions.

A Race Apart (reproduced courtesy of The Scots Magazine)

The Seeds of Evil

As with most mining areas in those days, life in Wishaw was hard Andra said, whatever the location. There were virtually no paved roads, little or no sanitation and no street lights. This was borne out when I referred to the *Statistical Account for Lanark* (1870) in which The Reverend George L.B. McAllister, in describing life in Wishaw at the time, wrote;

> *"While industry brought great prosperity, it also created vast problems. The herding of people together in large industrial towns, without proper provision for housing or sanitation or safeguards of health, caused a great deal of hardship. Long hours and small wages did little to compensate for the loss of better food and freer life of the country, from which so many had come. Malnutrition, disease and disablement took a heavy toll and caused much suffering. It was not unknown for workers to be forced to buy at stores provided by their employers. These years of rapid industrial development sowed the seeds of evil that will require generations to put right. There began the grim story of the miners' struggle for better conditions.*
>
> *In strikes, sometimes prolonged, they fought to gain some betterment, at times with a little success, but more often with none. That created a bitter, sullen spirit in the coal fields, as grievances became aggravated when not addressed. Trade unions were active in all branches of industry in the district.*
>
> *In these early years, many blocks of new, two-story tenements were put up to meet the expansion of industry and long rows of dismal rows of miners' houses were a feature inseparable from every colliery. Many were of poor quality and did not last very long, though they were still occupied years after they were unfit for human habitation.*
>
> *In the days before the growth of these large centres of population, sewage was deposited in front of each farm or house, where a local farmer would collect it as he needed it. This was still the only method used as the villages grew into towns but, with so many people gathered into a small area, this haphazard method became an acute danger to public health and, no doubt, aggravated epidemics. As a first step, the council began to use their own carts to remove the sewage regularly to the riverside, from where it was spread on the fields. About 1860 this gave way to the modern method of sewage pipes throughout the town, although this task took about ten years to complete."*

In the same vein, an anonymous historian of the times wrote that, *"It was a fact of life that miners and their overworked, downtrodden wives and children were, even in the supposedly enlightened Victorian days, regarded as almost a race apart from their fortunate fellow Scots. In their squalid hovels, which no amount of scrubbing or cleaning could make habitable, far less comfortable, they knew themselves to be ignored, initially abandoned and of no great concern to those in high office. How else could it be that, even on the Sabbath Day, miners and their families were frequently kept apart from the other members of the congregation and, in some documented instances, were even made to enter and leave the church through a different door and were denied the right to be buried in the church cemetery."*

Around this time also, an equally anonymous miner wrote to the Hamilton Advertiser saying, *"The Coal Masters horses have more comfortable habitations than their employees."* His letter also referred to the miserable, one roomed dwellings which passed as houses in the Wishaw area as being cramped and oozing with damp. With no back doors, bedrooms or closets and affording no decency or privacy for whole families.

The people, all so called pillars of society, who enforced these rules and standard of living on their fellow human beings, called themselves Christians! Is it any wonder that Andra, like many other victims of the system, eventually turned his back on religion and the church?

This then was the environment in which Andra spent the crucial formative years of his life and some of his earliest recollections were of being sent, several times daily, to fetch water from the communal water pump which dispensed brackish water that had been pumped from the pit bottom! Little wonder that there were frequent outbreaks of enteric fever and cholera amongst the workers, both of which are contracted from foul water. These outbreaks had a devastating effect on the people as there was only the one small local hospital at Dimsdale which was ill equipped to deal with the volume of patients involved.

The authorities were unconcerned at these regular outbreaks of disease among the working people and this point was clearly illustrated in the *Wishaw Press*, which reported on one such fever epidemic that, *'The sick were left unattended by indifferent medical authorities.'* Had the authorities been as concerned as they should have been about these constant outbreaks, they would have introduced legislation which would have forced the coal owners to, not only build better houses, but to ensure that a quality water supply was piped into each and every one of them.

Andra told me as he quietly puffed on his clay pipe that, although he didn't realise it at the time, these early experiences of living in such squalor, despite the unstinting efforts of his parents, obviously inspired him in later years to devote his life to fighting for better conditions for the miners and their families. As the anonymous miner had said in his letter to the Hamilton Advertiser, the coal owners made sure that their animals had a better standard of living than their workers and were completely detached from their ongoing living and health problems. Workers were there to be exploited and to do their masters' bidding without protest. Anyone who protested was quickly made an example of by, not only being dismissed from his job, but by having his family and himself literally thrown on the street by the owners' bully boys.

Miners Lamps (Courtesy of Joe McArthur of Fife Mining Heritage Society)

From School to Pit - In One 'Easy' Lesson!

The next milestone in Andra's life occurred a few weeks after his tenth birthday on New Year's Day, 1871 when his father Peter advised him that, as from the following Monday morning, he would be leaving school and going down the pit with himself and his brother Joseph. Andra, despite his tender years, was, like his brother Joseph before him and other lads in the same position, deemed old enough at ten to make a contribution to the family income and it seemed, both to his parents and himself, the natural thing to do.

In these modern times when children are not even allowed to deliver newspapers until they are about twelve, it is extremely difficult to imagine that such things were allowed to happen. The supposedly better educated classes of the time let this barbaric exploitation of innocent children take place, whereby they were sent down into the very bowels of the earth to work in dreadful conditions for up to twelve hours a day. The same people were equally culpable when, even after they grudgingly introduced laws which raised the minimum age of employment to fourteen, they failed to ensure that these self same laws were adhered to and they were in fact flaunted by the coal owners as and when they felt fit.

Andra recalled that the miners themselves had always been at the mercy of the harsh conditions and poor wages imposed on them by the coal-mine owners, who, secure in the knowledge that they also owned the apologies for houses that the downtrodden miners and their families lived in, still treated them more or less like serfs. The miners had always been exploited by what they considered to be the ruling classes. As they saw it, they had no alternative but to allow their children to go down the pit. Even the meagre pittance that could be earned by a child was an extremely welcome addition to the family income as they struggled for their very existence.

Had his father and others been paid a fair wage for the extremely hard and unhealthy work that they did on a daily basis, the necessity for this inhumane exploitation of innocent children would not have been necessary and their children would have had the opportunity to grow and develop, both physically and mentally, as other children of their era did. Fate decreed however that Andra, like the others in his position, was not only deprived of a proper education but was not able to enjoy the normal pursuits of better off children, both in and out of school. His lot in life was to be confined underground breathing in coal dust while they were running around in the fresh air much of the time, especially during school holidays. One of his abiding memories was that, because it was winter time, in the early months after he started work he only saw daylight on a Saturday afternoon and on a Sunday. Let us not forget he was then ten years old!

Against this background therefore Andra became a working miner and in his own words, *"took to it like a duck to water."* As he related this part of his life to me I was amazed that, despite the seventy five years that had passed since his first 'shift' down the pit and everything that had happened in between, he still had almost total recall of the first day of his long working life.

In the middle of the night (Andra thought it would be around 4 a.m.) he was roused from his sleep and after hurriedly dressing and eating a bowl of porridge made by his mother, who had obviously been up even earlier to light the fire to cook it, was soon accompanying his father Peter and brother Joseph as they squelched in the dark through the eternally muddy underfoot conditions towards the pit-head which was almost two miles away.

With only a thin jacket and trousers to protect him from the effects of a cold, blustery January morning, he said he was glad of the hand-knitted muffler, wrapped round his neck by his mother before he left home. This motherly gesture betrayed the concern she still felt for him as a child despite the fact (or because of it) that she must have known, immediately he stepped through the door that morning, his childhood like his brother Joseph's before him would be gone forever never to return.

His father and brother and others that they joined along the way spoke little as they bowed their heads against the stinging sleet that blew into their faces. The effect of this was that, even before they reached the pit-head to start their work, their clothes were quite wet. Before he had time to feel sorry for himself however, he found himself crushed into a cage with other miners to make the bumpy descent to the pit bottom and was immediately, because of his diminutive stature, the subject of many humorous remarks by the miners. He recalled his father 'defending' him by telling the men that, despite his size, he would still do the work of any two of them!

Waiting to descend

Once they reached the pit bottom however the jokes, for the moment at least, quickly came to an end. Although he had been primed by his brother and friends what to expect when he got there he told me that he would never forget his first walk from the pit bottom to his place of work.

After allowing the other miners to spill out of the cage and set off to their workplaces in the depth of the mine, his father led the way followed by himself with Joseph bringing up the rear. By the light of their 'tally' (tallow) lamps he was amazed at how low the roof was at places, which caused his father to stoop to make progress. Being very small he didn't have that problem but he did encounter one when they branched off the main road into a side road and came to a short section which was partially flooded. Being confronted with this minor hazard he said, his father, no doubt not wishing him to get any wetter before his first shift, had given him a 'piggy-back' through the water. He enjoyed the joke when I questioned the need for this, bearing in mind his comment about his duck-like abilities!

As they made their way through the pit by the glittering, smoky flame of their 'tally' lamps they passed through a couple of doors, each of which was opened and closed by a boy who appeared to be of his own age. The boys were hunched into little alcoves which had been hewn out of the coal at the side of the doors and were holding a short piece of rope which was attached to the door by means of a large nail, which had been bent over to make the rope secure.

The opening and closing of these doors was an absolutely vital operation, as it helped to control the current of air which was being pumped down and through the mine from the surface. As they passed through each of the doors his father told him to pay particular attention to what the trapper (as the youth was called) did, because the lives of everyone in the mine depended on it being done correctly and consistently. Nowadays it is difficult to comprehend that such an important job would be entrusted to a child of ten but this was the responsibility that Andra was to be given at a similar door further along the road.

Eventually they arrived at this self same place and the boy who was crouched there, John Macmillan, whom he knew from the street they both lived in and whom he was replacing, wasted no time in handing over the rope to him. John's joy at being relieved of this particular job was plain to see as he set off to his new job, working with the pit ponies at another location in the pit. Andra at his father's bidding, still clutching the rope, immediately squatted in the little alcove. His father and Joseph stayed with him for only a few minutes until the first time the doors had to be opened and, on seeing that he had apparently grasped what was required of him, left him, advising him that they would 'collect' him at the end of the shift.

Nothing, he said, could have prepared him for the emotions that ran through his mind as their flickering lights disappeared from his vision. Instantly, the full implication of his situation engulfed him, as he realised that he was going to have to hunker down here in this dark, cold and extremely eerie corner for the rest of the shift.

Although several of his young friends had described their working baptisms to him, nothing, he said, could have prepared him for the grim realities of the situation. Two days previously he had sat in a relatively comfortable classroom with the companionship of his peers around him. Now he found himself on his own, his clothes still wet from the walk to the pit and with only the intermittent company of those miners who required to pass his way, as they played their particular part in getting and taking the coal to the surface to make the mine owners even richer.

He wasn't completely on his own of course, the ever present rats which he could hear scuttling about in the dark recesses of the tunnel were a constant reminder of that and, as can be imagined, their presence did nothing to boost his confidence. Although he was used to rats in and around the area that they lived in, this was different. Above ground they could usually be seen and chased by throwing stones at them but here, as they scurried around just out of range of the light from his tally lamp, they were a bit scary until he got used to them as the days passed. In the meantime, he contented himself with lobbing lumps of coal in the direction of their squeaks.

As the morning progressed however, he said that the initial tension and fears that he felt gradually lessened, and this was in no small measure due to the good-natured banter of these selfsame miners as they passed through, particularly the ones who knew himself and his family. Realising how apprehensive he must be feeling, he said they went out of their way to bolster his spirits and, as he grew older, he came to understand that this was no isolated incident but rather the natural 'all for one' attitude of the working miners. An attitude that was to reveal itself to him on many, many occasions in the future.

Another event that day that he remembered well and one that was to become a regular feature both in that pit and others, was his brother Joseph, bottle of water and 'piece' in his hand, appearing at his side to spend his brief break time with him. Their father had sent him along to see how Andra was faring and, short though their time was together, he appreciated having his company as they ate the 'pieces' that their mother had prepared for them, stopping occasionally to open and shut the doors as required.

On Joseph's departure he carried on as before for what seemed like an eternity but, just as the misery of the cold and wet conditions were getting to him, groups of miners began to pass through on their way to the pit bottom, indicating to him that his first shift was coming to an end. In the last of the groups were his father and Joseph and, tired and hungry, he wearily followed them to the pit bottom to await their turn to enter the cage to be taken to the surface. This time, when they reached the flooded passage, his father and Joseph forged ahead leaving him to negotiate it as best he could. As far as they were concerned he was now on his own. On entering the cage he recalled that the men, visibly exhausted by their strenuous efforts in the dire conditions, were noticeably quieter than they had been in the morning. At the end of what had been an eventful first day at work for him, none were quieter than himself.

On reaching the surface they were, of course, faced with the walk back to their home in their sodden clothes. With a wry smile he said he could still remember, as soon as he stepped into the house, squeezing past the tin bath full of hot water which was in front of the blazing fire so that he could get closer to the warmth of the flames. The steam, which he said immediately began to rise from his clothes, bore silent testimony to the events of the day.

As a special concession, and due no doubt to his mother's influence, that night and for the rest of that week, he was given first chance to strip off and immerse himself in the hot tub to scrub the coal dust from his weary body with rough carbolic soap. Thereafter, his day's work completed, the pattern was quickly set whereby he arrived home from the pit about five o'clock, often soaked to the skin, waited till his father and Joseph had preceded him in the pecking order, and then bathed himself in the tin bath in front of the fire. When the men had finished bathing themselves his father and Joseph carried the heavy bath outside and emptied the dirty water into the gutter, as was the common practice in the community.

Communal water tap

At this point in his story he was lavish in his praise for the contribution made by his sisters to this daily ritual. He said that, immediately they returned from school, their first task was to fetch buckets of water from the communal tap outside the house, which then had to be boiled in a large pot on the fire, prior to being emptied into the tin bath. As this procedure was being duplicated by other miners' families up and down the street, they constantly had to wait in queues at the communal tap to collect the water. The mud underfoot was always inches deep in the area immediately around the tap and this, of course, was trailed into the house on the girls' feet each time they carried in a bucket of water. This inevitably led to more cleaning work for the girls every day, which they just accepted as part and parcel of living in this environment.

Washing completed, he joined his father and Joseph at the kitchen table for the hot but simple meal that his mother had prepared for them. In addition she, of course, had spent the last few hours supervising the collecting and boiling of the water for the daily washing ritual. While they were eating, she and his sisters were arranging their discarded working clothes in front of the fire, to ensure that they were dry for the next day's toil (on some occasions they had first to be taken outside to have mud scraped off with a knife.)

One can only imagine how steamy the atmosphere then became and how uncomfortable and unhealthy that must have made the atmosphere in the house for all concerned. As he described this to me, Andra struggled to remember a winter's day when there were no clothes draped in front of the fire.

By this time it was nearing seven o'clock but his daily work was far from over because, although his father had instigated his early departure from school, it wasn't his intention to allow him to stop his education completely. Accordingly he had made arrangements for Andra, after the long days working underground in dreadful conditions, to attend a nearby and somewhat makeshift (Andra's words) evening school to ensure that he continued to learn as much as possible of the three R's. This, as far as he could remember, cost his father three-pence a week plus the cost of the necessary books. Andra told me the return from this expenditure could never be properly evaluated because, basic though it was, the grounding he gained at this improvised school inspired him for the rest of his life to continually seek to increase his knowledge, by whatever means were available to him at any given time. He said that the more he learned and understood the more it increased his awareness of the vast gulf between the living standards of the ruling classes and the working people on whose efforts their wealth was accumulated. His thirst to educate himself also enabled him in later life to express himself, both verbally and literally, in the direct no-nonsense style that was to become his trademark.

With the above average intelligence that he possessed, had he been born in a privileged background he would quite conceivably have been given the opportunity to have a university education. Who knows what he and many others like him would have gone on to achieve in life, if this had been possible in those unenlightened days. The fact that he achieved all that he did in life speaks volumes for his determination to succeed in spite of the class distinction that prevailed and the obstacles that were placed in the path of himself and others like him.

Inglorious Mud

Little Boxes

Andra's comments about the dreadful living conditions in Wishaw in 1870 were augmented when I researched this particular aspect of his narrative. One would have expected that things would improve with the passage of time but, sadly, this was not to be the case. Fifty years later owners were still culpable of building equally sub-standard housing for their hard working employees.

The increased population of these economic immigrants created serious problems as far as accommodating them was concerned, as described by my friend Jim Rouse on his excellent Coal-mining Web-site (www.mcpitz.com). Jim was born and raised in Blantyre, Lanarkshire but now lives in Tasmania, Australia. Jim describes the condemned house he lived during the 1950's as having been one of 42 single-roomed houses and 41 double-roomed houses which had been built by William Dixon Ltd in 1892 to provide shelter for 492 people. These dwellings when built had no wash houses or coal cellars (coal would be stored indoors) no running water, had an open sewer behind 12 door-less privies and two drinking fountains. By the time Jim lived there there had been some improvement including, as depicted by Jim, the luxury of piped cold water!

Jim's research goes on to remind us that, in most cases, the coal and iron masters were responsible for the erection of their own workers' houses. They were therefore 'tied houses' meaning 'tied' to their jobs; the sack and eviction therefore went hand in hand, thereby punishing a worker's wife and children very harshly should he be deemed guilty of industrial misconduct.

The exact location of a row was determined by the owner's desire to have it as close to the mine as possible, since he would not need to buy additional land for his workers' homes. It also meant that he could keep tight social discipline over his work force, being able to inspect the condition of their houses, collect the rent, check up on absentees and, if necessary, carry out evictions of the families of 'troublesome workers.' For the worker himself it meant he endured a condition similar to that of George Orwell's nightmare of the future, '1984', in which the state (Big Brother) has full knowledge of the personal and social life and thus effectively controls the individual. Over a century before 1984 the mine owner and his overseers were just such 'Big Brothers' to countless thousands of workers, since their family life and leisure activities were conducted only yards from the workplace. For the miner's wife it meant not only insecurity in the family home but a constant battle against pollution from smoke and grit, of the house, the furniture and the washing.

The need to mass produce cheap workers' housing led to monotonously similar houses arranged in long lines – the essential rows: in these, the open spaces between were cluttered with common wash houses, dry toilets (with no flush) and middens (waste dumps). The actual construction of the houses was usually of the lowest quality: the possibility of a mine having a short life meant that they were not built to last. The investment in the capital equipment of the works was seen as being far more important than investment in the human equipment, i.e. the workers and their families.

One example recounted by Jim was the Carnbroe Rows built and owned by Merry and Cunningham in 1938, which consisted of three single storeyed rows running along the steep bank of the River Calder, Blantyre. The most westerly row, known locally as the Monkey Row, consisted of twenty back-to-back single ends containing two hole-in-the-wall beds – 'those cubicles of consumption' as one commentator described this feature. The other two rows were room-and-kitchens.

These rows, which stood well into the 20th century, were served by dry toilets, one common water pipe, and open sheughs (drains) until 1923, when a rude brick scullery with cold water and a toilet with unfinished inside walls and bare rafters were added to each house. It was into the 1930's before gas was led into these rows, replacing paraffin lamps for lighting: electricity never managed to get there before the bulldozer. Poor construction expressed itself in peeling wallpaper, rotting floorboards and repeated burst pipes in winter.

Throughout their existence, the workers' rows were visited by recurrent eruptions of cholera and enteric fever (both contracted from polluted water and food) typhus fever (from body lice) or endemic typhus (from the bites of rat fleas). The eradication of these came with the provision of piped, clean water, housing improvements, rubbish collection and personal hygiene in the 20th century. But it was well into the 20th century before such basic rights were won.

Miners houses at Quarter, near Hamilton

The fact that Jim actually lived in one of these houses gives so much more credence to his research on this subject and he concludes by informing us that, as late as 1912, The Royal Commission, reporting on Housing in Scotland, made the following submission regarding Rosehall Rows, which, although they had been built in 1837, were still being used to accommodate the unfortunate workers and their families:

*'They consist of four long parallel rows of single storey hovels. Most of them have no roves to carry the rainwater from the roof. Rainfall simply runs down the roof and then runs down the walls or falls down by chance as the wind decides. Coals are kept below the beds. The closet accommodation is hideous. A number of these hovels are built back to back. The closets outside are not used by the women. In some of the rows seven or eight people occupy a single room. The sanitary conveniences were in a state of revolting filth.' ***

The response by John T. Wilson, County of Lanark Medical Officer to reports like these was, not unexpectedly, cool to say the least. For example, my own research on this subject revealed the following extracts from the *Second Report of the Royal Commission of Mines (1910)*. They should have left him in no doubt as to the appalling living conditions of the miners but, as will be seen from his response and, as discovered throughout my research, miners were often treated as some form of sub-culture by people like him who were in a position do something to improve the miners standard of living;

*"The housing of miners, though an interesting subject, is not included in our terms of reference, but we feel it is incumbent on us to mention the statement made by some of the representatives of the Scottish miners that there are still mining villages in Scotland in which many of the miners' families live in single-roomed houses. Two of us took the opportunity when in Scotland, to inspect some of these cottages, and the conditions we found were extremely unsatisfactory, and in many cases the common privies and co; in connection with these dwellings were in a revolting and unsanitary condition. It is beyond the scope of this Commission to make any recommendations in this matter, but we wish to point the moral that for men and women living in such surroundings facilities for cleanliness are non-existent, and it is scarcely possible for the men returning from the pit to wash themselves completely without a breach of the common decencies of life."***

Mr. Wilson's response to this was as follows;

> "No doubt the Commissioners had in view the desirability of providing washing facilities at the pit-head, but the statement may well be questioned. Consider the social relations among the class of workmen. Miners marry early in life and the birth rate is high. Now is a one apartment home not a suitable dwelling for a young couple and might it not be considered suitable even for the first five years of married life? It should be remembered that the greatest strain upon the family resources usually takes place after ten years of married life. The clothing and feeding of, say, six children from the source of income requires thrift and careful management. It is very desirable that the public mind should be cleared of any sickly sentiment as to the supposed evils of the one-apartment house. There can be no doubt that a real demand for such houses exists. Many are the happy and healthy homes found in one-apartment dwellings. There is no doubt that the personal factor is by far the most important in securing a healthy home. Give many housewives four walls and a roof and she will make it look like a modern dwelling. The floor may be defective, but it is covered in linoleum. The internal walls and ceilings may be defective and even damp, but the walls are covered with paper twice or three times a year and the ceiling is lime-washed. The recessed beds are fitted with modern wire mattresses and with hair mattresses. The wall alongside the bed may even be draped with a suitable cloth. If the coals are stored beneath the bed, the height of the mattress is sufficiently high to allow of someone getting access to the remotest parts of the space below the bed. A beautiful pawn hangs in front, keeping the coals from view. The furnishings are very complete. If there is no wash-house or scullery, the washing and cleaning up is done at a time when the confusion caused will be least noticed. The question of occupancy is one of the very utmost importance in making a dwelling comfortable and wholesome. The structural arrangement is no doubt a matter of great moment, but occupancy is the most powerful factor and should never be lost sight of.
>
> The subject of privy middens (outside dry closets) constitutes the most common form of nuisance dealt with by the Sanitary Inspectors and in some localities is a danger to health. Miners are a class of migratory habits but this is particularly marked in some localities. The more changeable the population the greater is the liability to introduce an infectious disease. When typhoid has been introduced there is a great difficulty in controlling the spread of the disease where foul privy middens are in use. Once the disease is fairly widely disseminated it is apt to become endemic. Blantyre is a locality that has suffered in this respect. Before the water-carriage was introduced into tenement properties it was no uncommon sight on a warm summer day to see children walking through excrement refuse on the floors of privies or deposited round the ash pit. Notwithstanding all the researches of recent years showing how infection may be retained in the human body, there can be no doubt that common conveniences, whether of the privy midden type or the water carriage type, are much more liable to spread infection than where a convenience is provided for each house."*

Mr. Wilson then described a privy midden situated to the rear of an old three storey tenement property at Blantyre Works.

> "The elevation shows a stone structure that would do credit to any builder of a modern dwelling house. The midden occupies a central position and the household refuse can be thrown into it via two openings. There are four groups of privy seats. The detailed drawing of seats show a great deal of ingenuity to avoid soiling the person. There is a seat for adults and a seat for children, so designed that the only part of the seat to touch the body is a portion of about three inches square on either side of a semi-circular front. The whole seating arrangement is formed of iron, except two rests for the buttocks, which are covered with wood. No doubt when these structures were erected about one hundred years ago they would be considered models of perfection and, if properly used, no serious nuisance might arise. At the present day however the midden is not only a receptacle for dry household rubbish, but for liquid slops of various kinds. The result is that instead of the excrement refuse being covered with dry ashes from the fireplace, it mingles with other liquid refuse and becomes a fermenting, offensive mass."*

Stonefield Road, Blantyre

I had to reread the above report several times to make sure that I wasn't imagining some of the remarks made by a County of Lanark Medical Officer. The rosy pictures painted by him re the desirability of such hovels are a shining example of how easy it was for the coal owners and their like get away with almost anything. It also explains why so many of the mining people went to an early grave.

"Now is such a one apartment home not a suitable dwelling for a young couple and might it not be considered suitable even for the first five years of married life?" he says. What he really means is that it was suitable only because the young couple were mining people and it was good enough for them. It is an absolute certainty that no child of his, if and when he or she married and was seeking suitable accommodation to begin their married life with their partner, would be influenced by his sad attempts to embellish the squalor that prevailed in these dingy slums by writing, *"The question of occupancy is one of the very utmost importance in making a dwelling comfortable and wholesome. The structural arrangement is no doubt a matter of great moment, but occupancy is the most powerful factor and should never be lost sight of."*

If there is such a thing as reincarnation, I'm sure that a great career as an estate agent awaits John T. Wilson in our present generation. Anyone who could write, *"The internal walls and ceilings may be defective and even damp, but the walls are covered with paper twice or three times a year and the ceiling is lime-washed"* and/or *"The floor may be defective, but it is covered in linoleum"* as if these were virtues, would surely prosper in the lucrative property market of today.

Miners had a great sense of humour despite the hardships they endured. (photo by kind permission of Guthrie Hutton).

The Truck Act

On another day, while talking to me about everyday life of the miners and with more than a hint of disgust in his voice, Andra recollected that, apart from the inadequate housing, another instance of the coal owners greed and the manner in which they attempted to control the miners lives was evinced in the arrogance they displayed in ignoring the Truck Act.

The Truck Act, he explained, forbade employers paying their workers with either goods or tokens but in many instances the act was totally disregarded by the employers. As an example, Andra explained that miners who obtained employment with a new master had 'lie time' on their wages during their first period of employment. During this stage workers were obviously compelled to apply for an advance in their wages but, instead of being given cash, they were issued with credit slips or tokens which could only be exchanged for goods at the company store. Placing the worker immediately in their debt of course, ensured that in many cases the system perpetuated itself. The store was usually next door to the pay office and many of these company shops short weighed the customers and sold them goods that weren't up to the standard of similar items which were on sale in local shops. The goods were usually dearer as well but, despite this, the miners were not allowed to buy from these sources. Indeed, they were often threatened with dismissal if they attempted to do so. As this meant that they would also be evicted from the company house, the threat was usually enough.

Andra said that Alexander McDonald M.P. who was a great champion of the miners, highlighted this abuse of the Act in the Houses Of Parliament on several occasions, as he endeavoured to eliminate the exploitation of working people. Seeking confirmation of this I read The Navvy In Scotland, by James E. Handley. In this he alluded to McDonald giving evidence to a Select Committee of Mines in 1866 that;

> 'the Truck System held the heavy industries of Scotland in a vice. Though monthly or fortnightly payment of wages were the rule, the workmen could receive subs daily, or even twice daily, providing such advances were spent at the stores, which sold "everything but coffins". Even to such a trifling commodity as buttermilk, a popular thirst-quencher with miners, the stores contracted with the farmers of the district for all their supply and the worker therefore, if he sought a beverage other than water, had to go to the stores for it.

> Beer and spirits were also on sale at most of the stores and influence was often brought to bear on local Justices of the Peace to induce them to refrain from granting licences to outsiders. The owners of the stores were often magistrates themselves. The credit book of the workman was continually scrutinised by the store-man and the pay clerk, and any attempt to funnel the cash into his pocket instead of into the store or, as the slang of the day had it, 'slope the store' put an end to his chance of further subs. Moreover, he received first an admonition for his misdemeanour and then dismissed if he remained obdurate.'*

McDonald concluded by telling the committee that the whole system of Truck was a grievous vexation for the miners and kept continuously aflame a spirit of bitterness against their employers, but harbouring resentment was all that they could do. Strikes against it invariably petered out.

Alexander McDonald M.P.

Subsequent to McDonald's intervention, Commissioners questioned two Procurator Fiscals in Lanarkshire about the pursuit in law of infringements of the Truck Act but found that no measures were taken. From one, they learned that the Procurator Fiscal took his instructions from the Commissioners Of Supply, who administered the financial and other affairs of the County. That body was composed of the leading proprietors in the County, a large number of whom were mine-owners. In modern terminology this was obviously par for the course!

* Source: National Library of Scotland

Family Grief

For Andra, the few years after he commenced working passed quickly he recalled and, in 1874, by which time he was fourteen, he was working alongside his father and brother at the coal face as they lay on their sides and hewed and shovelled coal by the ton. His father, he recalled, always had to fold a couple of sacks to lie on to protect the area of his back that had been scorched in his last accident. Their mates, in typical miners' fashion, made him the butt of many jokes about sleeping on the job etc.

1874 was also an eventful year for the workers in the mining industry and they were embroiled in many disputes with the coal owners after swingeing cuts in their daily wages, some as much as 40%. Strikes were frequent but the miners were disunited and, as several attempts in the preceding years to form unions had foundered, their actions were uncoordinated. The management were usually dealing with small, individual deputations of men who knew that they were likely to lose not only their jobs but their homes as well if they upset the management too much. The coal owners took advantage of this weakness and remained resolute during several months of scattered strikes.

'Lie Time'

During this time, the miners and their families suffered great hardships and, as if things weren't bad enough for the McAnultys, on the 8th May of that year Andra and the rest of the family were devastated when, apparently after only a short but painful illness, their mother Catherine died. Andra said that, because of the nature of the illness, she must have been suffering considerable pain for some time previously but the family had never heard her complaining. She was only 42 years of age and her death certificate reveals that cause of death was cancer of the womb.

Speaking of his dear mother's death, Andra recalled that his father was inconsolable but his sister Agnes, who by this time was almost eighteen, immediately gave up her job and quickly assumed her mother's role in the household. Fourteen year old Mary, although employed locally, was an able part time assistant to her sister as they performed all the chores that were necessary to feed and care for the family. Andra said that much of their time was, as before, taken up with the seemingly never-ending need to wash and dry the men's working clothes on an almost daily basis. Bridget, now nine years old, had already inherited the task of fetching and carrying the family's daily water requirements from the communal tap.

This situation prevailed until the middle of 1877 when, in quick succession, two other incidents transpired which caused further upheaval in the household. Agnes, who was by

Glasgow Road, Blantyre

now twenty one years old intimated that, with Peter's blessing, she wanted to get married. However, while the family were coming to terms with the thought of losing her from their midst, the second and altogether more serious incident occurred. Seventeen year old Mary, described by Andra as a bright and cheerful person, contracted one of the fevers which were prevalent in the community and succumbed to it in only a matter of days. The family were stunned and Andra recalled that Agnes was reluctant to go ahead with her marriage, which was due to take place just a few weeks after the funeral, with Mary as her bridesmaid. His father persuaded her that this was the right thing to do and so she duly got married and left the family home to go and live with her collier husband. During her discussion with Peter and because, by this time, Agnes was a mother figure in young Bridget's eyes, it was decided that she would go and live permanently with her and her new husband after the marriage. In view of subsequent events this proved to be no bad thing.

Now that the family was reduced to the male members only, Peter decided to make a fresh start in the expanding mining district of Blantyre, Lanarkshire and soon thereafter he secured employment for himself, Joseph, Andra and William with Messrs. William Dixon Ltd. At No. 2 pit, in High Blantyre. This was to prove to be an ill-fated move.

Dixon's No. 2 Pit

The First Explosion

The family's new home was at 57 Hall Street, Blantyre, in what was commonly known as Dixon's Rows. The name Blantyre is thought to have been derived from the Gaelic Bla'-an-tir which translated means 'a warm retreat'. Apt though this name for the village might have been in the days before the first pit shaft was sunk, things had obviously changed drastically by the time the family arrived there, so much so that Andra described Blantyre at that time as being, "A village of a kind but, as a matter of fact, it was nothing better than a clay-hole." There were practically no paved roads and of course there were no street lights.

End House Of Dixon's Rows

Five companies had sunk pits in Blantyre, the three large ones being Merry & Cunningham, William Dixon and William Baird. In total, eight pits were sunk and to accommodate their employees the coal owners constructed rows of houses adjacent to the various pits. *These of course were very basic and living in the cramped quarters with their cold stone floors was extremely stressful,"* said Andra, *"at no time has Blantyre been distinguished for its beauty but in those days it really was a dreary and dismal area."*

Indeed soon thereafter, a Herald reporter who came to the village said that, like many colliery communities, High Blantyre was to all but the most fervent local patriot an unlovely sight, The village straggled 'with no attention to order' and was a somewhat shapeless settlement of buildings 'of all shapes and sizes' where new roads were added 'just as a whim of the proprietors (might) dictate.' Indeed, the reporter could not forbear mentioning his need to thread his way through 'a maze of the dirtiest and most intricate ways and byways that the country can boast of.'

The fact that approximately sixty years later, my mother, who was born in Blantyre in 1900, still referred to Victoria Street in Blantyre (which links High and Low Blantyre) as "The Clay Road," is probably indicative of what it was still like underfoot in some parts of the village in her early days.

Amidst these harsh conditions, between 7 and 8 a.m. on Monday the 18th of August, 1877 an event occurred that, tragic though it was, was only the precursor of an even greater tragedy. In an interview with the *Weekly Record* in later life Andra described it thus:

> *"We had not been in our new surroundings (Blantyre) long when disaster overtook us. My elder brother Joseph (22), my younger brother William (15) and myself, then*

WEEKLY RECORD, JUNE 16, 1928

World Famous Pit Disaster	Heroes Of Great Calamity

MY MEMORIES OF BLANTYRE DISASTER WHEN HUNDREDS MET DOOM.

VILLAGE THAT WAS DESOLATED BY LOSS OF FATHERS AND SONS - GRIM MEMENTOES DEARLY TREASURED.

BY ANDREW McANULTY, IN AN INTERVIEW

Although many years have passed since the greatest pit disaster in the history of Scotland, many people can still recall the harrowing details of the Blantyre calamity, and in this interesting article Mr. Andrew McAnulty, High Blantyre, relates the story for the benefit of "Weekly Record" readers, revealing some new and remarkable details of the dread drama.

To the present generation the Blantyre pit explosion is but an item of history well nigh forgotten, remarked Mr. Andrew McNulty when a "Weekly Record" representative called upon him at his home in High Blantyre. There are still a few people left in the district who are able to recall that fateful Monday morning – the 22nd day of October, 1877 –when a message flashed from end to end of the country that nearly two hundred and thirty miners had lost their lives while earning their daily bread.

The magnitude of the catastrophe seemed to completely stagger the whole country and although over fifty years have elapsed since its occurrence, the whole circumstances of that dread time are as visibly impressed on my memory now as if they had happened only yesterday.

17, were down Dixon's No.2. My brother Joseph had a contract for working out the stoops (stoops were 50ft square pillars of coal left behind to support the roof as the underground roads advanced). We had been laying rails from 6 a.m and, about 8 a.m. there was an explosion of gas at my naked light and Joseph and I were severely burnt, William, who was some yards away was unharmed. My brother Joseph died at 10 o'clock that night. I was burnt on my hands, feet, arms and back, the scars of which I still carry to this day. All of the persons about the place were using naked lights and no one had told us to be careful with lights because there was gas in the mine."

Expanding on the contents of this article, Andra remembered vividly being blasted off his feet by the force of the explosion and the feeling of complete disorientation he felt as he struggled to come to terms with what had happened. It was pitch dark but he didn't require light to know that he had received serious injuries to his head, eyes, arms and right foot in particular. The agonising groans from his brother Joseph betrayed the fact that he too was seriously injured, but he was somewhat encouraged to hear William's voice as he endeavoured to reassure Joseph and himself that help would soon be forthcoming. After what seemed an interminable period of time help did arrive and his next memory was of the pain he endured while he and Joseph were being carried to the pit bottom by his work-mates and thereafter to the surface. On reaching the surface, he and Joseph, who were both almost naked because their clothes had been shredded by the force of the blast of flames, were laid on the back of a flat, horse-drawn wagon which then trundled to the local railway station. Bearing in mind the previously documented condition of the road surfaces, one can only attempt to imagine the further agony and discomfort this short but terrible journey inflicted on their already pain-racked bodies. To compound the suffering, this was followed by a jolting train journey to the Central Station in Glasgow, followed by an equally uncomfortable hand cart journey through the streets of Glasgow to the Royal Infirmary. Remember, Andra was sixteen years old.

His father, whilst working at the coal face in another part of the pit, had been informed about an hour later of the accident and quickly made his way to the surface. Still in his working clothes he hurried to the railway station and made his way to Glasgow and the Infirmary. On his arrival there he was immediately confronted with Joseph's naked and scorched body lying on top of a bed, his almost jet black, charred body in stark contrast to the white sheet below it. Peter, hardened as he was from personal experience to such injuries, knew instinctively that Joseph couldn't survive the almost 100% burns to his body. Because his lungs were also scorched, Joseph couldn't speak to Peter but the fear in his son's eyes betrayed that he too knew that he was finished. Realising that death was imminent, Peter stayed with Joseph until mercifully, several agonising hours later, Joseph's damaged lungs breathed their last. He was twenty one years old.

Later that night, while Andra was still receiving treatment for his own appalling injuries, his heartbroken father had the unenviable job of telling him that his brother had died. Peter told him that Joseph had suffered such horrific burns that his premature death was, in every sense of the word, a blessing.

Andra himself was badly burned, particularly on his right arm and shoulder and only a few hairs remained on his scorched head. When the bandages around his eyes were being changed he discovered that he was almost completely blind in his right eye and had blurred vision in his left. At this time also, although he couldn't see for himself because of the bandages round his leg, he was advised by the Matron and his father that three of the toes on his right foot had been blown off in the explosion. In spite of this catalogue of injuries he still felt lucky to be alive.

Andra said that Peter stayed with him for at least three days and nights until he was assured by the doctors and the Matron that Andra was going to recover, albeit in a damaged condition. During this time he snatched a few hours sleep now and then in a large chair which the Matron had placed at the side of Andra's bed. Andra was, even at this great distance in time from the event, still visibly affected by the affair as he spoke to me of the caring and compassionate manner in which the Matron, who was aware of their grief at the loss of Joseph, had dealt with himself and his father. She no doubt broke or bent a few of the rules when she ensured that, not only was Peter fed during his vigil but was also allowed to bathe and be given some clean clothes to wear, no doubt to preserve her white bed sheets from his soiled working clothes! The aforementioned working clothes were also washed and cleaned for him to take home with him when he went.

After a period of time during which he was given further treatment in the Infirmary, Andra was removed home, again by handcart and train. Following his return home, he told me that later he was to give evidence that, although a policeman had subsequently called to see him on two occasions to tell him that Mr. Dykes, the Procurator Fiscal of the Upper Ward of Lanarkshire, wanted to see him in Hamilton regarding the circumstances surrounding the death of his brother, no one from the Dixon's Pit management came to see him at any time thereafter, to inquire after his condition or to discuss the incident. As he was of course still suffering badly from his injuries, he wasn't able to make the four miles or so journey to Hamilton to comply with the heartless fiscal's request and he never heard from him again.

At this juncture Andra opined that it suited the powers that be to quietly forget a serious accident which had killed one miner and badly injured another. The sight of his scorched right arm with its shriveled sinews which he then showed me and the foot, minus three toes, which he revealed when he removed his right boot, bore silent testimony to the severity of those injuries. That memory has stayed with me until this day.

In that the incident was also not recorded by the colliery management in their official accident book (a contravention of the Mines Act of 1872) as was subsequently revealed at the Public Inquiry into the later, greater disaster, The Establishment had effectively closed ranks. Such was the value that was placed on the lives of members of the mining community in those harsh days.

As he spoke to me about his brother's horrific death and the callous manner in which it was dealt with by the authorities, his voice betrayed the hurt and anger he still felt almost seventy years later. This had been compounded by the fact that, because of his injuries, he had been forced to remain at home propped up in bed while the other members of the family attended Joseph's funeral. He recalled how depressed he had been for days afterwards and had always been grateful to their neighbour Mrs. Cox who lived at number 54 Hall Street and who, in keeping with the great community spirit which prevailed in the street, came in several times daily throughout his incapacitation to administer to his needs.

Another daily visitor during his convalescence was Dr. Grant, a medical man who was greatly esteemed by the local people and who was to become even more so as a consequence of tragic events still to come. Andra said he had mixed views about these visits to say the least. On the medical side this meant the daily removal of the bandages from the dreadful burns he had received, to allow Dr. Grant to treat them. Although he said it in a matter of fact way, as I entered these simple comments in my notebook the mere thought of the pain he must have endured on each of these occasions sent shivers down my spine. On the positive side, however, he said that after Dr Grant had finished the medical requirements of his visit, he sat at the foot of the bed sipping a cup of tea which had been provided by the kindly Mrs. Cox and spoke to him about his hopes and desires. Andra said that this thoughtful gesture was not only his first real contact with someone from out-with the mining community but also the first indication in his short life that some people of Dr. Grant's status in the community did care about the working people.

Their discussions were not only therapeutic to Andra but he said they taught him the lesson that the somewhat jaundiced view he had previously held about the middle classes, influenced no doubt by his perception of the dogmatic attitudes of the coal owners and managers, required some rethinking on his part and that he should henceforth treat everyone on their merits, whatever their position in society.

Despite his youth Andra must also have made a profound impression on Dr. Grant regarding his thirst for knowledge because, after a few days, he started to bring some books for him to read and thereafter discuss with him. This meaningful gesture was, Andra said, a turning point in his life, as it gave him access to authors and subjects, judiciously chosen by Dr. Grant, of whom he had never even heard and which inspired in him an appreciation of amongst other things, a love of the poetic works of Robert Burns and Shelley. He was also greatly inspired and impressed by Burns' championing of the working classes. Dr. Grant must have been sufficiently aware of the impact that the books he had chosen were making because he told Andra on one of his visits that he could, if he wanted, call at 'Croftpark House' his residence in Broompark Road, after he recovered from his injuries and chose some books from his extensive personal library on an ongoing basis.

This spontaneous and generous offer was to be fully honoured in the course of time and was never forgotten by Andra. He said that the treasure-trove of books that he was given access to helped him to educate himself far beyond his wildest hopes.

I know from personal experience that this love of books and reading was to stay with him until he died, because another of my chores was to be sent once a week to the local library, which at that time was in High Blantyre School, to choose, with the assistance and guidance of Quentin Smith the headmaster, several books at a time on various subjects. These, despite his weak eyesight, he pored over from morning to night - sometimes with a little help from me!

Dr. Grant (W. Bolton Collection)

Catastrophe

Due to the administrations of Dr. Grant and greatly comforted by the reading material provided by this kind gentleman, Andra was soon making satisfactory progress towards recovery. He was at the stage when he was able to walk (or stagger as he called it) but still had limited use of his arms, when, several weeks later, on the 22nd. October, 1877 a catastrophe which horrified the whole country took place. Andra described it to me thus;

"My father left for work as usual about six o'clock in the morning, after making me a cup of tea and leaving me some porridge for later. As he walked out of the door without a backward glance, I did not realise that I would never again see my father - alive or dead. Shortly thereafter my brother William came home from the night shift in No. 2 pit, where he had been working since the accident that he and I had been involved in. Had he still been on the day shift he would also have perished in the tragic event which was to unfold. He had just gone to bed after having eaten some of the porridge made by my father, when an explosion occurred between eight and nine o'clock in the morning and its effort was similar to a dull concussion with a slight trembling of the ground. The atmosphere became quite dark, due no doubt to the great volume of coal dust thrown up by the explosion.

Bad news travels quickly and in a short space of time men, women and children, including myself and William, had gathered in excited crowds in the vicinity of the colliery. My arms were still heavily bandaged and due to the fact that we had hurried from the house instinctively, William and I were only wearing the thinnest of shirts. It was very cold and there was a trace of sleet in the air but, ourselves and many of the others who were also unsuitably attired were, initially at least, oblivious to the cold. Many of the scenes which followed were painful in the extreme.

The explosion was attributed to an accumulation of gas and originated on the south side of No. 2 pit. There were several men working on the north side at the time but they escaped as they were what I might term out of the "vent." There were really four pits, known as Nos. 1, 2, 3 and 4. Nos. 2 and 3 were both on the same ventilating lead. No. 2 being what is known as the "downcast" and No. 3 being the "up-cast". When the explosion occurred everything was blown towards the "up-cast" pit and, very speedily, the shaft of No. 3 pit was completely filled up with tubs, trucks, dead bodies, and debris of all descriptions.

Some men who were putting on a cage at No.3 pit at the time were severely burned and this, notwithstanding the fact that No. 2 pit was one hundred and fifty fathoms in depth and was fully half a mile distant. That alone gives one an idea of the intensity and volume of the fire.

The rumble of the explosion had hardly died away when the men who had dashed to the pit head, immediately and without question, offered themselves as rescuers. My brother William was among these and he and the others were soon joined by the men from Nos. 1 and 4 pits, who had quickly been brought to the surface immediately after the explosion. I trust I may not be considered prejudiced when I say that the spontaneous offer of help and succour to a suffering comrade seems to be peculiarly characteristic of the miner and, on this occasion as on many others of a similar nature, it was really magnificent to see those men begging to be permitted to descend. Engineers and other competent judges however decided that to allow the men to go down would simply mean adding to a death roll which was already appalling, but the men in their anxiety were difficult to appease."

His words, which were spoken to me in a hushed voice, are borne out by newspaper reports at the time which spoke of no fewer than 2,000 miners from the neighbouring pits marching along the road towards Blantyre, determined to descend the ill-fated mine en masse to look for survivors. At the same time

Alexander McDonald, M.P. who lived nearby, having heard of the calamity, was also rushing towards the scene. Reporters at the scene noted that, on seeing this mass of humanity on the march and hearing of their intentions, he at once stopped and addressed the men and pointed out to them the folly of endangering even more lives. With his reputation for reasonable conciliation, his impassioned plea finally convinced the miners who, albeit reluctantly, were dissuaded from their act of bravery. Even so, the very fact of their spontaneous attempted action to help the already doomed miners, shows not only the empathy for their fellow workers but also their unflinching bravery.

The newspapers also reported seeing another assembly of heartbroken people wending their way to the pit-head. Streams of women and children were issuing from the rows of houses adjacent to the colliery, while from High Blantyre and farther away groups of men and women of all ages, many still scantily attired and all with the same fearful expressions, came hurrying towards the pit. According to their knowledge of the whereabouts of friends and relations, they made their way to No.2 or No.3 pit, surrounded the shafts and enquired after fathers and brothers, sons and husbands.

The crowd was not, according to reports, without a dangerous element of anger and only the strenuous efforts of the local ministers and parish priests brought comparative calm to the situation. Most of the anger was directed towards the management who, they considered, had failed to learn a lesson from the recent accident involving the McAnulty brothers. There was an unwillingness by the survivors and relatives to accept that 'no one was really to blame'.

All Ye Young Miners: Blantyre, 1885, written by The Reverend Stewart Wright, explained the importance, *'which the bereaved always attach to the quick recovery of their dead in mining disasters. In this particular case the mood of the village and perhaps the surrounding colliery settlements, fanned no doubt by the previous incident regarding the McAnulty's, was also one of outrage and anger. It was strongly felt that management was in some measure to blame for such catastrophes. The embers of an old and bitter resentment could so be easily fanned into the flame of riot and lawless desperation. The seeming inefficiency of recovery operations, which could be interpreted as callousness, might so easily provide the draught to produce a conflagration of reckless passion. Few were the mining communities without old scores to settle against the coal-owners; fewer still those without a general grievance about the indifference to human life of 'the authorities.'* *

Panic

Alexander McDonald, M.P. continued to play his part in cooling the obvious but natural displays of anger and frustration although, according to some reports, he himself accused the district inspector of gross neglect over a period of time and told the colliers that he would not rest until a public inquiry was held; (other reporters on the scene alleged that he had called the colliery owners and their managers *murderers* but he later publicly refuted this claim and said that he had referred only to the disasters themselves). He promised that, if the crowd would break up peacefully, he would try and expose whatever negligence there had been by means of a Public Inquiry. This anger, easily fanned into flame, was, as we shall see, a distinctive feature of the disaster and its aftermath.

The night that followed was described by the *Herald's* reporter as,

> *'the most grievous in Blantyre's history, when fierce squalls of sleet and rain drove away the merely curious; but lowering under hedgerows or whatever slight shelter they could obtain, many anxious ones continued to hang about the scene, eager to receive any scrap of news'.* Further that, *'only the genuinely bereaved or concerned were in evidence. No idle sightseer would have braved such a night.'*

This scene was to change drastically the next day however as was recorded also in 'All Ye Young Miners: Blantyre, 1877'.

> *'Sensational news, as we have seen, draws the multitude. Throughout the day the Strathaven railway line did a record amount of business. The trains were crowded to a degree never previously experienced and conduct at the station varied from the indecorous to the unruly. The weather remained wet and miserable, reflecting - though only imperfectly - the gloom and despair of the village. Local pubs did roaringly well, catering for drenched sensation-mongers, while the hundred constables on duty were kept fully occupied, dealing by turns with distressed relatives and drunken sightseers. The representatives of the press recorded their impressions, including a faintly resentful feeling that they were being accorded something less than courteous treatment by the authorities. Reporters found the colliery managers unwilling to give any but the most meagre information about the state of operations underground.'*

The main frustration for everyone, management and colliers alike, was the fact that fire was still raging in No. 3 shaft and an attempt to use No. 2 to attain access to No. 3 via the underground 'roads' had, despite the fact that a team of men had made some headway, been abandoned because of the continued presence of gas which had overcome one of their number and the perceived danger of a second explosion. Hugh Brown, an older workmate and close friend of my great grandfather and grandfather, and who

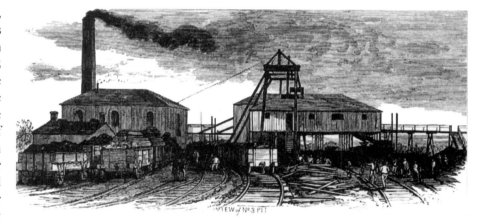

Dixon's No. 3 Pit

was one of only a few who escaped from the no. 2 shaft immediately after the explosion, later told reporters that this initial enterprise had been led by Mr. Dickinson, the Chief Inspector of Mines and three of his assistants. He also had with him ten or twelve colliery managers from neighbouring collieries, Doctor William Grant and several colliers including Hugh himself. After being lowered, three at a time, into the No. 3 shaft in the 'kettle' which was a barrel-like vehicle used in sinking pits and which, from its shape, would go down or up a shaft where a cage couldn't go; and after making several attempts over a period of time to make progress into No. 3 pit which was blocked by tons of debris and full of smoke from the still raging fires underground, it was the unanimous opinion of these brave, experienced men that no further attempts via this access could be made until the fire in the shaft was extinguished. Hugh said that it was the only possible decision under the circumstances. In view of this, No. 2 shaft which was also badly blocked with debris was again thought of as a means of access and this further effort by these brave men was described in the Hamilton Advertiser thus;

> *'Not more than three men could get into the kettle at a time and, ultimately, the explorers found themselves unable to make much headway down the blocked shaft. They heard the faint shouts of some poor fellows below, but it was agreed amongst the men that, until they saw some surer prospect of gaining access to the mine, it would be needless to excite them by raising vain hopes, and no response was given to the cries for help.*

Steadily and perseveringly the work to clear No.2 shaft went on. The day, which had been cold and wet, was succeeded by the darkness of night, whereupon the fires in the great iron braziers threw a ruddy glow over grimly silent men, whose set faces bespoke determination to proceed on the mission of mercy. On every hand were crowds, eager-eyed but also silent, except for the groans which escaped the lips of the women. The search parties, relieved at brief intervals, were busily at work in the blocked shaft. When a batch of those who had been relieved made their appearance, the beads of sweat on their faces and the knotted veins of their hands told of the severity of their exertions. Withal the work was protracted and slow; for the soft metal in the sides of the shaft bulged in, filling up the shaft and rendering the work so dangerous that it was found necessary to renew the lining. When they eventually reached the bottom of No.2 there was no shortage of volunteers to penetrate the dangerous depths below.

The members of the selected party led by, among others, Mr. Charles Thompson, one of the partners of William Dixon and Company, general manager Mr. Frederick Duncan and Mr. Anderson, manager at Auchenraith Pit, extended in a line within calling distance along the whole extent of the workings between the two pits. Of course, the reason of this arrangement is obvious, for if the deadly damp should overtake any section of the party, these would be able to make the fact known to their comrades.

The searchers on all sides met a sight too awful to put into words, which at once demonstrated the terrible nature of the explosion and the utter hopelessness and the expectation that many, if not all, could be alive in the mine. The intelligence that the party had penetrated to No.3 elicited a cheer from the crowd gathered at the shaft. During the hour which followed, the excitement increased in intensity and, despite a pitiless rain, driven by a strong wind, the number of persons continued to gather at the scene of the explosion.'

Ultimately, the *Hamilton Advertiser* reported that a few bodies, badly mangled and burned, were found and conveyed to the pit bottom with great difficulty and subsequently to the surface but, after several of the men who had recently been below had fancied that they could discern the flicker of fire against the face of the coal in some of the workings into which they had peered and after one of their party was overcome by the deadly gas, the decision was made by the proprietors of the colliery, reluctantly, to take the precautionary measure of closing the mine until ventilation was restored through the clearance of No.3 shaft. This was accordingly done and after half-past six in the morning *'no one was suffered to descend'* according to the *Advertiser*.

It was almost twenty four hours after the original explosion therefore before the sad but necessary decision was made to pump water down the No. 3 shaft to quench the flames which still raged below and to disperse the gas. This necessary decision was for the onlookers a tremendous blow. During the preceding day and night they had endured the cold wind and sleet as they huddled together for warmth, kept going in most instances by the thought that there would be some survivors and that their loved ones would be among them. Andra said that, when the pumps starting pouring water down the shaft, a silence descended on the massed crowds of people as they realised, finally, that there could now be no survivors. If by some miracle a few had survived the explosion, the water would now claim them.

Miners Lamp

When the fire was finally declared out, small three-men teams (again including Andra's close friend Hugh Brown) descended in the kettle and began to clear away the debris to make a passage to allow the air to go down into the workings below. It took some considerable time to clear away enough debris to allow the kettle to go down through it, before they could begin the horrific task of bringing up those bodies or, even more horrific, parts of bodies (and there were many) that they could find.

Hugh Brown later revealed to my grandfather that, when they first descended in the kettle, they plunged into water at the pit bottom which was about four feet deep. After they recovered from their immersion they were horrified to see, by the dim light of their flickering lamps, about thirty bodies floating on the surface of the water, their clothes having been burned off by the fire. This was, Hugh told my grandfather, the beginning of a period that would be etched in his mind forever and that he, like most of the others involved, had to be freely fortified by refreshments (as he called them) of whisky at regular intervals to enable them to carry out the gruesome task which they had volunteered to perform.

To retrieve the bodies they had witnessed at the pit bottom they had first to construct a platform at the bottom, big enough to hold six bodies at a time. Having done so, wading in water up to the waist, they recovered each body, wrapped it in a white sheet and laid it out on the platform. It was agreed that the best way to take them up to the surface was to put one of the bodies into the kettle standing straight up and that two of the volunteers would stand on the outside of the kettle, one on either side of the body, while they guided the kettle up the shaft. This was necessary because it required very careful handling to guide it through the narrow hole which was in the middle of the shaft.

Hugh Brown said that when his two work-mates got into the kettle with the first body and gave the signal for the engine-man to raise them up, he was left alone with the other bodies on the platform until they returned. He said that, while he didn't believe in ghosts, he was most unhappy during their absence. This gruesome procedure continued until all six bodies had been taken to the surface, at which point they again had to wade around and collect a further six victims to repeat the process.

Rescuers (back row, left to right); John Nelson, William Watson, George Watt, William Gilchrist, Donald Morrison, John Bowie, Thomas Forrest, John Henderson, Dougal McNicol, John McKinlay, Daniel Hendry, James Brown (front row, left to right); William Struthers, John Pickering, Hugh Brown, John McMullen, Robert Peel, Walter Nelson, Thomas Cook, John White, Thomas Laidlaw. Hamilton Advertiser, 22 October 1927.

Once they had cleared the initial pit-bottom area the task of extending the search began. This however could only be accomplished after the ventilation system, which had been destroyed by the explosion, was replaced and the many roof falls cleared. This, inevitably, took a lot of time as the teams of men involved worked under extremely hazardous and difficult conditions. In addition, stoppings (roof supports) had to be renewed and much of the stoop and room system had to be cleared of pockets of gas before they could get to other areas of the pit to seek further dead bodies.

Three weeks or so later, just when their grim task was coming to an end, Hugh and two others had to endure more horrors when first they came upon the bodies of three intimate friends of his, one of whom, John Dobbie, had been best man at his wedding. Hugh told my grandfather that he didn't think he would have had much trouble identifying such close friends but, so badly swollen and disfigured were they by the damp, he was only able to recognise them by their clothes and their names stamped on their tools.

The final and worst case that Hugh had to deal with was that of the Brown family who came from Law, near Carluke. There was the father and three sons and they had by this time been dead for three weeks and the smell emanating from their corpses was dreadful. Hugh said that he and the men who were with him, despite all that they had witnessed previously, shrank back in horror and refused to handle them but their leader, John Pickering, appealed for one of them to assist him to roll the bodies on to the sheets. Bracing up sufficient courage to undertake the work, Hugh helped Pickering to roll the bodies on to sheets and then laid them upon the stretchers. The other men then helped them to carry the bodies to the pit bottom.

At a later date Hugh, in a letter to the Advertiser, revealed that he and others felt that himself and the other brave, non-management men involved would have been suitably rewarded by the colliery owners for not only the long and arduous duty that they had performed but for the ongoing fortitude that they displayed while doing so. Not surprisingly, given the contempt that the owners had for the working miners, although the leadership and bravery of some of the managers etc was recognised in a tangible manner, the often gruesome work of the lowly colliers involved was taken for granted and it was left to the National Bible Society of Scotland to recognise the humane task that Hugh Brown and the

Volunteers

others had performed in such inhumane circumstances. Hugh and each of the other volunteers was given a copy of The Bible with an appropriate inscription on it from Mathew's Gospel; *"Inasmuch as ye have done it unto one of these my brethren, ye have done it unto me."* As Andra told me this, he made the point to me that this inscription could equally have been directed at the Colliery owners for the manner in which they had failed to recognise the colliers fortitude in an appropriate way!

My grandfather went on to describe the non-stop horrors that he and the others endured while these necessary operations were taking place. Because of the masses of people who were milling about in the immediate vicinity of the colliery, cards had been issued to the immediate families and friends of the missing miners, which allowed them within the enclosures at the pit-head. At this close distance therefore, over several days and nights in dreadfully cold and wet conditions, they watched the bodies which Hugh and his colleagues had recovered being conveyed a hundred yards or so to the weigh-house, a rough wooden building about a hundred feet long by twenty feet wide, which had been hastily converted to serve as a mortuary. Here the mangled and broken bodies were laid out on straw and the anxious relatives, himself and William included, were invited to inspect them for identification purposes. This arrangement was under the charge of Mr. Neil Douglas who was William Dixon & Co.'s cashier. The caring and compassionate manner in which this gentleman, who was later to become Chairman of the Blantyre Parish Council, conducted himself on their behalf in this unenviable task was never forgotten by my grandfather or the rest of the people of Blantyre.

Not everyone however was as compassionate as Neil Douglas. Hugh told my grandfather that Mr. Douglas had observed that on one of the bodies when it was brought to the mortuary was a silver watch and sometime afterwards he saw a suspicious looking person extract the watch from the pocket of the dead man, so he laid hold of him and handed him over to the police. The crowd, on hearing of this despicable action, wanted to lynch him but the police would not allow them to interfere with their prisoner. How anyone could perpetrate such a mean and heartless theft in these circumstances is beyond belief.

The procession of relatives round the mortuary was one of the most melancholy spectacles it is possible to picture, especially when identification was being established. Andra told me of his own personal anguish as, on each and every occasion that a body or bodies were brought to the surface and laid out in the makeshift morgue by some of the large staff of undertakers who were in attendance night and day, he followed the lengthy procession of people as they entered the dimly lit interior of the building and made their way past the wooden benches that had been hastily erected to hold their grim displays of broken humanity. The large number of coffins piled up at the end of the building did little to alleviate the misery.

Each body, or, in many instances, parts of a body, had to be closely scrutinised by himself and the other relatives to ascertain if it was that of the one(s) they were seeking yet, at the same time, dreading to find. Imagine the horrific memories Andra must have had when he spoke of many of the bodies, the majority of which were badly burned and mutilated, being unrecognisable, and their identity could only be established by their belongings - belts, knives or some other article.

On each occasion, almost as soon as he entered the building, he had to share the grief of those who had found loved ones but, being the close-knit community that they were , even amidst their own distress they were quick to comfort others alongside them who had also identified one of the mutilated victims. His personal recollection of this was of himself, a seventeen years old youth, trying to offer comfort to Mrs. Cox, who had so faithfully tended him during the last two months. Not only had she lost her husband John, who had walked to the pit every morning with his father Peter and was indeed his closest friend but their only son Drew (16), who was an equally close friend of Andra, had also perished. She had just identified the body of her husband by means of a darn that she had put in one of his socks a few days previously but her personal agony was to be prolonged for several more days until the badly burned body of Drew was recovered. Andra said that, not surprisingly, Mrs. Cox never really recovered from the shock of seeing the burned and battered state of the bodies of her husband and son. Subsequent to the disaster, having apparently lost the will to live, she herself was to die less than two years later at the age of 41. For some therefore, there was the doubtful consolation of at least finding their loved ones. For others, including my grandfather and his brother, even this consolation was to be denied them.

One cannot start to imagine the lifelong effects it must have had on themselves and the other relatives as they were compelled to view body after body in their often vain search for loved ones. Despite the length of time that had elapsed since the event, Andra's voice still visibly lowered as he recounted this portion of his life. Only now, having researched independent reports of the disaster, have I been able to fully comprehend the reason why. For instance, in reporting the scenes in the makeshift morgue, the *Hamilton Advertiser* noted that;

Reading the list (reproduced courtesy of The Scots Magazine)

'The bodies conveyed to the morgue were washed and dressed as decently as the circumstances would permit and then handed over to the care of families and friends. It is to be noted that the bodies recovered almost all had the marks of injuries by burning. Some were contorted in the most dreadful manner, with the faces as black as the coal they had been shovelling. Others were torn and bruised, with dark crimson streams of blood trickling through their mud-covered and dust-begrimed clothes. A few had shreds of their pit clothes torn away and were battered and bruised in a shocking manner. The small number who had, apparently, succumbed to the choke-damp, wore a peaceful expression as if in sleep and those, when found, were discovered lying on their faces in the levels, as if they had been making haste to the pit bottom when overtaken by the deadly, suffocating gas.'

Some people were fortunate, if that's the correct term in the circumstances, to identify a loved one in the early days after the disaster (whatever their condition) but, because their loved ones were never recovered, Andra and many others had to endure the close inspection that was required by them of almost every one of the bodies that were recovered, in their vain search for their own kinfolk.

During their three weeks or so vigil and nine days after the explosion, a mass burial of the majority of the victims of this terrible disaster took place at High Blantyre Cemetery. At the appointed hour literally thousands of people filled the roads in the immediate vicinity of the cemetery as they jostled with each other to gain an appropriate vantage point to witness the proceedings. Many of them were people who had been arriving and departing daily by the trainload to gawp at the drama which was unfolding, literally in front of their eyes. Then and no doubt as there would be now, many undesirable types also descended on the village to look for easy pickings among the stricken families and/or empty houses. Quite a few of these opportunists, when discovered, were dealt with by the miners in what was to them an appropriate manner and a number of others beat a hasty retreat before they too endangered life and limb at the hands of these self-appointed guardians of this close-knit community. Most of course, were well intentioned people who, touched by this terrible tragedy, had come from far and wide to give moral and spiritual support to the local people on this tragic occasion.

As if they hadn't enough problems to contend with, this unprecedented influx of people to the area created further problems for the villagers. The condition of the unpaved muddy roads in and around the village quickly deteriorated and soon became almost impassable in some instances. On the 31st October the *Glasgow Herald* noted that:

'Visitors to Blantyre during the past week have had unpleasant experiences of the state of the roads in the locality but, impassable as these have been hitherto to all but the most resolute pedestrians, then conditions today absolutely defies description. Suffice to say, that one floundered amidst accumulations of mud until he became quite regardless of consequences and, simply shaping his course for the particular point he wished to reach, he directed his whole attention to the matter of arriving at it, no matter through what sort of 'glaur' (mud) he was obliged to wade. Around the pits, the water gathered in large pools and filled up the tracks of the service lines leading to the colliery.'

Amidst this background therefore the funerals took place. At the north eastern portion of the cemetery, two trenches upwards of 50 yards long, 3 yards wide and 2 yards deep had been prepared and, one by one, the coffins bearing the remains of these ill-fated miners were lowered to the bottom by their families and friends. Andra, because he knew so many of the victims intimately, would ordinarily have been involved in a number of these but because of his previously sustained injuries he was unable to do so and all he could do was to attempt to comfort their grief stricken families as best he could. He said that many of them were still in a state of shock and acted as if they were in a trance throughout the lengthy proceedings.

It was a long and fretful day for all of the families who had been involved but at least they had the satisfaction of seeing their loved ones laid to rest. Others, like Andra, were still in a state of limbo as they resumed their vigil with, by now, only a forlorn hope of seeing their loved ones recovered from the depths of the mine.

Occasionally, as the days passed, a body would be found in some corner of the mine and brought to the surface. There it would be washed and dressed and placed in a coffin to await identification by one or more of the waiting relatives. On one such occasion a body was discovered in the north workings of No. 3 Pit. The body, despite being badly burned, was subsequently identified as John Crow (22) 19 Miller Street, Blantyre, by his widowed mother, Jane Crow and his fourteen years old sister, Mary Crow. They were able to do this by means of a long blue scar on his left forearm. This incident had been witnessed by Andra and he described it to me in great detail because of its relevance to his and my personal life.

John Crow had befriended Andra's older brother Joe when the family came to Blantyre and he had been most distraught when Joe had been killed just weeks earlier. Since Joe's death he had come to visit Andra almost every day after work, and had been a great source of comfort to him. Now he too had been killed in horrific circumstances and Andra said that he felt that it was almost as if he had lost another brother.

He then told me that, as he comforted Jane and Mary, little did he or they realise that he and Mary would become man and wife six years later and that John, by a strange quirk of fate, would therefore become his brother-in-law (deceased).

When I sought the documentation to support the notes I had taken of this conversation with Andra, I quickly learned that John Crow's death had inadvertently created a mystery for the many people who have, over the years, attempted to collate the facts and figures of the disaster. The recovery of John Crow's body, almost six weeks after the explosion, was well documented in the newspapers and Andra later attended his funeral at Dalbeth Cemetery, Glasgow on the 31st of October. His burial was thereafter recorded in the cemetery internment book.

So far so good. Unfortunately, to their consternation, none of the researchers were able to find a death certificate for John but, because they had proof via the newspapers that he had been recovered and buried, they confidently added him to their final total. What they didn't realise was that they already had him on their list, albeit under another name!

The reason for their confusion was really quite simple, but it was only because of the family connection that I was able to succeed where all of the others had failed. Initially, like everyone else, I too was baffled and I spent fruitless hours searching for the elusive death certificate. The mystery was finally solved when, during research for my family tree, I discovered that his mother, Jane Crow (my great grandmother) had, at the time of John's birth, been married to a James Cavanagh. John's birth certificate revealed that he was actually registered as John Cavanagh and, having subsequently discovered that John's father James was killed four years afterwards, I can only assume that his mother thereafter reverted to her maiden name once more. Whatever the reason, John Cavanagh thenceforth was known as John Crow.

Armed with this new information I was able to quickly locate John's death certificate at Blantyre Registrar's Office registered under his true name of John Cavanagh, usual residence 19 Miller Street, Blantyre. This death certificate clearly shows his parents as James Cavanagh and Jane Cavanagh, m.s. Crow.

Previous researchers correctly recorded John Cavanagh from this death certificate when compiling their lists, but were mislead by the newspaper reports and the Dalbeth Cemetery internment book into adding John Crow's name to their list also. Indeed, looking at some of the lists of the victims which are available, you can actually see both names, almost side by side, both with the same address in Miller Street, Blantyre. From these previous sources the number certified as killed in the Blantyre Explosion was given as 216. In view of my finding, I suggest that the correct figure was therefore 215.

As a postscript to the events surrounding the aftermath of the explosion, a fitting tribute to the many unsung heroes who risked their own lives as they endeavoured to rescue the hapless 215 victims was contained in the following *Daily Telegraph* report;

"The British miner can fight with as much 'strength and majesty' as the British soldier. If one falls in the imminently deadly breech, another coolly takes his place and carries on the assault with a sublime unconsciousness of any odds that may be against him. So it was at High Blantyre. When a disabled hero (rescuer) was brought back to bank and carefully covered with earth to free him from the influences of poisonous gas, ten more were eager to descend into the depths and risk a similar fate, or worse. We are glad to think that there are thousands upon thousands of men in these islands who know that they themselves would have done the same had they been present, yet few are able to realise the circumstances amid which the noble Scotsmen proved their bravery and devotion.

A battlefield is ghastly enough, and its horrors might well appal those who look upon them. The soldier, however, has all the excitement of personal conflict, and sometimes a burning thirst for revenge to sustain him; whereas in the High Blantyre mine, the rescuers struggled against an invisible foe, who's distinctiveness was evidenced on every side in the most horrible forms.

In due course of time, when the two hundred plus bodies shall have been brought up, and consigned by loving hands to their last resting place, the cause of the disaster will receive attention and the Government Inspector will make his report. But all of this has been done before and we seem as far off as ever from the ability to protect our miners against the dangers that surround their calling."

Group of Dixon's Miners c 1880

The Inquiry

While all of this was ongoing, Andra had to face another gruelling experience. In the aftermath of the explosion the miners had demanded a Public Inquiry and at a meeting in Hamilton a few days later chaired by Alexander McDonald M.P. miners' delegates from all of the Scottish Coal fields made it quite clear that they would settle for nothing less. The authorities duly acceded to their demands and the Inquiry was convened to take place in the Lanarkshire County Hall on the 11th of November, 1877.

The Government commissioners were Joseph Dickinson, the Mines' Inspector and Robert McLean, advocate. Alexander McDonald M.P. represented the Miners' National Association while an advocate from Edinburgh, Mr. Strachan, had been briefed by a number of the relatives of the deceased. In all, forty eight witnesses were examined, ranging from the colliery's manager and oversmen down to individual colliers and day-men. Because of their involvement in the previous explosion, the latter included Andra and his brother William.

Mr. McLean, opening the Inquiry, stated that,

> *"The occurrence was so appalling in itself and so deplorable and calamitous in its consequences, involving as it did so great a sacrifice of human life and rendering desolate the inhabitants of a whole district of this county, that it was judged right that there should be a searching investigation made, in order, if possible, to ascertain the cause of the catastrophe."*

He then *invited* all persons who had a knowledge of the subject to give their assistance and co-operation, in order that it might be as full, complete and satisfactory as possible.

This simple statement which appeared to reassure the victims that all of those involved, owners and miners alike, would make themselves available for cross examination, was immediately 'blown out of the water' by a statement from Mr. Timothy Warren a Glasgow solicitor who was representing the owners of the mine, Messrs. Dixon. He declared,

> *"I am merely here to watch the proceedings on their behalf. Messrs. Dixon, after due consideration, have resolved that it was their proper course in the meantime to take no active part in the inquiry, reserving to themselves, if they think fit, to be represented by counsel afterwards. In making this statement, however, I am anxious that the Commissioners should understand that Messrs. Dixon have every desire to afford them every facility and opportunity in order, if possible, to ascertain what the cause of the explosion was."*

This statement was immediately accepted by Mr. McLean and thus the sham that the Inquiry was to become was immediately highlighted for all to see.

Were an accident of such magnitude to occur in today's world where workers are protected by acts covering Health And Safety at Work, it is easy to envisage the furore there would be if the company involved was merely *invited* to attend the inevitable Inquiry that would follow - with the option to decline the invitation if they so wished. Such was the way society was organised to safeguard the interests of the ruling classes at this time however. Mr. Warren had chosen his words carefully in advising the Inquiry that Messrs. Dixon reserved the right to appear *'if they think fit.'* What he was saying in effect was that, even before the Inquiry had got under way, they accepted no responsibility for the actions (or lack of it) of the managers, firemen etc, who were employed by them to maintain a safe environment for the miners to work in. By his judicious use of words he was letting both those who were conducting the Inquiry and the miners know exactly where they stood as far as culpability was concerned.

The importance attached to the earlier explosion involving the McAnultys was evinced by the fact that almost the first person questioned in the Inquiry was Mr. Frederick Duncan. He was asked by Mr. Strachan, to produce the statutory report books relating to No. 2 and No. 3 pits. Mr. Duncan, after admitting that not all of the books were available, produced some of them for examination. Inspection of these revealed that in the three months period covering both explosions there were quite a number of days where no reports were entered, including of course the day that Joseph was killed and Andra badly injured. According to official management records therefore, which by the Act passed in 1872 was supposed to indicate all such incidents, there had been no gas, no explosion and no one had been killed or injured. There was also no record of any gas having been seen in the pits during the three months prior to the disaster. *"Is it not the fact that there was some and that it exploded with fatal results,"* he was asked. *"Yes, I believe so,"* he replied.

The next witness, John Pickering the oversman at No. 3 pit, had a simple explanation for this. According to him, on the days that had no reports entered and were unsigned, the firemen involved were *'off badly'* and the firemen who had assumed their responsibilities had merely neglected to enter the reports and sign them as well as their own. What he neglected to say and wasn't even asked was that, as oversman, he was ultimately responsible to the manager J. Watson for ensuring that these report books were correctly filled in every day. What he also neglected to say was that, if the presence of gas in general or the earlier explosion in the stoops been noted in the report books, according to the Act of 1872 the following procedure should have been complied with thereafter,

> *'No powder shall be taken into the mine or be in possession of any person in the mine, except in accordance with the following regulations:- During three months after any inflammable gas has been found in such mine and if the said inflammable gas issued so freely that it showed a blue cap on the flame of the safety lamp, it shall only be used when the persons ordinarily employed in the mine are out of the mine or out of the part of the mine where it is used.'*

John Pickering, J. Watson and others involved knew that there was gas in this part of the mine and that there had been a fatal explosion several weeks prior to the disaster. Despite this, he/they knew also that thereafter powder was not only taken into the mine on a daily basis but that it was often carried in wrapped in newspaper, as was testified by a number of later witnesses. He/they also knew that shots were fired indiscriminately by miners themselves, as and when they liked. The real reason that this part of the Act was ignored by one and all was simply one of expediency, i.e. production.

Had the Act been complied with in respect of moving the men out of the mine or part of the mine while shots were fired by competent people, coal output would have been reduced accordingly. This would not have suited Watson in particular as he was ultimately responsible to the owners for production. The callous owners of course were only interested in profit. They cared little about everyday working practices and would have quickly replaced Watson if they thought he wasn't managing to extract the maximum amount of coal from the pit on a daily basis. The miners too, who were ill paid to begin with and who were in the main totally ignorant of the safety rules, were for their part intent only on filling as many hutches as possible. To them fewer hutches filled meant less wages.

This, as far as the miners were concerned, however should not have been the case, if one considers the testimony of a miner called George Speirs who had lost two sons in the explosion. He told the Inquiry of a conversation he had overheard between the fireman Willie Black and the contractor called Peter Carlin about the danger of further explosions in the stoops where Joseph McAnulty had been killed. Black had told Carlin that he should stop using powder in that area because of the, 'great danger'. Carlin had replied that if he had to stop blasting in that area he would have to be paid a better price for extracting the coal without the use of the explosives. Black had then advised him to go to the oversman Joseph Gilmour who was responsible for fixing the prices that the workmen got for the coal. Unfortunately Black, Carlin and Gilmour all lost their lives in the explosion so were not available for questioning on this matter. This "production at all costs mentality" allied to the slack procedures in the mine ensured that the disaster was literally an accident waiting to happen.

Further proof of this slackness was forthcoming in the testimony of fireman J. Little who, when questioned, said that no one in management had called his attention to the Act regarding procedures to be adopted in the event of gas being in the workings but he had read them. He said that he had understood the rule but agreed, when further questioned that the ordinary working people were not sent out of the mine when the shots were fired at two levels. He was then asked if any competent person e.g. himself, was appointed to examine the places before the firing took place and who in fact fired them. He replied that he had never been authorised to fire them and that the men went and lighted them as they liked. The Act had never been complied with in the pit as far as he knew.

Because of their involvement in the earlier explosion Andra and his brother William were called for questioning by Mr. Strachan on the 15th. of November, this being the fourth day of the Inquiry. Bearing in mind that Andra (who was still suffering from his injuries) was still eight days short of his seventeenth birthday and William had reached a mere fifteen years old only six days previously and that, in addition, their minds were still in a state of turmoil as they waited and wondered if their father's body was going to be recovered, this must have been a further traumatic experience for them both.

Andra told me that he was asked to sit in a hard chair facing a table at which sat the Government commissioners, Mr. McLean the advocate and several of their entourage.

At the prompting of Mr. Strachan the miners' advocate he stated;

> *"I live at Dixon's Row, Stonefield, Blantyre and I am sixteen years of age. I was down one morning in No.2 pit, Blantyre with my brothers Joseph and William. He had a contract for working out the stoops. I was laying rails with my brother Joseph when the gas exploded at my naked light. We were both severely burned. I was burnt on my hands, arms and back and my brother was so badly burned that he died at ten o'clock that night. I have been unable to work since the accident because the sinews of my arm are contracted. All the persons around the place were using naked lights because no person had ever told us to be careful with naked lights. I have never been back at the pit since then and no person from the mine has come to make an inquiry about what had happened that day. A policeman came to me twice to tell me to come to Hamilton because the fiscal wanted to see me."*

Andra also testified that no one from the colliery had called to see him after the explosion. Mr. McLean did not seem interested in this revelation. Tellingly, he only had one question of this key witness. All he wanted to know was how far away his brother William had been from the blast and whether he too had been burned.

His brother William, when questioned by Mr. Strachan confirmed that all of the men were using naked lights and that William Black the fireman was working near them when the explosion took place. He had said nothing about fire, nor had anyone else. William further stated,

> *"The second day after the explosion the Government inspector came down the pit. I had not seen him before and he did not speak to me. The day before he came we were put to work with gauze lamps given to us by William Black the fireman. The men who got the lamps were at the stoopings but about twenty yards from there open lights were still used. Blasting went on regularly at The Stoopings until I left there. The powder was taken into the mine by Peter Carlin the contractor. He sometimes took it in a paper and sometimes in a can. He took it loose and the men made it into cartridges where the lamps were trimmed. Shots were frequent and on firing we all came outside The Stooping. The fireman fired the shots and he always used an open light to fire them.*
>
> *There was always gas lying in the waste about us and we were told once by Mr. Pickering when he was the fireman there not to lift our lights, as if we lighted it up it would kindle. Mr. Black was not there at that time. About six weeks ago we could not get in on account of it. It was well known to all of the men that there was gas lying about the waste and Mr. Gilmour the oversman was often there.*

Mr. Watson (the manager) I only saw there once or twice the whole time I was in the pit. I left The Stoopings because I was getting afraid. The gas was a constant subject of conversation amongst the men who worked there."

Mr. McLean, who let us not forget was conducting the Inquiry, asked several superficial questions about how long his brother Joseph had had the contract to work in the stoops (three or four months) and whether or not there had been any other explosions before the one involving his brothers. The only pointed question, again of a key witness, was when he asked him to confirm that Pickering had told them not to raise their lights in case the gas kindled.

Working at the Coal Face

Both of the brothers had now told the Inquiry of many contraventions of the Act before the disaster and Mr. McLean had miserably failed in his duty by not asking these two youths to clarify any of the points made by them, so that he might have as clear and objective a view of what the *real* working practices were in the mine. Andra told me that if he had been truly interested in finding out the facts he would have asked. He didn't ask so Andra and William, despite their tender years, were astute enough to draw their own conclusions.

Andra could not understand why those conducting the Inquiry were not interested in the fact that no one from the colliery had contacted either of the brothers since their fatal incident. There had been widespread anger amongst the crowds in the immediate aftermath of the main explosion about the failure of the owners and management to learn lessons from the McAnulty incident. This anger had only been stemmed by the intervention of Alexander Macdonald the miners' leader when he assured them that he would demand a comprehensive inquiry into *both* events. Clearly, despite this demand, this was not happening.

All of this had been widely reported in the national newspapers and the coal owners and the Government inspector must have been fully aware of the inferred connection between the two incidents. The Inspector of Mines had apparently gone down to the scene of the explosion involving the McAnulty brothers three days after it happened but hadn't deemed it necessary thereafter to question either of the two people who had survived the incident. William, after all, was at the scene of the incident when the inspector visited it. Why then did he ignore him as testified by William?

According to Andra, William and his fellow workmen had been astonished that the Government inspector had failed to speak to him about the accident when he visited the scene. In light of future events it is highly possible that had the inspector conducted a more thorough investigation into their incident and the causes thereof, the greater tragedy which cost the lives of over two hundred men might have been avoided. His failure to speak to either William or Andra was bad enough but there was, in my opinion, an even more blatant example of the irresponsible manner in which he carried out his investigation, namely his failure to consult the record book.

It had been shown quite clearly at the beginning of the Inquiry that the record books for the period covering the McAnultys' incident contained no entries relating to the explosion or indeed to the presence of gas in the area. If the inspector was conducting a proper investigation into the incident he would surely have consulted the record book to see what description of the matter had been written therein. Examining such books to see if the 1872 Act was being complied with was, after all, part of his job. Had he looked at the book, of course, he would have seen only a blank page for the day in question as was witnessed at the Inquiry. That this page was still blank at this time can only lead me to one conclusion therefore. Either he had looked at it and was unconcerned that the explosion hadn't been recorded or, as is the more obvious reason, he had failed to examine it as he was required to do so by law. Whichever of these is true it seems to confirm how superficial his investigation was. The report of the accident that he submitted was subsequently referred to at the Inquiry, the gist of which was that, 'there had been some laxity.' This begs the question, laxity by whom?

To any fair minded person this failure by the inspector to search out the truth regarding the incident, which would appear to have been a precursor to the later disaster, would appear to be a major cause for concern. Mr. McLean in his opening statement had assured everyone that a *'searching investigation would be made to ascertain the cause of the catastrophe'.* Fine words indeed but his abject failure to pursue this point with the inspector was yet another indication of the direction the Inquiry was going. Little wonder that the miners and the relatives of the deceased were already beginning to suspect that the Inquiry was for cosmetic purposes only. Andra said that when he and William returned to their vigil at the pit head after taking part in the Inquiry the consensus of opinion amongst the mining community was exactly that.

A succession of witnesses came and went and most told similar stories of how lax the discipline was in the mine both before and after the incident involving the McAnultys. One man, William Eadie, whose father had been a roads-man in the pit and who had perished in the disaster, told the Inquiry that his father had spoken to him several times of the gas that was in the mine and that he had never seen such carelessness in dealing with it before. He said his father had told him that he had spoken to Joseph Gilmour the oversman about the carelessness of those in management in the pit and that he believed that there was not a competent fireman there who knew anything about working with gas. According to his father Mr. Gilmour had said that he could not ask a competent man to work for the wage that was being paid.

Another witness, A. Gardiner, was asked if he remembered when Joseph McAnulty was killed in the pit and if he'd had a conversation with Black the fireman about gas being in the pit before that explosion. In reply he stated,

> *"Black and I had a crack about it after it was over and he told me that he had been telling Joe Gilmour (the oversman) about this gas and he did not see how they could come upon him (Black) after he had reported the thing to Gilmour."*

He was then asked if he understood that he was saying that Black had told him that he had reported to Joe Gilmour that there was gas in the place *before* the death of Joseph McAnulty. *"Yes,"* he replied. He also confirmed that Black had told him that he thought he had done his duty when he reported the gas to Gilmour and that Mr. Ralph Moore the Government Inspector, who was present at the time of the conversation, could confirm that this conversation had taken place. This testimony would seem to confirm the evidence of G.Speirs earlier regarding the conversation between Black and Gilmour. It is significant also that Mr. Ralph Moore was never asked about this conversation, which allegedly took place in his presence.

Witness John Neil said that he used powder every day that he had bought in the ironmonger's shop and brought into the mine, loose in his pocket. He said he only saw the oversman Joe Gilmour about once a fortnight and that, on one occasion when they had gone down the pit, Gilmour had told them that there was gas in the place but *'not much of it'* and that they should *'give it a wee bit of a "dicht"* (wipe) *with our waistcoat or our bunnet (cap).'*

Neil and his neighbour had left the pit the next day because they didn't like the gas that was about. They also considered that they weren't being properly paid for the work they did.

Various experienced witnesses thereafter provided a lot of technical information regarding, amongst other things, the ventilation system that was in operation at the time of the disaster and the bratticing (screening) system that was in situ to control the direction of the flow of air. Reading transcripts of their testimonies it would appear that the consensus of opinion was that, because of the vast and complicated spread of the underground workings in what was the deepest pit in Lanarkshire, with its labyrinth of rooms and stoops and the miles of roadway connecting these, it was far from ideal.

Plans that were shown and discussed indicated that in some instances the air current was first sent through areas that were known to be gassy, picking up gas as it went along, after which it passed through 'clean' sections on its return journey. There were also many instances of bratticing having collapsed due to roof falls and other reasons. There was also evidence of miners having built screens around areas that were being worked by them because they considered that the current of air was too strong for comfort on occasion.

Almost the last witness to be interviewed was the colliery manager, Mr. James Watson. Mr. Watson was represented by Mr. Robertson, a solicitor from Glasgow. Before giving any evidence to the Inquiry Mr. Watson was advised that previous evidence given had implicated the management and that anything that he might say could be used as evidence against him. 'Could' turned out to be the operative word.

Mr. Watson said he had been working with several others at the pit-head installing a new cage into the mouth of the shaft when the explosion occurred and had himself received burns to the face and arms. He had been unable to work since that time.

Prompted by his solicitor, Mr. Robertson, he testified that he had been the manager of the colliery for six years and that in that time approximately 882,430 tons of coal had been taken out of the four pits that had been sunk. He was asked by Mr. Robertson to state to the Commissioners how many fatal accidents, if any, had occurred in working this quantity of coal. He replied that the only fatal accident had been that of Joseph McAnulty.

He said that the accident had been caused by an explosion of firedamp and that he had gone down to the scene of the incident the same afternoon and discovered that some of the roof had fallen. He had found evidence of firedamp emanating from the hole in the roof and was sufficiently concerned to issue instructions that closed gauze lamps should be used in that section thereafter. The chief fireman in that part of the pit was William Black but his assistant John Sharp had been detailed to look after the lamps and see that no one approached near The Stoopings with a naked light. Sharp had later been succeeded by another fireman, Robert Eadie.

Mr. Watson, questioned further by his solicitor Mr. Robertson, said that he had not seen evidence of gas in any quantity in any other places in the pit as to render the use of naked lights as dangerous. He was then asked if he had ever spoken to the firemen about the absence of any reference to firedamp in their reports. He replied that he had frequently spoken to them about it and that he had never heard of anyone being told to "dicht" the gas out of places they were working in and would not have allowed such a thing to be done. Since the McAnulty incident he had only had one verbal report from Gilmour the oversman about a sufficient quantity of firedamp in The Stoopings to cause the men to be withdrawn from their place of working (but not from the pit) but in a short time they had been able to resume their work again as the firedamp had cleared away.

At this point in the proceedings it was reported in the *Hamilton Advertiser* that Mr. Robertson complained that the witness under examination was being disconcerted by the gestures and remarks of Mr. Alexander Macdonald M.P. who was present at the Inquiry. He said that Mr. Macdonald's position at the Inquiry was anomalous. Mr. Macdonald responded to this by stating that he had a perfect right to be there and make any gesture he liked. The Act of Parliament was plain, clear and unmistakable and every effort had been made on the part of the gentleman who had just spoken to get the witness he was examining to evade the Act - to make light of it.

As the Inquiry continued Mr. Watson, was cross examined by Mr. Strachan who was acting on behalf of some of the bereaved families. When questioned about the rate of wages paid to the oversmen in comparison to other pits, Watson said that they were paid about a shilling a day less than those employed by *coal-masters* but Messrs. Dixon were *iron-masters* (so called because they owned iron/steel works) and their rates compared with other iron-masters . (Considering that they were removing coal from the pit this seemed like a good arrangement for Messrs. Dixon!) Despite the lower wage, he said, they had no difficulty in getting thoroughly efficient men for the wages that were given. He said that the roads-men and firemen were generally appointed by the oversman but they were required to acquaint him with the man so that he could be satisfied that he was a competent person.

Mr. Watson, when asked if abstracts of the Act and special rules were supplied to the oversmen, stated that they were and they were instructed to distribute them amongst the firemen and other officers that required them. He also said when questioned that the Government Inspector and Assistant Government Inspector frequently inspected the mine. They had never thereafter made any complaint to him regarding the mode of working.

When asked how often he was down in the workings in the course of a normal week, he said that he was sometimes down every day but that on average he was down about four times a week. He usually went down about half past six in the morning and was down for about three or four hours at any one time. In answer to various questions, he said that every part of the workings was familiar to him from personal examination and it was his special object that everything which care and skill could do for the safety of the workmen should be attended to. He had prohibited the blasting of powder in the stoops *about a week after* the McAnulty incident and, when questioned specifically on the point, stated that powder was always taken down the mine in canisters and that he had no knowledge of it ever being taken down any other way. He considered the pit to be very well ventilated and considered the mine to be a safe one in every way.

Mr. Watson said that at the time of the explosion he had been working at the pit-head with several others installing a new cage in the mouth of the shaft. Before commencing this operation they had placed four wooden planks over the pit mouth, each plank measuring eleven inches in width. This was a safety measure to prevent anybody from falling in to the shaft while they were working and they had been placed there about thirty minutes before the explosion. Lower down the shaft, three planks each measuring twelve inches in width were also placed across the shaft.

He was then asked if it ever occurred to him that the ventilation was in such a state that it might be affected by these two sets of beams. He replied that he considered that there was still sufficient area not covered to allow plenty of air to go through. He was then asked if he was aware that previous evidence had indicated that, at the time of the explosion, only one of the two underground ventilating furnaces was operating fully, the other having only a small fire at the back of the grate while it was being cleaned. He replied that he had seen this reported in the newspapers and agreed that this would decrease the ventilating power but the decrease wouldn't amount to a great deal. It was then pointed out to him that two sources of decreased ventilation had now been revealed and was asked if he could think of any others. He couldn't.

Mr. Strachan, in continuing his cross examination, then attempted to verify information that he had received that Mr. Watson was paid a smaller salary than was paid to other managers at other collieries. Mr. Watson's solicitor objected to this and the question was not answered. Mr. Watson was then questioned about the statement he had made about his firemen being paid the same wages as firemen in other collieries in the district. He replied that what he had said was that the wages were the same as were paid in other collieries owned by *iron-masters* but he had to agree with Mr. Strachan that Dixon's was purely a coal mine. Because, however, the owners termed themselves *iron-masters* they followed the common practice of paying a lower rate in coal mines owned by them than was paid in mines owned by *coal masters*. This unfair practice carried out by Messrs. Dixon was further indication of their greed and also their attitude towards their work force.

Mr. Strachan then subjected Mr. Watson to some rigorous questioning about his previous statement that there had been no previous accident in the pit arising from firedamp before the McAnulty incident. First he was asked if he knew about the deaths of two men called Robert Pollock and John Kerr who had been killed in a firedamp explosion four years previously when they were sinking a shaft. When he replied that he did, he agreed that he had not mentioned this the day before when questioned.

He also agreed in answer to another question that, prior to the McAnulty incident, a man named Morrison had been killed when he had fallen down the shaft of No. 2 pit.

Mr. Watson was then asked if he knew that a book had been produced which had commenced on 15th. February, 1876 and which contained copies of notices sent to the inspector of mines, which indicated that there had been fourteen accidents in the pit, several of which were fatal. The accident in which Mr. Morrison was killed was not however one of those recorded in the book. Mr. Watson said that he was unaware of this book and was then advised that all of the reports had been signed by him. When asked to examine the book he then stated that he, *'knew all about these accidents'.*

Questions were then put to Mr. Watson regarding the evidence given to the Commission by John Pickering the fireman. When he was asked if he was aware that Mr. Pickering had stated in his evidence that on three occasions when acting as fireman he was compelled to prevent the men from going down in consequence of the presence of gas in the mine, he replied that he had read his evidence. Why then, he was asked, had he stated previously that he had never heard of gas being present to any extent before this in No. 2 pit? *"I do not remember,"* was his answer. When asked if he remembered seeing entries made in the book at that time about these instances he said that he had. Why then, if he remembered this he was asked, could he now say that he had no recollection of these things having taken place? *"It might have escaped my memory,"* was his lame reply.

He was then invited to comment on evidence given by various people about gas being in the mine and in particular one statement that men had been sent away from the stoops only one week before the disaster because of the presence there of a quantity of gas. He said he was unaware of these things and that the only explanation he could give was that the men must have been keeping the information from him. When asked if there would have been any motive for the men keeping such a serious matter from himself, the certificated manager of the mine, he said he reluctantly agreed that he did not think they would.

Questioned about his statement that he inspected the workings four times a week, he was asked if he was aware that his fireman John Pickering had testified that he, Mr. Watson, was only in the pits once a fortnight. He said that he was not aware that this had been said. When questioned about this further he said that he had read in the newspapers that another two of his firemen, Mr. Little and Mr. McCall had also told the Commission that he was only down the pit every two or three weeks. After being told that several other people had said similar things he was asked how this reconciled with him saying that he was sometimes down there every day. *"It is quite possible that I might have been in the pits without being seen by these persons,"* he replied.

50

When it was put to him that these men were constantly down the pit from six in the morning till four in the afternoon and that it didn't seem possible that they would not see him during this time, he said that possibly he was following them or they might be following him. Asked if he ever went round with John Pickering he said that he had on many occasions but when prompted he was unable to say how often.

Mr. Strachan then asked Mr. Watson if he thought that a person who had never read or knew the regulations in the Act of Parliament, or the special rules of the pit, was a proper person to discharge the duties of a fireman. Mr. Watson replied that he did not think that any of the firemen would be ignorant of these. Mr. Strachan stuck to this point and asked him again to comment on their suitability for the job if they were ignorant of the Act. Mr. Watson then agreed that they would not be suitable if this were the case.

He was then asked if he was aware that four of his firemen, Simkin, Wood, Hendry and Sharp had all stated before the commission that they were in that position. Mr. Watson's reply to that was that it was the oversman's duty to supply them with the special rules. He was then asked if he withdrew his statement that he had personally reassured himself that they were competent to do the job before they were appointed. This he declined to do, insisting that they would know the nature and extent of any danger. When it was put to him again that these men, who never knew the regulations in the Act of Parliament and who had never read the special rules of the pit, were not properly qualified men to act as firemen, he stated, *"No. They could not do it properly."* When Mr. Strachan then asked him if these men were therefore unfit to discharge the duties for which he had appointed them, Mr. Watson's solicitor (Mr. Robertson) complained that this was not a competent question to put to him. This interjection caused Mr. Dickson the Commisioner to rule that, if the men were unacquainted with the rules and the Act, they were, in Mr. Watson's opinion, not properly qualified.

The questioning by Mr. Strachan then moved on to the incident when Joseph McAnulty was killed. He stated that the accident had occurred at The Stoopings but when it was put to him that Joseph's brother William had stated that he was about eight yards from The Stoopings when the explosion occurred Mr. Watson replied, *"I hardly think that he would be that."* When asked if William had any reason to tell anything but the truth he replied that, *"he doubted if William McAnulty was telling the truth because it would have been a very serious matter if gas had been lying about as far back as that from The Stoopings."* When asked if he had heard of this before he said that he hadn't and that he was under the impression that William McAnulty was in close at The Stoopings at the time of the explosion.

This last line of questioning and the answers given by Mr. Watson were, perhaps, the most significant in the whole Inquiry. Here we have the manager of the colliery who had supposedly investigated the incident thoroughly and submitted a report on it to the Government Inspector, revealing that he was under the impression that William McAnulty was in close at The Stoopings at the time of their explosion when, in fact, he was at least eight yards outside them as he had testified.

This was an undoubted admission that he had not spoken to William McAnulty about the incident at any time. Had he done so of course he would have realised that the gas, far from being confined to the stoops area, was in other areas outside of them in large quantities. Having realised this he might just have taken more positive action regarding the ventilation of that section of the mine. He might also have considered extending the area in which closed gauze lamps only were meant to be used. One or both of these actions could, conceivably, have averted the major disaster which followed.

When questioned about the ventilation method used to supply a current of air through the stoops in question he said that this was done by means of bratticing (screening) but admitted when questioned that the bratticing originally only controlled the air passing through two lower stoops. Bratticing for the upper stoop area was only fixed after the McAnulty incident. *"Did that explosion which killed McAnulty result from a defect in the ventilation or what was the cause of it?"* asked Mr. Strachan. *"I could not give an opinion as to that, further than by saying that if the place had been so ventilated at the time to carry off the gas there would have been none there,"* replied Watson.

Following this ambiguous answer Mr. Watson was then questioned about the fireman Sharp whom he said he had appointed to superintend the area after the McAnulty incident. He was asked if he had read in the papers that Sharp had admitted that he never knew the regulations and the Act of Parliament about working in dangerous places. Mr. Watson said that because Sharp had previously been a fireman in another colliery, he assumed that he knew the regulations.

When it was put to him that he had previously stated that Sharp had only been authorised to trim and lock the lamps and see to the safety of the men when fireman Black was not around, he agreed that he had said this. *"Why then,"* he was asked, *"had Sharp further testified that part of the duties he was given was to look after the blasting and discharge the shots."* Watson replied, *"I say that if there were any shots fired after the explosion when McAnulty was killed, it was in contravention of my imperative orders."*

When advised that Sharp and all other surviving persons who had worked in the stoops area had testified that blasting was carried out regularly in the area from the time that McAnulty was killed and that these shots had been fired by firemen Sharp and Eadie, he said that he was unaware of this activity. The following exchange then took place between Mr. Strachan and Mr. Watson;

Mr. Strachan	*"If this mine was under your daily supervision could this have gone on and you not known?"*
Mr. Watson	*"Yes, I believe so."*
Mr. Strachan	*"Was it not your duty as manager to see that those persons whom you had appointed to that place had discharged their duties?"*
Mr. Watson	*"I did that by appointing an oversman there who was constantly in the mine for the purpose of seeing that these other officers did their duties faithfully."*
Mr. Strachan	*"Did you think you had discharged your duty by appointing Sharp?"*
Mr. Watson	*"Yes."*
Mr. Strachan	*"And you had nothing whatever to do with looking after him or seeing that he did discharge his duty?"*
Mr. Watson	*"I had decidedly to do with him."*
Mr. Strachan	*"What had you to do with him besides appointing him?"*
Mr. Watson	*"If he was not doing his duty I could have removed him and put another in his place."*
Mr. Strachan	*"You knew that that was a dangerous part of the mine?"*
Mr. Watson	*"Yes, I considered it a dangerous part."*
Mr. Strachan	*"And you knew that this man Sharp was discharging dangerous duties there. Did you think you were discharging your duty as manager by simply going there once a fortnight?"*
Mr. Watson	*"Yes."*
Mr. Strachan	*"If Sharp did carry on that system of blasting and firing shots all that time it was a dangerous thing was it not to fire shots with a naked light in a place where men were working with gauze lamps?"*
Mr. Watson	*"If I had not thought it dangerous I would not have forbidden the use of powder."*
Mr. Strachan	*"Was the system of ventilation adopted in the colliery devised by yourself alone?"*
Mr. Watson	*"Yes."*
Mr. Strachan	*"It has been suggested that the air in No. 2 and No. 3 pits had too far to travel and that it became impure before it came to the up-cast shaft. What is your knowledge with regard to that subject?"*

Mr. Watson	*"My knowledge is that it is not impure after travelling that distance."*
Mr. Strachan	*"You are aware that it has a considerable length to travel?"*
Mr. Strachan	*"Yes, I am quite aware of that but the current was good and the quantity of air was quite sufficient to dilute any gas that might escape."*
Mr. Strachan	*"What did you do to improve the ventilation after McAnulty was killed."*
Mr. Watson	*"We did not require to improve the ventilation further than to put up a little brattice to prevent any accumulation of gas taking place in the place where it was supposed to have accumulated when the explosion took place."*
Mr. Strachan	*"And was that all you did?"*
Mr. Watson	*"That was all. We had plenty of air to render harmless any gas that would be coming off."*
Mr. Strachan	*"You say you went to the place once a fortnight after McAnulty was killed?"*
Mr. Watson	*"Yes, I was there at least that."*
Mr. Strachan	*"When were you last there before the major explosion on the 22nd of October?"*
Mr. Watson	*"About a fortnight before it."*
Mr. Strachan	*"Then from your knowledge you cannot tell us what was the state of the ventilation or the state of the gas in these stoops for a fortnight before the explosion?"*
Mr. Watson	*"Not from my own knowledge."*
Mr. Strachan	*"You have read the evidence which has been given here by witnesses Docherty, McIver and McAnulty as to the large quantities of gas which were met with at the stoops prior to the explosion on 22nd October?"*
Mr. Watson	*"Yes."*
Mr. Strachan	*"Then if these witnesses are telling the truth, there was a failure of duty on the part of the fireman or those whom you had entrusted with the management of that part of the pit?"*
Mr. Watson	*"Yes, decidedly."*
Mr. Strachan	*"And of Gilmour the oversman?"*
Mr. Watson	*"Yes."*
Mr. Strachan	*"There could not have been such an accumulation of gas in the stoops unless there was a serious defect in the ventilation?"*
Mr. Watson	*"There must have been if such a thing had taken place."*
Mr. Strachan	*"Did you ever hear that Black, your fireman, had told Carlin the contractor for the stoops that he would require to give up blasting as the place was so dangerous?"*
Mr. Watson	*"No, not until this Inquiry."*
Mr. Strachan	*"Can you explain how that state of matters could have existed there and those things going on that the witnesses speak of, assuming them to be true, without coming to your knowledge?"*
Mr. Watson	*"I cannot tell."*
Mr. Strachan	*"Was it your practice when any men did speak to about matters connected with the pit to tell them to go to Gilmour?"*
Mr. Watson	*"No, it was not my practice. I have told several perhaps to go to Gilmour but it was not my regular practice."*
Mr. Strachan	*"Have you heard him swear to the men?"*
Mr. Watson	*"I have heard him give a bit oath occasionally but nothing very serious in my presence."*
Mr. Strachan	*"Do you or do you not know that he was in the habit of swearing at the men when they made any complaints to him or asked anything from him?"*
Mr. Watson	*No."*
Mr. Strachan	*"Did you ever hear of men having been dismissed for refusing to work at the stoops?"*
Mr. Watson	*"No."*
Mr. Strachan	*"Could that have been done by Gilmour without your knowing?"*
Mr. Watson	*"Yes. He had full power to employ or discharge workers."*

Any reasonable analysis of Mr. Watson's performance during cross examination would suggest that there were many inconsistencies in his testimony. For instance, is it credible that he could have been down in the pit four days a week for up to three or four hours at a time and not have been seen by so many people? Several of the people who testified that he was only down about once a fortnight were his own firemen, with whom he would presumably have interacted when he was underground. Why would each and every one of them lie?

If, as he claimed he only went to the stoops once a fortnight, is it not a likely supposition that this visit to the stoops was made during his actual fortnightly trips underground? If he had been down as often as he claimed is it not reasonable to assume that he would have visited this site oftener given the problems that he said he knew were there? By his own admission he knew that this was a dangerous place and one would have expected any responsible manager would, if he had been down as often as he claimed, have visited it regularly to ensure that all was well and that his instructions were being carried out.

When questioned about the ventilation in the area he at first said this was adequate. If it was adequate why then did he then state that, *'we did not require to improve the ventilation further than put in a little bratticing to render harmless any gas that that would appear?'* If he considered this action would eliminate the problem, why then did he instruct that closed gauze lamps be used thereafter and that no shots should be fired in the vicinity? There would surely have been no need for either measure if the gas accumulation had been eliminated. If, as he said, his correcting the problem with a *little* bratticing was enough to control the air current, why then did he thereafter agree that there could not have been such an accumulation of gas in the stoops unless there was a serious defect in the ventilation? This was surely an abject admission on his part that he had failed miserably to eliminate this virtual time bomb in the very heart of the mine.

Reading again the last part of his cross examination, one gets the distinct impression that Mr. Watson appeared to have left most of the day to day management of the mine workings to his oversman Joseph Gilmour, who sadly perished in the disaster and was not there to give his version of events leading up to the tragedy.

Based on what many witnesses had said, Mr. Strachan seems to have been implying that, on many occasions, when miners approached Mr. Watson with a problem he passed the problem to Joseph Gilmour. The oversman unfortunately seems to have been verbally abusive to the miners in many of these instances, which left the miners in an unenviable position. If they were to attempt to stand up to him there is every likelihood that they would have been dismissed for their troubles as had been testified. This, of course, not only meant the loss of their jobs but would result in them being immediately evicted from their company owned houses. In fairness to Joseph Gilmour it must be remembered that he too would possibly be under a lot of pressure to ensure that as much coal as possible was extracted from the mine in as short a time as possible. Any failure on his part to comply with instructions would no doubt have led to his demise as oversman.

One man who hadn't made himself available for questioning at the Inquiry was Mr. Charles Thompson, one of the partners of William Dixon (Limited). The manager (Mr. Watson), had testified that Mr. Thompson supervised his work by coming to the colliery occasionally to see how he was getting on and to consult with him about future operations that were to be carried out. Mr. Thompson had instructed him as to how the pits were to be sunk and the size they were to be. He further testified that there had also been proper consultation about the connections between one pit and another and the overall system of ventilation that was adopted in the colliery, which had been devised by himself (Mr. Watson) and had been approved of by Mr. Thompson before it was done. They consulted the plans about every six months to ascertain how the coal was to be worked out from the different seams. These plans showed the different workings and the air courses laid down to each extension and Mr. Thompson had never voiced any objection to them.

Tellingly, Mr. Watson revealed under questioning that Mr. Thompson had only been down No. 3 pit once since it opened nine months previously and was only down No. 2 pit *once or twice in the year.'* Here then we have a gentleman who, to all intents and purposes was in overall charge of supervising the running of the colliery on behalf of William Dixon (Limited), clearly quite happy to carry out this responsible task by merely looking at plans every six months or so. Theoretically he may have known what was going on but, in practical terms, by going underground only once or twice a year he could have known virtually nothing about the work (mal)practices that prevailed.

The Inquiry, which had opened in the County Hall in Hamilton on the 12th. of November ended on the evening of the 23rd. of November and Mr. McLean the advocate who had conducted the Inquiry, together with Mr. Dickinson, Inspector of Mines, retired to consider the evidence.

Miner with tally lamp (reproduced by kind permission of Guthrie Hutton)

The Aftermath of the Explosion

My grandfather Andra and his brother William had given their testimony on the 15th. and 16th. of the month respectively, following which they had resumed their vigil at the pit head as they awaited news of their father. During this time they, like all of the other families in a similar situation and indeed the whole village, had followed the proceedings in the Inquiry by means of the national and local newspapers. Andra said that the reports were the main topic of conversation at many a street corner and that he and other witnesses were avidly questioned about their experiences at the Inquiry when they returned to the village. Nothing that was revealed on a daily basis by the press or the witnesses did anything to alter the opinion of the villagers that the disaster had been caused by serious neglect on the part of the owners. From past experience however, they held out little hope of any blame being apportioned to them.

As they awaited the official report on the disaster, finally and inevitably after another week or so, it became obvious to themselves and everyone else that all of the unaccounted for miners must have been at the seat of the explosion and that, consequently, they must face the fact that all trace of them had been obliterated by the force of the blast. Mercifully their deaths would have been instantaneous and unlike many of the others, painless.

On the 6th. of December, 1877, after 45 days and nights of unimaginable anguish and little sleep as he watched and waited in vain to see if his father's body would be recovered (all this at a time when he should have been at home resting and recuperating from his own terrible injuries), Andra was given a certificate by another hero of the disaster, his mentor Dr. Grant, which stated officially that his father had been declared killed by an explosion of fire damp on the 22nd. of October, 1877. Peter, having successfully survived three previous personal disasters in other coal mines, had finally run out of luck. Dr. Grant, because of their previous acquaintance, once again demonstrated what a compassionate man he was, by spending some time with him as he attempted to reassure him that his father's death would have been instantaneous and that he would not have suffered in any way.

Later that day, assisted by close friends Patrick McQuade and Willie Lamont, he made the painful train journey to the Registrar's Office in Hamilton to present this death notice to have the death officially recorded. On the way back he told his friends that, having lost his mother and father and also his brother Joseph in such a short period of time and not even knowing where he and his brother William might be able to live in the future, he was entering the unknown as far as the rest of his life was concerned. Little did they, or indeed he, realise what an eventful and worthy life that would prove to be!

The final death toll of the disaster was given as 216 (see list at end of book) with a further 40 recorded as injured. Only 23 miners managed to get out alive. These depressing numbers, large though they were however, concealed the other victims of the disaster, the immediate relatives. According to the *Hamilton Advertiser* there were 105 widows and widowed mothers; 27 other adults whose breadwinner was killed in the accident; 255 children of widows, who were under 13 years of age; and 52 children of other aged and infirm parents; making a total of 439.

Andra said that the local community were quick to respond to their plight, as indeed were people throughout the country and the *Hamilton Advertiser* reported that a local Relief Committee was quickly set up in Blantyre, The Reverend Stewart presiding, which immediately received donations of cash from many quarters including a donation of £100 from Mrs. William Dixon. Simultaneously, at a meeting in Glasgow organised by the coal masters, a national relief committee was formed and first subscription lodged was one from the coal owners W. Dixon (Limited) for £1,000. This was followed by another for £500 from coal owners Merry & Cunninghame. Her Majesty, Queen Victoria donated £100.

From these two relief sources, Andra said that help was quick in coming and almost immediately the families concerned were each given a ticket for groceries for the current week to the extent of 5/- (25p) for each widow and 2/- (10p) for each child, plus 1/- (5p) for coals to provide heating in their homes. The *Advertiser* also reported that at a meeting held in the Blantyre Parish Church to procure mourning and ordinary clothing for the wives and families of the bereaved, the platform in front of the pulpit was piled high with dresses, bonnets and other items from various quarters and that a letter was read out from Lady Hamilton of Dalzell who was prepared to supply 90 mourning dresses, besides shawls, for widows. Other sources revealed that Queen Victoria had, in addition to a monetary donation, also donated lengths of black material to be distributed to the widows so that they could have them made into dresses or skirts. Two ladies were then assigned to each district to visit the destitute families and procure the requisite information as to their wants.

The enormity of the disaster stunned the nation and donations, large and small, poured in from towns and villages throughout the land. In all the magnificent sum of £48,137 was raised and the Relief Committee appointed a superintendent to inquire into the circumstances of each family involved to enable the committee to judge the amount of allowances that should be given to those who had been left unprovided for by the accident.

In their wisdom the weekly allowances awarded to individuals by the Committee was as follows;

A widow who had lost her husband and who was unable to work was given 7/6d (37 p);
> to a widow with one child, 9s (45p);
> to a widow with two children, 11s (55p);
> to a widow with three children 12/6d (62p);
> to a widow with four children, 14s (70p);
> to a widow with five children, 15s (75p);
> to a widow with six children, 16s (80p).

Based on a report by an actuary, it was estimated by the committee that by setting these amounts of compensation, the fund would continue to support the widows in their lifetimes and would sustain the children *until they reached the age of thirteen years*. Any widow unfortunate enough to have children who had already attained that age or were near to it was in an unfortunate position to say the least. Presumably the children who were that age or above or who would attain it in the near future were expected to be able to work to keep themselves!

Besides these allowances there were at the outset a number of cases to which temporary relief had to be given - to those who had been injured by the accident and were subsequently unable to support themselves.

This latter category is an interesting one because Andra, despite having been severely injured as a result of the previous explosion of gas, which everyone then and later acknowledged was a precursor to the disaster on the 22nd. of October, was advised that he wasn't eligible for an allowance from the fund. He was informed that the Executive Committee could make no exceptions to the rule that only those men who had been injured in the main explosion and were unable to support themselves qualified for relief. They said that his explosion was nothing to do with the main one and that, although he had lost his father, his brother William was able to work and so, in theory, was he!

Able to work of course he wasn't and indeed he was unable to return to work for a further three months. This wasn't his only immediate problem however as he and William had to find someone to take them in as boarders and, as he wasn't earning any wages, this was no little problem.

In these early days Andra said that it was unheard of for single people to live on their own even if they could have afforded it. When a single man of any age arrived in the village to start a new job his first task was to find board and lodgings. This was seldom difficult because most of the families were poor and they were only too pleased to augment their income by taking in a boarder. The fact that they were probably overcrowded before he arrived wasn't even considered and he himself would expect to have to share a bed with one or more of the males in the family anyway!

Andra told me that his fears were soon found to be unwarranted because his problem was quickly solved when he discussed it with his close friend Patrick McQuade. After a quick word with his mother Catherine, whose husband had been killed in a pit accident in the previous year and left her a widow at the age of thirty four, he said that she was more than willing to take William and himself in despite Andra's situation.

Including Patrick she had four children in the house already but she said that by using the 'hurley beds' for the two younger children, they would cope. When I asked Andra what 'hurley beds' were he said that they were low set wooden framed beds with small castor wheels attached to the base. This enabled them to be wheeled in and out from under the set in beds in the house.

I already knew what set-in beds were because I had seen them in my aunt Nellie's house in Baird's Rows in Low Blantyre. There were two of these which, as suggested by their name, were wooden framed beds which had been built into recesses in the side wall of the house on wooden battens and were approximately two feet above the stone floor, which was covered in waxcloth. The space underneath these beds usually had one or two trunks or boxes which held the families few clothes and possessions. No fitted wardrobes in those early days!

Mary Crowe, author's Grandmother

Jean Crowe, author's Great-Grandmother

The Whitewash

Andra recollected that he and William had barely had time to settle in to their new surroundings when, on the 22nd. of November the first of two reports about the disaster were published.

The first such report, of which Andra still had a well thumbed copy (which is now in my possession), was prepared by the Government Inspectors of mines, namely Messrs. Ralph Moore, T.E. Wales and James Willis. Most of their report was technical but towards the end they deduced that,

> *'shot firing was stated to be prohibited but there seems to be no doubt that gunpowder was used at the stoops. It seemed also to have been freely used in other parts of the pit where naked lights were used. The shots were fired by miners instead of by a competent person appointed for the purpose and the powder was taken into the mine in canisters instead of in cartridges, as directed by the Act. Both from their inspections and from the evidence given at the Public Inquiry, they were of the opinion that gas was always present at the stoops and they considered that shot firing there, under such circumstances, was most dangerous and ought not for one moment to have been allowed. Upon the whole, the discipline of the mine was loose and the orders which the manager says he gave, as to shot firing in particular, seemed to have been neglected altogether. The pit had been too speedily opened up and this had necessitated great lengths of bratticing. This was common to all new pits but it should be practised as little as possible. The distances by which the air is to be conveyed to the 'coal faces' by bratticing should be reduced.*
>
> *Keeping in mind those matters and especially the present great calamity, we recommend that the present mode of working with naked lights and leaving the stoops comparatively unventilated be discontinued. Shot firing should be prohibited.'*

Although this report purported to be objective, it should be noted that Mr. Ralph Moore, the Government Inspector whose name was appended to the report had himself been down pits No. 2 and 3 on many occasions prior to the disaster, once notably immediately after the death of Joseph McAnulty. Bearing this in mind if, as was asserted in this report, - the mine had been opened up too speedily necessitating great lengths of bratticing - gas was always present at the stoops - there seemed to be no doubt that gunpowder was used at the stoops - the discipline in the mine was loose, questions have to be asked as to why this gentleman never took the appropriate action to have some or all of these highly unsuitable and even dangerous practices stopped.

If as he stated in the report, the pit had been opened up too quickly and there were great lengths of bratticing throughout the workings he couldn't possibly have failed to notice this on his trips underground. If so, why did he not use his authority to compel the management to develop the workings in a slower, safer manner?

If as stated in the report, gas was always present in the stoops which were in his words comparatively unventilated, why did he not use his authority to compel the management to have the area properly ventilated to prevent the accumulation of gas?

If as stated in the report, he was in no doubt that gunpowder was used at the stoops and that discipline in the mine was loose, is it not fair to assume that he had had a perfect opportunity to discover both of these facts in the immediate aftermath of the Joseph McAnulty fatality. The reality was that, almost unbelievably, when he accompanied the manager Mr. Watson to the scene of this incident he failed to question any of the workmen at the scene, including William McAnulty.

Had Moore done so and ascertained that gas was always present and that, despite this, naked lights were being used and shots fired by all and sundry, he might just conceivably have ensured thereafter that the appropriate preventative measures were taken to ensure that further explosions would be avoided. With the benefit of hindsight, I wonder if he ever thought of this in the aftermath of the disaster which followed several weeks later.

I personally consider that this man, by his negligence, was almost certainly to blame for the Blantyre Disaster, as it was known. Watson the manager and others were also culpable but, it could be said in their defence that they were under extreme pressure from the owners to obtain maximum production. Moore had no such pressures, in addition to which he had the power to enforce the necessary safety measures which would have averted the disaster. He failed miserably to do this.

When the report was published Andra said that he and the others in the village were divided in their opinions as to what it would achieve on their behalf. Some felt that there were sufficient criticisms made of the management and the working practices in the pit to ensure that the owners were held liable for the disaster. Others including himself were not so sure that this would be the case and decided to wait for publication of the main Inquiry Report before they formed an opinion. They were however not hopeful that it would attach any great blame to the owners and find in favour of the miners. In the event, their pessimism was fully justified when this report was published on the 21st of December by Mr. James McLean, the advocate who had conducted the Inquiry on behalf of the Government.

The direction the report was going in was highlighted almost immediately when reference was made to the qualifications and duties of the colliery manager Mr. James Watson. According to the report, Mr. Watson had, as required by law, presented himself to the examiners appointed by the Board for Examination of Colliery Managers and obtained a certificate of competency in 1872. So far so good.

The report then stated that Mr. Watson's practice was to be at the colliery regularly. He had surface duties as well as below ground to attend to. He daily met the oversmen of the different pits at breakfast time and was himself on average below ground about four times a week, the visits being sometimes twice a day when needed and depending considerably upon the reports made to him by the oversmen.

A special fireman, or competent person under the Act, was stationed at a part of the pit called The Stoopings where accumulated firedamp had been met up with.

How Mr. McLean, an esteemed advocate, could have listened to the evidence that was placed before the Inquiry and interpreted it in the above manner is almost beyond belief. Almost without exception, every witness had testified that they only saw James Watson down the pit every two or three weeks. Several of these witnesses were firemen who had been appointed by him and had no reason to lie. Despite this Mr. McLean chose to accept the manager's version of his activities.

He also opted to enter in the report that a special fireman or competent person under the Act was in charge of affairs at The Stoopings. This same fireman, J. Sharp had actually testified at the Inquiry that he was ignorant of the regulations in the Act as was his colleague Robert Eadie, so the discrepancy between the reality of the situation given in evidence and the conclusion reached in the report is difficult to comprehend to say the least.

The ventilation of the pit was described in detail in the report and at one point noted that,
> *"the working places or rooms had bratticing or temporary partitions for sending air through the coal faces. These were very numerous and consequent upon each stoop not being completed or cut round before driving in advance and commencing others, the length of bratticing was extraordinary. There was a total length of 2,271 yards, or more that a mile and a quarter of temporary bratticing."*

My interpretation of this is that, because the pit was being opened out too quickly the ventilation system was struggling to keep up with it and too many temporary, inadequate means of ventilation were being used.

When reporting on the lighting and blasting in the pits Mr. McLean observed that open oil lamps were ordinarily used in working and that safety lamps were used where much firedamp had been met with. At the part of the colliery known as The Stoopings where accumulated gas was being met with, safety lamps had been in use at the time of the explosion. Blasting was allowed in the lower part of the seam but it is said by the manager to have been forbidden by him at The Stoopings, but it was practised there and the shots were fired by the special fireman.

Here then, we have an acceptance by Mr. McLean that although safety lamps were being used because of gas, shots were being fired in the area. He qualifies this by stating that these shots were being fired by the special fireman whom we have already noted had confessed that he was ignorant of the special regulations covering these situations.

Mr. McLean then reported his findings on the firedamp which was ordinarily given off in the mine in general. He stated that when the miners were beginning to drive out the south level from the shaft of No. 2 pit, the ordinary issue of gas was such as to overpower the ventilation and apparently no means were taken to prevent this, either by lessening the speed of driving or by widening the places so as to give more air at a velocity safe for the safety lamp. The return air, after leaving the gassy Stoopings area, passed through several places where persons were working with naked lights.

The main thrust of this section of his report concentrated on the gas in the stoops area. He first alluded to the explosion which had killed Joseph McAnulty and said that an accumulation of firedamp had occurred when a section of the roof fell and this had ignited at the open lights being used by the McAnulty brothers who were working nearby, fatally injuring one of them. Gauze lamps were put in use there next day and a special fireman who was a competent person was appointed to take charge of The Stoopings. The Government Inspector had visited the place on the third day after the explosion and in his official report he stated that, 'there had been some laxity.'

Mr. McLean noted that firedamp was found at times in high volumes. Two entries of gas appear in the firemen's books but other evidence showed that gas was oftener met with than that. It was well known to the miners that there was gas about. The issues from the roof coal were often such as to get lighted and small accumulations near the roof were common and had at times to be batted or wafted out, called "dichting".

Based on evidence given at the Inquiry, Mr. Mclean concluded that Mr. Gilmour the oversman had been spoken to about the gas and he had replied, *"There was no danger, there will be not a man fallen in the pit."* In fact it kept getting worse. On Friday, three days before the explosion, things seemed to be coming to a crisis so Black, the head fireman, spoke to Carlin the contractor at The Stoopings as to the great danger of blasting there. He asked him to arrange with the oversman Mr. Gilmour a price for working the coal without blasting.

Partial stagnation of the air then ensued and a steam or mist is said to have set in. Sharp the fireman said it was powder smoke but the men said it was not. Sharp or Eadie, the other fireman fired the shots, opening their safety lamps to do so, *"watching a chance to fire the shots."* Neither of them liked the job. Eadie absented himself from it on the Friday and Saturday before the explosion, in consequence, as was stated by his son, of his apprehension of danger which he had named to him and which statement his son said could be confirmed by his mother and his aunt. His father said *"there was gas enough to blow the whirleys or pulleys off the pit-head frame".* The head fireman, Black, called at Eadie's house on the Saturday evening. As a result of this visit his father had returned to work on the Monday morning of the explosion and he and Black were amongst the dead.

So here again in this report we have confirmation the pits had been driven out too speedily and that necessary safety measures were neglected at the expense of production. The report freely acknowledges that the preponderance of evidence proved that gas, often in high volumes, was frequently there and that the men often had to comply with the instruction to, *"bat or 'dicht' it out with their waistcoat or bunnet."* Out to where one has to ask! The evidence also showed that it was pointless complaining to Gilmour the oversman because of his indifference to the danger. It is worth noting also that the special, competent firemen were, despite their apprehension, still firing shots with naked lights.

In view of this section of Mr. McLean's report, it is again difficult to comprehend why he acknowledged all of this as being evidence honestly given as to the real working practices underground but still prefaced his report with an acceptance of Mr. Watson, the colliery manager's testimony that he was down this pit at least four times a week for three or four hours and sometimes as often as twice a day. Did he really believe that Watson could be there almost every day and not smell or see the gas which was often evident in large quantities? Did he seriously believe that Watson could be down so often and not, even on the odd occasion, hear or see the shots being fired? Could Watson be there so often and fail to see the mist which was hanging in the air? Not many fair minded people would think that this was credible.

The miners from the firemen down were clearly anxious about the dangers but any protests that they might make would, once again, be tempered with the knowledge that if they overstepped the mark they could forfeit not only their jobs but their homes also. How fortunate was Andra's brother William who, as he had testified, left The Stoopings about two weeks before the disaster because he was afraid. He had gone to work on the night shift in another part of the underground workings and providently had come up from there about two hours before the blast.

The report by Mr. McLean, when describing the actual explosion, stated that it had extended throughout miles of the workings and was of the most violent kind. The gas in a large portion of the workings had been mixed in a most explosive state. The force seemed to have been most violent in No. 2 pit especially in the area of the stoops which had been one of the noted places for yielding gas. Some human bodies were torn asunder. Props were driven out and air or trap doors and wooden bratticing shattered and tramways torn up. Rails, sleepers and debris being mixed together as if they had been fired from a gun.

In respect of the causes of the explosion, Mr. McLean stated that having apparently gas likely to have been in existence sufficient to account for the explosion, it might be assumed that it was needless to look for other causes. It was alleged however by some that, had the ventilation been in the state described, the explosion would probably have happened sooner. Exceptional circumstances were then surmised. These consisted of the possibility of an outcome of gas, escape of air such as might occur from the leaving open of a trap door or the fall of roof in an airway. All of these were considered but there was no direct evidence to support any of these theories.

The contributing causes that would have had an effect in leading to the explosion were indicated in the report as being;

(1)   The mine had been opened out too rapidly. One of the oversmen had stated that he had never seen a colliery so rapidly opened, whether non-fiery or fiery. It appeared that in stoop and room working, it was an old rule in Scotland to have each stoop formed before beginning others beyond. This in order that one stoop-length only may depend on bratticed air. Here

rooms were driven in advance before the 'througher' or cut through had been completed. Work was opened out as speedily as possible in every direction from both pits, the thought appearing not to have occurred that in a fiery mine the openings should be few and, unless the surplus ventilation is great, driven slowly to allow the gas time to get vent.

(2) The excessive bratticing consequent on a large number of places being worked and the additional lengths consequent upon the rooms not being cut through as described. The bratticing seems to have been well attended to but it is scarcely within human power to keep a pit safe and clear of gas with more than a mile and a quarter of bratticed air, without counting the north side of No. 2 pit.

(3) The fallen coal at The Stoopings at times hindered the air.

(4) Men also had on a few occasions been found with screens put up to shelter themselves from the air current. This to some extent interfered with free ventilation.

(5) Four planks were put across one of the three compartments into which No. 3 shaft was divided and they had remained there during the half hour immediately preceding the explosion. These planks went across the 8 foot width of the shaft, each plank being 11 inches in width, making an area of 26 feet 8 inches, to which extent they blocked the air. There was still an area of 165 square left. The restriction being at the entrance would also increase the suck or pull of the furnace upon the mine and therefore cause more firedamp than usual to be drawn out of the coal and from the accumulated gas at The Stoopings. In a mine with the ventilation closely verging on the explosive point, *this may have turned the balance.*

(6) At 7.15 a.m. on the morning of the explosion the cubeman (man who tended the furnaces used for ventilation control) cleaned one of the two operational furnaces. To do this he first pushed the fire far back, throwing on a little fresh coal to keep it in.. He then cleaned the bars and filled the fire up with fresh coal to get the fire into active operation again. Having finished this fire he was repeating the procedure with the second furnace when he was blown away from the fire by the blast of the explosion. One of the fires was thus, at the time of the explosion, not in full operation.

The involvement of the firemen immediately before the explosion was then examined in the report. Apparently the day firemen had gone down the pit on the fateful morning a little before 4.30 a.m. which was later than usual. Their task was to check that the working places and travelling roads were safe before the miners descended. Besides travelling from the shaft to the far ends and back again, each fireman had to inspect a large number of places, most of which were bratticed. Fifty minutes later at 5.20 a.m. they signalled for the miners to descend.

John Pickering, the oversman of No. 3 pit, who had previously been a fireman in one of these rounds in No. 2 pit, had told the Inquiry that it usually took him 80 minutes and that if on this occasion 50 minutes only were taken it would have to have been done running. Another important witness had said that it would take two hours to do the inspection properly.

The explosion happened at 8.45 a.m. so time enough had elapsed for the miners to be fully at work but whether every working place had been visited and found safe and miners put to work in them, there was no survivor to tell.

Two minutes after the firemen reached the surface, the explosion took place. The manager was at the top of No. 3 shaft supervising the putting in of a new cage above the shaft mouth and got badly burned by the flame which came up the shaft. He afterwards told the oversman, *"Surely you had left something desperately wrong."* *"No, everything was right,"* was the answer. The firemen also denied that they had come up early in consequence of any apprehension of danger.

Under the heading of discipline, skill and care Mr. McLean's report indicated the discipline seemed to have been of a mixed kind. The manager, he said, was down in one of the pits at least four times a week. Some of the witnesses had testified that they only saw him down there once a week, others once a fortnight and some not at all for five weeks.

The abstract of the Act and the special rules were posted up at both of the pits in question. The Government Inspector and his assistant had been frequently at the colliery and made no complaint but suggested that the miners should avail themselves of their power to make inspection. On the other hand, representations of danger by the miners were said to have been rudely received by the oversman James Gilmour.

Batting or wafting gas out, disavowed by the manager, was carried out. Powder, where inflammable gas had been met with in the preceding three months, was allowed to be taken in paper parcels.

The miners could scarcely have been expected to foresee that the whole system of the ventilation was breaking down but some of them were participators in most of the acts of omission and commission enumerated.

In his final summing up of the disaster Mr. McLean stressed, *'that no blame could be passed to the Government Inspectors.'* He then listed a great number of their responsibilities, which he concluded made it impossible for them to control the changing circumstances in a colliery without the co-operation of the staff and miners working under them. Opinions of those having knowledge of the subject all agreed that responsibility for a colliery can only centre on the owner, agent and manager. The colliery manager is exceptionally responsible, even beyond what some persons qualified to give an opinion on the subject believe to be just. Repetition on this point might seem tedious he stated but at times *a portion of the public appear to require to be reminded of it*. Every miner was also required by the special rules to report to his superior anything likely to be dangerous which comes under his notice. The miners, he stated, as a body are an intelligent and unobtrusive class of men. When they see things going wrong they think offence might be given by naming it to their superiors. It is a duty they owe unto themselves.

Clearly then, McLean stated that the Government Inspectors were absolved from any blame and that responsibility for these pits lay with the owners, agent and management. He also stressed the part the miners were required to play in reporting problems. Had he forgotten his previous comments about the rebuffs the miners got from their superiors when they did bring things to their attention?

Mr. McLean concluded his report by stating,
> *'no penalty that could be imposed under the Coal Mines Act would be at all appropriate to this awful catastrophe. It presents to some extent an exceptional state of things. The owners supplied everything that was required. Nearly every man who had any share in the occurrence lost his life. The manager was at his post of duty and got burned. The oversman and all but one day fireman lost their lives in one pit and those of the other pit only escaped by the skin of their teeth. Notwithstanding what occurred, of all who knew the mine but one or two seemed at all apprehensive of what might ensue. The Inspector of Mines and his assistant had frequently visited the mine and never complained except to suggest that the men should inspect for themselves. The owners are severe sufferers by the wreck of property and the expense of the delay in restoration. The oversman who lost his life whilst underrating*

the danger, as has now been proved, stated but three days before the climax, "There was no fear. There will not be a man fallen in the pit." The surviving sufferers have to be relieved. All are required to join heartily to prevent the recurrence of such a disaster. Anything that might interfere with this should in our opinion be carefully avoided.'

In the final paragraph of his report, Mr. McLean acknowledged the help given by the local authorities in Hamilton in arranging the Inquiry, the owners of the colliery and those connected therewith and the representatives of the miners, mining engineers and the coal masters and others who gave evidence. The evidence, he stated, was sifted probably in every way that was possible under the circumstances but, in considering it, *'it was to be borne in mind, that the owners took no part in the Inquiry and that it was only on the last four days that the manager was represented.'*

When this report was published, Andra said that there was another explosion in Blantyre. This was an explosion of fury, which erupted when details of the report reached the village. The anger that the people had exhibited in the immediate aftermath of the disaster was, he said, nothing compared to the displays of outrage he witnessed when the surviving miners and the bereaved families of those who had died were made aware of the contents of this, as he described it, iniquitous report.

A mass meeting of the villagers was hastily convened which was addressed by Alexander Macdonald M.P. and several prominent people in the village. Alexander Macdonald was clearly as angry as anyone involved in the tragedy and pledged that he would do his utmost to have the feelings of the locals about this shameful report placed before Parliament.

Andra told me that the main ground for complaint about the report was that, not surprisingly, it had singularly failed to recommend any punishment under the Coal Mines Act, of Messrs. Dixon and Company the owners of the colliery and/or their management The local people at the meeting wanted to know why the author of the report Mr. McLean could, on the one hand, list so many examples of gross mismanagement and dangerous working practices in the colliery which had been clearly proved beyond any shadow of a doubt and thereafter state that no appropriate penalty could be imposed.

Several speakers at the meeting challenged Mr. McLean's statement that punishment of the owners, whose absence from the Inquiry had to be borne in mind when sifting the evidence, was not appropriate. Neither, according to Mr. McLean, was any censure of the Government Inspectors an option. They, he stated, had frequently visited the mine and never complained except to suggest that the men should inspect for themselves. This meant in effect that although, for instance, the Inspectors might observe one and a quarter miles of ventilation bratticing on one of their frequent trips underground, it was not for them to advise the colliery management that this was potentially dangerous. According to the Inspectors this should be done by the miners themselves, despite the proven difficulties they encountered when they tried to do so. Based on this premise, any fair minded person would wonder what exactly was the purpose of having Government appointed Inspectors in the first place.

The fact that Mr. McLean had also stated in the report that, *'the owners are severe sufferers by the wreck of property and the expense of the delay in restoration'* incensed the families of the victims of the disaster. The lifestyle of the owners, who lived in their grand mansions and were witnessed every day driving around in their carriages had, to all intents and purposes, been totally unaffected by the disaster. Compare this to the miserable situation the relatives of the deceased found themselves in as they struggled to survive on the meagre pension allotted to them. *Their* lives *had* been wrecked and they knew that, based on previous experience, their tenure in their miserable homes would be short lived and they would soon, literally, find themselves out on the street.

Andra's abiding memory of this assembly was the fact that it was the first occasion that he had stood up and addressed a public meeting. When I asked him what he had said, he told me that after reading out the remark made by Mr. McLean, *that a portion of the public appear to require to be reminded that the regulations for the conduct of mining rest with the owners and management of the colliery*, he had made the point that Mr. McLean would, if he had taken heed of his own advice, have reached a much different conclusion. That, of course, would not have suited the self-styled ruling classes.

Having since read the Inquiry notes and both reports of same in great detail and with the benefit of hindsight of Andra's intuitive analysis of them, I suspect that this was the day that Andra McAnulty, campaigner for miners' rights, was born. He himself was probably unaware of this at the time but there is no doubt in my mind that, the mental scars he was left with, more than matched the many physical scars on his body. With the passage of time the physical scars (but not the disabilities) would heal but the mental scars would remain with him until his dying day. Few would disagree that, given the horrific circumstances, this was inevitable.

Proud men (reproduced by kind permission of Guthrie Hutton)

Uproar in the House

The miners, quite rightly in my opinion, still considered that William Dixon and Co. should be held to account for the disaster and that Watson, the manager, should be stripped of the certificate that allowed him to hold such a position. Their only hope of seeing these wishes fulfilled rested in the promise that Alexander McDonald the Member of Parliament had made, to raise the matter in the House of Commons at the earliest opportunity.

Mr. McDonald kept his word and, after failing to have the matter brought before the House in the session immediately after the disaster, he resorted to more direct action in the next session. The following extract from Hansard, as highlighted in the *Hamilton Advertiser*, reveals the outcome of his initiative when he did so:

Mr. McDonald asked the Chancellor of the Exchequer if: *'considering the loss of life in the mines of the United Kingdom, he would arrange for the discussion of the resolutions on that subject some day before the Easter holidays?'*

The Chancellor of the Exchequer: *'I very much wish I could, but I am afraid, in the present state of public business, I cannot.'*

Mr. McDonald asked the Home Secretary whether his attention had been called to the evidence given before the Court of Inquiry into the colliery explosion at Blantyre, showing frequent violation of the provisions of the Mines Regulation Act?

The Home Secretary - said the 32d section of the Regulation Act was a useful one and he had frequently, at the suggestion of the Inspectors of mines, put it in force, in order to show the managers of mines that they had something of the same responsibility as attached to captains of ships.

Still the Secretary of State could only act upon information which he received. In this case a Special Commission was appointed to inquire into the explosion, and the Commission consisted of an eminent advocate and a chief inspector of mines. When they made their report to him they made no mention of the 32d section, and thinking this was a case in which their attention ought to be specially called to it, he did so. *The Commissioners, however, replied that in their opinion it was not a case in which any action ought to be taken.*

Mr. McDonald - felt it was his duty to take the extraordinary course which he was about to take in consequence of the answer just given by the Chancellor of the Exchequer. He should move the adjournment of the House (Uproar). If hon. gentlemen opposite would give him their attention he would promise to detain the House only a few minutes, but if they interrupted him, he should -

Mr. Ritchie rose to order. He wished to ask The Speaker whether he had not, under similar circumstances, already ruled that a member dissatisfied with the answer to a question could not raise that question again by moving the adjournment of the House?

The Speaker - *'I have said that such a course is highly inconvenient. I cannot say that the hon. member is not within his rights in doing so if he thinks proper, but at the same time I am bound to observe that the hon. member in using language of a threatening character, is out of order.'* (Cheers.)

Mr. McDonald - said that, *'if he had used words which were in the slightest degree out of order, he would withdraw them at once.'* The hon. gentleman then said, *'that in accidents which had taken place since the Mines Act came into operation a total number of 535 lives had been lost, every one of which had been lost in consequence of violation of the rules laid down in the Act.'* He ventured to say, *'that to call them accidents was a prostitution of language. The only proper name for them was a scandalous waste of human life. He should call them murders in mines; nothing short of that would do, but what he had to object to was this - they could discuss trivial matters day after day, but they couldn't find time to discuss the loss of 535 precious lives.'*

The Speaker - *'The hon. member has already given notice that he will bring the matter before the House, and I am bound to say that his observations are altogether irregular and out of order.'*

The Home Secretary - said that the hon. member had attacked him more than once upon this question and he had assured him that the inspectors were doing their very best to enforce the Mines Regulation Act. Mr. Moore the Inspector, in his written answer to the Home Secretary, had stated that, *"I just want to say again, that unless a complaint is made to me I have no reason to think that the rules are being neglected. I do not consider that it is my duty at all to go into a mine to ferret out complaints."* The miners he would point out, had considerable powers under the Act in calling in inspectors, and he could answer for every one of the inspectors that there had never yet been a complaint, whether unanimous or otherwise, which had not received immediate attention.

This exchange of words clearly indicate that, not unexpectedly, The Establishment were doing what they normally did in these situations, closing ranks. Andra opined that once again the miners, both in Blantyre and elsewhere, had been fobbed off by being told that it was more or less their fault for not complaining about contraventions of the Mines Regulation Act. This despite overwhelming evidence of what happened at local level if they did so. In effect they were faced with what was more or less Hobson's Choice - complain and risk losing their job and their home or keep quiet and risk losing their life.

At various times thereafter Alexander McDonald attempted, in similar fashion, to persuade Parliament to take action against William Dixon and Company but was out-manoeuvred by the machinations of government on each and every occasion.

While researching this part of my story, I thought it would be interesting to find out something about the types of people who were Members of Parliament and who sat in the House of Commons in these days. This I duly did and perhaps my findings will give some insight into why working people like the miners faced an uphill battle to receive justice at their hands.

In one such Parliament of the day, of 611 members, there were:

157	Manufacturers	115	Landowners	102	Lawyers
61	Insurance Directors	50	Ex-Army Officers	30	Shipping Directors
28	Bank Directors	17	*Coal Directors*	12	Ex-Naval Officers
10	Doctors	10	Brewers	4	Oil Directors
15	Others				
				Total	611

Many long years were to pass before members who were elected to the House truly represented a cross-section of the populace, and that only after a lot of self-sacrifice by people like Andra and others who devoted their lives to fighting for justice for all. The imbalance indicated above would seem to indicate that they had every reason to do so.

Rough Justice

While reading the *Hamilton Advertiser* article about the discussion in Parliament of the Blantyre Pit Disaster, my attention was drawn to an article in an adjoining column of the newspaper. This was a report of another fatal accident at William Dixon's No. 3 Pit which, with No.2 Pit, had reopened on the 1st of December.

The report stated that:

'on Tuesday, a cage containing seven occupants was being raised to the surface when, by what is known as over-winding, it was drawn over the "whorles" and wrecked. Six of those within being precipitated down the shaft and killed, and only one man escaping, singularly enough without a scratch.

Everything pointing to the culpability of the engine keeper, Arthur Clelland. Mr. Watson the manager immediately appraised the police of this suspicion and Clelland was taken into custody. On Wednesday he was judicially examined before Sheriff Birnie and committed to prison, pending further investigations, on a charge of culpable homicide or culpable neglect of duty.

Mr. John Miller, Depute Procurator-Fiscal, accompanied by Mr. Paterson, Sheriff-Clerk Depute, visited the colliery immediately after the accident, and made the necessary official investigations. On Wednesday Mr. Ralph Moore, Government Inspector, visited the colliery, and inquired into the circumstances of the occurrence.'

The report concluded by stating that, while in Scotland over-winding seldom occurred, in England over-winding had been a fruitful source of accidents, leading to much discussion and, in many instances, the adoption of mechanical means whereby a repetition was prevented.

On reading this report I was immediately struck with the contradiction of the swift 'justice' that was applied in this instance compared with, both the initial fatality involving Joseph McAnulty and the calamitous disaster which followed several weeks later.

As described earlier, when Joseph was killed the Procurator Fiscal wasn't really interested in finding out if someone's negligence was a contributory factor in his death. Was this because, if searching investigations were instigated, the person or persons responsible might prove to be management/owners?

It's difficult to discount this theory when one compares this inaction with the immediate action taken when one of the miners, the unfortunate Arthur Clelland, was suspected of a criminal act. No less personages than the Depute Procurator Fiscal, the Sheriff-Clerk Depute and the Government Inspector descended on the scene of the 'crime' *immediately.*

As indicated, there had been many accidents of this nature previously and steps of 'mechanical means' had been taken to prevent a recurrence. In that the said 'mechanical means' were eventually installed in the winding gear at every pit, this surely is an indication that inadequate equipment was to blame for the deaths of the six miners at Dixon's and not the miserable engine keeper. Despite this, the wretched man was eventually sentenced to six months imprisonment for *'culpable neglect of duty.'*

I doubt if any further comment from me is necessary re this incident. I'm quite content to let readers form their own opinion.

Life after Death

While the members of Parliament were deciding what not to do, Andra and William were confronted with the same problem that faced most of the families in Blantyre: survival.

Andra told me that it was like waking from a nightmare only to discover that all the terrifying things which had occurred in the nightmare were in fact real. All of the houses in the immediate area were owned by William Dixon and, almost without exception, each household had lost one or more of its male occupants in the disaster.

One of the side effects of this was that the well trodden streets between the rows of houses were eerily quiet, especially early in the morning and the late afternoon. Normally at these times hundreds of miners would have been making their way to and from the pit, their voices echoing from the rough walls of the houses. Now only a few of the surviving miners who were involved in restoration work at the pit made this daily journey and their conversations were, understandably, muted.

Andra said that the many widows in this close-knit community were united in their grief but most of them were still too stunned by the dramatic changes in their lives to even begin to know where to start to get their lives back into some semblance of order.

Their entire lives had revolved round the necessity to ensure that everything that had to be done was done in ensuring that their husbands and sons were able to go to work every day in the pit to provide the means for the family to survive. Now, for most of them, that need was gone and they were floundering in the vacuum that had been created in their lives by the disaster.

Daily, in the early days, Andra witnessed small groups of these women standing outside of their houses speaking in hushed voices, most of them with black shawls wrapped round them as barriers against the prevailing cold, dreary, winter conditions. Although he was not privy to the subject of their discussions, he surmised (correctly) that their main concern would be the inevitability of the eviction notices which would be served on them by William Dixon & Co. as soon as the callous owners deemed it necessary. This was common practice and everyone knew, that despite the enormity of the disaster, the owners would not allow any family to live in one of their houses who did not have at least one male member who was employed in their pit.

Andra and his brother William had, of course, moved in with his friend Patrick McQuade's family and were slowly coming to terms with sharing a confined space with the various members of the household. Catherine, the head of the family, was acutely aware of the agonies that they were enduring due to the dramatic events of recent weeks and Andra told me that she made every effort to make them feel like an extension of her own family.

Initially at least, Andra and William's needs were slightly different. Andra was still not fit for work but William, or Wull as he was commonly known, was involved in the restoration work at the pit, as was Patrick the oldest member of the family. Catherine therefore required to see Wull off to work every morning with Patrick, making sure that both of their water bottles were filled and that they each had a small package of oat cakes or bread and jam, which was the miners' staple diet in those days, to sustain them while they were underground. When they returned from work, of course, she had to have hot water ready for the bathing ritual which was part and parcel of the daily routine of a mining family. Speaking of the bathing routine, Andra remembered with a wry smile Wull's embarrassment on the first few occasions that he had to strip and bathe in front of everyone. Wull was by nature a shy man and bathing in front of his own family was one thing but having to do so in front of Catherine and her family was another. Fortunately he soon overcame his initial shyness and soon began to 'race' Patrick for first turn of the clean, warm water.

As far as Andra was concerned Catherine quickly assumed a 'mother' role in their lives and he spoke of her with great fondness. Because of his long vigils at the pit-head waiting for news of his father he had not been eating regularly and, in his own words, become rather gaunt in appearance. This state of affairs was to change rapidly due to Catherine's ministrations as she *bullied and cajoled* him (his words) to eat the basic but wholesome meals that she provided and he soon began to feel a lot better, both physically and mentally. Dr. Grant, who still called on a regular basis, told Andra that, although he had 'turned a corner' in some respects and would, if he maintained his improvement, soon be able to return to work. However, there was a huge question mark in the doctor's mind about what type of work he would be able for.

Andra told me that he had already been giving this a lot of thought himself and wondered what the future had in store for him. Since the explosion he was involved in the sinews in his left arm had shrivelled and he had very little use of the arm. In modern times he would have had the benefit of skilled surgery and, no doubt, several skin grafts on the arm, followed by intense physiotherapy sessions to regain some of the mobility in the limb and rebuild its strength. In the times we are talking about, despite the administrations of Dr. Grant, Andra said that the muscles which had developed in his arm because of the hard work he did down the pit just seemed to waste away in front of his eyes at an alarming rate.

Although the condition of his arm was concerning, Andra also had other debilitating injuries. In addition to the severe burns he had received on his arms, his hands and a large area of his back, he had lost three toes from his right foot. Inevitably the latter injury affected his balance when he was walking and he told me that he had great difficulty in not only coming to terms with this but the necessity to develop a new 'style' of walking.

All these years later I was still able to witness the areas of his body which had been burned and it was extremely obvious that they must not only have been severe but must have been very painful. I was also acutely aware of the problem he had with walking, a problem which had been exacerbated by the passage of time. Wherever he went, he required one of our family to walk beside him (more often than not my mother) so that he could hold on to our/her arm for support.

One day, as I observed the extent of his injuries, I told him that I was astonished at the objectives he had achieved in his life in spite of them. His riposte to that was that: *'his body had been injured but, fortunately, his mind had remained intact.'*

Changing Partners

While Andra was fighting his battle with the after effects of his injuries, events were moving on in the village. New winding gear and cages had been installed and gradually the underground workings in the pit were being cleared of the debris created by the explosion. This was a laborious task but Andra said that William Dixon and Co. were putting every effort into restoring the pit as soon as possible. While the pits were closed they were not making money from them and they were desperate to reverse this situation.

All of this work required to be done by men and men were in short supply in Blantyre. 215 of the work force had lost their lives in the explosion and they required to be systematically replaced by Dixon and Co. as and when each area of the pit was ready to resume production. This could only be achieved by importing new labour from areas outside of Blantyre and Andra told me that, initially, Dixon and Co. had 'boxed clever' by employing only single men. Andra explained to me that the reason for this was really quite simple. If hired, married men would require to be given housing accommodation but the houses owned by the company, which would normally have been given to them, were occupied by the widows and families of the victims of the disaster. Dixon's knew that there would be a public outcry throughout Great Britain if they moved to evict these families immediately so they quietly *'bided their time'* (Andra's words) until they considered that the general public had lost interest in the affair.

Andra further explained to me that, by comparison, accommodating the single men was relatively simple to achieve. Many of the widows either did not have sons or, if they did, they weren't old enough to work in the pit. This meant that they were prime candidates for eviction when Dixon and Co. deemed that the time was right to literally cast them out into the street. The obvious ways for them to escape this fate was to (a) take in a lodger(s) who worked for Dixon and hope that this would be enough to prevent Dixon evicting them or (b) marry someone who worked for Dixon's. In some instances, human nature being what it is, (b) followed (a) in a natural way but in others there were different considerations.

According to Andra's recollection of events, there were quite a number of instances where men arrived in the village who had been beguiled by reading about the vast amount of money that had been donated to the disaster fund. These fortune hunters wrongly assumed that the widows were going to receive 'lump sums' of money in due course and they were determined, by whatever means, to acquire some if not all of it for themselves.

Living in our modern society, we cannot begin to comprehend the predicament that the widows found themselves in. If only a few miners had been killed the mining community would have rallied round them in traditional fashion but the enormity of the disaster precluded this. Nowadays the state and others would provide them with both practical and financial support and the tenure of their homes would not have been in jeopardy, but now is now and then was then. Mentally shocked as they were at losing husbands and sons in such a sudden and dramatic fashion, they were ill equipped to make decisions of any kind, let alone the major ones involving their personal lives that required to be made. Many of the widows being faced with the inevitable prospect of themselves and their children being, literally, thrown out of the homes so soon after losing their loved ones, felt that the only possible choice was to get married as soon as possible. Inevitably some who made this choice were easy targets for the wrong type of men and lived to regret their decision, well intended though it had initially been.

Others, faced with what can only be described as 'Hobson's Choice', chose not to have either lodger or new spouse, preferring to 'get by' on the pittance of a pension awarded to them. In the fullness of time they were to pay the ultimate penalty for this decision.

In the event, they didn't have to wait long. Andra told me that, approximately six months after the explosion the last of the widows had been evicted. The cold hearted manner in which this was done is described in the *Hamilton Advertiser,* 18th. May, 1878:

'Ejection of the Blantyre Widows - On Thursday, Sheriff Birnie had before him 34 summonses of ejectment at the instance of William Dixon, (Limited) against widows whose husbands were killed at High Blantyre Collieries in October (sic) last. Mr. J.D.Fairley represented the firm. It may be mentioned that circulars were without effect some time ago served on defenders, with the view of having them removed from their houses. They did not all appear on Thursday, but a large proportion answered when their names were called in court. Addressing the first who appeared, the Sheriff asked her the reason for not going out? Widow - I have no means to pay a rent with. The Sheriff - What do you propose to do? Widow - To go out after I was in a way to pay a rent. The Sheriff - You see I have no power if that is your only excuse. Why have you not means as well as others? Are you not getting from the Relief Fund? Widow - We are not getting enough. We cannot keep our families and pay the rent off what we get. Mr. Fairley said the firm did not wish to be hard. The Sheriff - I'm sure the firm will not be so. The ordinary time for leaving the house is five days; are you inclined to give more? Mr. Douglas, cashier to Messrs. Dixon, said some of the widows had taken other houses, and the firm were willing to give them until the 28th. the term day at Blantyre. The Sheriff fixed this as the last day of removal. Mr. Fairley asked and obtained decree for expenses, explaining that they would not be exacted. Widow after widow pled the same reason for not removing, and one said the firm should have ejected her on the day of the explosion, as the public would then have taken her by the hand. The Sheriff - It was out of kindness you were allowed to remain. Widow - They have taken a cruel way of showing their kindness. The Sheriff - You will see I am sitting here as a Court and cannot give way to feelings of kindness. But I can scarcely agree with you. I think both Messrs. Dixon and the public have been extremely kind and generous. Except where illness was involved, removal on the 28th. was decreed. The proceedings were of a painful character.'

The reporter's last sentence speaks volumes!

Barnhill, Blantyre

From Little Acorns

A frequent visitor to Andra during his convalescence was Hugh Brown, who had played such a valiant role in the aftermath of the disaster. Because of his bravery and the sensitive manner in which he had dealt with the bodies of so many of their relatives, Hugh was held in great esteem by the people of Blantyre. Andra told me that on each and every visit Hugh and he had an earnest discussion about what the future held for Andra because of his infirmity and one day Hugh put forward a suggestion to him that, unknown to either of them, was to change not only Andra's life but the lives and working practices of thousands of people in the years to come. Hugh suggested that he (Hugh) should propose him as a check weigh-man.

Andra explained to me that a check weigh-man was not employed or paid by the owners of a pit but by the miners themselves. His job was to work alongside the weigh-man who was employed by the owners to check, on the miners' behalf, the weight of each hutch load of coal as it emerged from the pit. This was credited to the miner who had filled the hutch at the coal face, his wages being paid on the cumulative total for each shift worked.

Merry's Rows, Blantyre

Individual miners were identified by a pin or numbered disc which they placed in each of the filled hutches (usually about half way down the inside of the filled hutch), the pins or discs subsequently being hung on a board in the weigh-man's office and tallied at the end of the day to determine individual wages.

When I asked Andra why it took two men to do this he told me that, before the miners won the right to have one of their own check the hutches, unscrupulous owners had cheated the men out of their due wages in several ways. Their man either deliberately recorded a lighter weight for each hutch or he declared that there was too much dirt amongst the coal in a particular hutch and refused to sanction payment for the coal content. This led to many disputes as miners, already being paid a pittance for their exhausting and dangerous work, demanded that they be paid the proper amount for their toil.

A further question from me as to why the pins or discs were placed half way down the filled hutches caused Andra's brows to furrow for a moment before he offered me the explanation:
'*This was necessary*' he told me, '*because*' and at this point he struggled to find the right words, '*it was a necessary precaution to prevent the most heinous crime that one miner could commit on another, that of exchanging his own pin or disc for that of the miner who had filled the hutch.*'

This was an extremely rare occurrence he told me but it did happen and, when discovered, the outcome was explosive to say the least. Without exception, he said, the perpetrator of this foul deed would initially be severely beaten by his fellow miners and reports of his malpractice would go round the village like wildfire. His job and house would also be forfeited because the coal-owners knew that not only would the miners refuse to work alongside him again but that he and his family would be ostracised by everyone in the village.

Consequently the family would be immediately evicted from their home and, if they knew what was good for them, they would leave the village as quickly as possible.

Hugh Brown was as good as his word and spoke to several of the surviving miners at Dixon's pit at the first opportunity. Andra told me that, according to Hugh, they were a bit sceptical at first because of Andra's youth but this was counterbalanced by their awareness at the 'wrongs' that the McAnulty family had suffered at the hands of Dixon and Co. For this reason alone the miners considered that he would ensure that the miners' rights were in safe hands. In addition, despite his youth, he already had the respect of his seniors for the articulate manner in which he had conducted himself at the frequent pit head meetings re working conditions etc, in the short time he had worked beside them. The average young miner of his age would usually sit back and let the problems be debated by the older men but Andra was different in that respect. On several occasions when discussions had become a bit heated he had given the first indications that he was capable of putting forward a considered point of view to bring matters to a reasoned conclusion. Accordingly, when Hugh's proposal was debated at a subsequent meeting, Andra was unanimously elected as the miners' check weigh-man, as and when he was fit to resume working,

In that the check weigh-man was paid by the miners the coal owners could not discipline him for speaking out, so this placed the check weigh-man in a unique position. Where ordinary miners had to be careful what they said during disputes with management, the distinctive position held by the check weigh-man meant that, by a simple process of evolution, he had become the person that the individual miners brought their problems to so that he could intervene with the management on their behalf. Unwittingly (or maybe not!), Hugh Brown had been the catalyst in the launching of the career of one of the greatest activists for miners' rights in the Scottish coal fields. Andra McAnulty was not aware of it at the time but he was about to take the first step on the road to becoming the 'Miners' Champion,' as he was referred to later in life.

Blacksmiths at Dixon's

Back to Work

When Dr. Grant was appraised of this turn of events he had no hesitation in giving his blessing to Andra's return to a working life. Andra said that the doctor had never put it into words before but he now admitted that he had had grave doubts about Andra's ability to go back to the strenuous work underground due, in particular, to his weakened arm. He expressed his pleasure however that Andra was now able to return to work in a less demanding role because he felt it would be good for him, psychologically at least, to be active once more.

Andra said that his return to work coincided with the partial resumption of production in the pit and he was therefore able to thoroughly acquaint himself with the requirements of his new job while the momentum of production built up. It also gave his body a chance to get used to the fresh demands placed on it after such a long spell of inactivity.

Andra recalled that the weigh-man employed by Dixon's was a tall man named Walter (Wattie) Park, who seemed slightly surprised that the miners had chosen someone as young as Andra to look after their interests. His attitude at the beginning of their working relationship was one of *'I'm in charge'* but Andra said that he immediately let him know that, as far as he was concerned, they were on an equal footing and he was his own man. This show of strength seemed to make an impression on Park because thereafter they had a fairly good working relationship.

There was, however, one local rule that frequently caused a little bother between them and that was the one which stated that, if there was more than 25 lbs. of dirt in a hutch then the miner concerned didn't get paid. This was later amended to a system of payment whereby the miner's lightest hutch was considered the average weight of all of his hutches and the amount he was paid was based on that principle. Andra told me that Wattie Park was a stickler where this rule was concerned and each perceived contravention of the rule generated much weighing and re-weighing of the offending dirt before a mutually agreeable decision was made (knowing Andra, I'm sure that he won more of these debates than he lost!).

Pit Pony And Hutches

Main Street, High Blantyre

Main Street, High Blantyre

Memorial erected by Dixon & Co., High Blantyre

High Blantyre Cross

Miners Banner (Courtesy of Scottish Mining Museum)

Blantyre Miners Welfare

Etaples Military Cemetery, France

Rededication Of Memorial At High Blantyre , October 2000 (Courtesy of Nigel McBain, Motherwell)

From left to right; Jim Cornfield, ?, Nicky Wilson (N.U.M. Secretary), Neilly McLaughlin (past President of Blantyre Miners Welfare), Robert 'Tucker' Anderson (President of Blantyre Miners Welfare), Alan Dick (past Lord Provost), Billy Maxwell, Andy Paterson (Author), John McNab (Secretary of Blantyre Miners Welfare)

First Encounter with Keir Hardie

Gradually, as Andra settled into his new job, he became more and more involved in both the minor and major disputes between the coal owners and the miners. This intervention at local level was necessary because, in the past, although many attempts had been made around the country to form unions both at pit-head and County level, none of these had lasted for any great length of time.

One man who was determined to organise the miners, not only at local level but nation-wide, was James Keir Hardie. When Andra started telling me about him it was plain to see and to hear that Keir Hardie, as he was commonly known, had been a very influential figure in his life. Andra told me that Keir had been born near Holytown in Lanarkshire but had lived most of his early life in Quarter, which is near to Hamilton.

The men had much in common. Keir, like Andra, had been working in the pits since he was ten years old but this hadn't deterred him from seeking to gain an education by attending evening classes after the day's work was finished. This thirst for knowledge was maintained as he grew older and by the time he reached 21 years he had gained a reputation in the Hamilton area for the articulate and straight forward manner in which he could explain to his fellow miners the need to organise themselves into strong unions.

Keir later told Andra that he was, invariably, always their spokesman in disputes with the pit managers and, such was his grasp of the economics of the coal industry, he was able to refute many of the false claims put forward by management as they sought to reduce the miners' standard of living to almost starvation level. Management were not used to having to deal with this level of astute representation and, at the age of twenty one, Keir and his brother George were not only dismissed by their then employers but were 'blacklisted' by them which, in effect, meant that they would be unable to gain employment in any other pit. Try though they might this proved to be the case. Their undeserved reputation as troublemakers and agitators had gone before them to all other pits in the area and they were given short shrift by prospective employers.

As Keir later told it to Andra, it was Keir's mother who came up with the idea which solved their dilemma. With a husband and two sons working she had managed to put a bit of money away for a 'rainy day.' In her opinion that 'rainy day' had come sooner than expected and it was she who suggested that they open a small shop in Quarter, right in the middle of the mining community there. At his mother's instigation therefore Keir's father, who was a carpenter, had quickly altered the premises and made a counter and some shelves for them at little cost. The brothers were well known in the area for the determined manner in which they had fought for the miners rights and that they had been blacklisted for so doing. His mother was sure that the miners would support them in their venture and this eventually proved to be the case. Not only that, the shop quickly became a focal point for the miners to get together and discuss the issues of the day. Far from diminishing Keir Hardie's influence the coal owners had inadvertently created an opportunity for him to further his cause of uniting the miners against them.

Keir Hardie M.P.

It was in this shop that Andra, by now in his twentieth year, had his first encounter with this charismatic man who was destined, in the not too distant future, to become a Member of Parliament. As Andra related it to me, having heard of Keir's growing reputation amongst the miners, he had walked the four miles from

Blantyre to Quarter to seek his advice about a local dispute he (Andra) was involved in between the miners and the owners of Spitallhill Pit in Blantyre. What he had thought would be a short meeting about this soon developed into a general conversation which lasted several hours and culminated in him being invited to stay and have supper with the family. This, said Andra, was the beginning of a lifelong friendship between himself and the Hardie family and their meeting inspired him to really get involved in the miners struggle to attain the wages and conditions that they rightfully deserved. Andra admitted to me that, from that day hence, Keir Hardie became his mentor.

This involvement eventually led him to assist Hardie in organising several meetings of delegates from the many pits in Lanarkshire, with a view to forming an official Lanarkshire Miners' Union. Another who was involved in this and whom Andra came to respect was Bob Smillie from Larkhall, Lanarkshire. He had been a close friend of Hardie's since they attended evening classes together and they were jointly determined to unite the miners in this fashion. Bob was also destined to become a close friend of Andra's in the succeeding years, as was another activist called Willie Small.

Significant though their Union activities were at local level, the most ambitious achievement of this small group was a political one when, under the guidance of Keir Hardie and Bob Smillie, they and a few others including Andra, founded the first ever version of the Scottish Labour Party in September, 1886. At this particular time, as Andra explained it to me, most miners who bothered to vote supported the Liberal Party. Hardie and Smillie it was who had sufficient vision to realise that the only hope that working-class people had of bettering their lot in life was to be represented by their own political party.

Andra told me that, despite their efforts and enthusiasm, they discovered that a sufficient number of the then working classes weren't convinced enough to immediately support this radical attempt to alter the face of British politics forever. Consequently the Party only lasted for seven short months but this was only a temporary setback and, on August 25th 1888, the Party was re-launched and Keir Hardie stood as the Scottish Parliamentary Labour Party candidate for the constituency of Mid-Lanark, with the support of Willie Small and Andra who acted as his election agents.

Hardie came last in the poll but he and like minded people around the country were not to be denied and by the time the next elections took place in 1892 and he offered himself up for election as the Independent Labour Party candidate in the West Ham South constituency of London, he was victorious. He thus became the first true representative of the working classes in British history, and served immediate warning of his intended role in the House of Commons by appearing among the top hatted and tail-coated members on his first day, wearing a cloth cap and a tweed suit.

A tight squeeze (reproduced by kind permission of Guthrie Hutton)

The implications of this historic success at the polling booths were obvious and I could tell that Andra was justifiably proud of the small part he had played in the long struggle to achieve it.

Hearts and Minds

Following this historic meeting with Keir Hardie, Andra's contribution to the miners struggle for survival in those austere times has been widely chronicled by writers much more knowledgeable and competent than myself to do so. R. Page Arnot and Alan Campbell in particular spring to mind. In the conclusion of R. Page Arnot's book,

'The History of the Scottish Miners' which many consider to be the definitive book on the subject, he writes, '*All these activities of the Scottish miners at the present day have been sustained and carried forward, not only as a response to material needs, but by the strength of an idea. The idea of a Socialist society has been the common outlook of thousands of miners. It has been part of all their history since Keir Hardie, William Small, Bob Smillie and Andra McAnulty began their propagandist and organising efforts three-quarters of a century ago. It is the idea of Socialism that nerves and sustains the most active and leading spirits among the Scottish miners today.*'

A great number of other books and countless articles in old newspapers also bear witness to the self-sacrifices these four and others of their ilk endured in their constant quest for justice for their colleagues in the mining industry. During the last couple of years it has been a humbling experience for me as I've learned more about the hardships and injustices which were part and parcel of their daily lives, especially when I compare it to the lifestyle enjoyed by myself and the majority of people in our society today.

Unfortunately, too many of us are blissfully unaware that the working and living conditions which most of us enjoy in our modern era, in all walks of life and in all occupations including 'white collar' ones, are a direct result of the sacrifices made by people like Andra and his peers, who dedicated their whole lives to the struggle for justice for all. Their achievements, in the face of seemingly insurmountable odds, cannot be over emphasised.

In this context however it should not be forgotten that there are at present millions of people in our society, especially in third world countries, who are *still* being exploited by others as they struggle for their very existence. Most of this exploitation of the poor and the weak is, as it was in Andra's day, profit driven and a phrase from The Bible, '*the love of money is the root of all evil*' is as true today as it was when it was written. Sadly, to misquote George Orwell, '*some people are (still) more equal than others*'.

The general theme running through most of the books and articles re miners of that era is, of course, one of continual confrontation between the miners and the mine owners and/or the politicians of the day. The criteria for drawing the battle lines was simple. The mine owners expected to make a certain (high) margin of profit irrespective of the means necessary to achieve it, be this the working conditions in the mines or the fluctuating price of coal in the market place. Their disregard for safety in the mines owned by them was highlighted earlier and they were completely indifferent to the continual loss of life in their greed for money. This meant that, when the price of coal decreased at the point of sale, they were not prepared to accept a cut in their profit margins. When this occurred they maintained the profit status quo by simply reducing the price per ton paid to the miners for extracting the coal from the bowels of the earth, or reducing the hours worked per week - or both! They did not, of course, simultaneously reduce the rents paid by the miners to live in the squalid houses provided by them, this sum being deducted from the reduced wages before the miners received them. When their wages were slashed, the only things the miners and their families could reduce to compensate was the amount of food purchased by them. There was little or nothing else they could economise on.

Understandably, the miners attempted to resist this inhumane treatment on many occasions but the odds of success were usually stacked against them. Individuals or small groups who spoke out against the injustices were given short shrift by the mine managers. Quite simply they were given two choices. Keep quiet and get on with the work or, continue to protest, lose their job and be evicted from their company owned house with immediate effect. This latter edict was swiftly enforced by 'heavies' employed by the owners who dragged the few pieces of furniture owned by the family into the street. Anyone in the community who attempted to stop this cruel act were afforded the same treatment. This well known practice was a simple but effective deterrent. Andra articulated to me that it was a common sight to see families who had been so treated, living in makeshift tents made from old pieces of tarpaulin and wood on the outskirts of the village. This, he said, was an even more heart rending sight in the winter time as the families were observed huddled around fires burning in home made braziers, the coal used in these having been scavenged from the nearby pit bings by the unfortunate people.

On finding himself in this situation the miner concerned knew that it would normally be a waste of time applying for a job in the immediate area because he knew that he would have been immediately 'blacklisted' by the manager who had dismissed him i.e. his name would have been passed to other prospective employers as a malcontent. His only option therefore was to move to another area and use an assumed name when he applied for work. In that this was the only possible chance of him obtaining employment this was common practice in these circumstances. This latter custom of name changing has however, in recent times, been the cause of a lot of head scratching amongst family descendants as they strive to uncover details of their ancestors lives. Quite a number of entries in birth certificates and census forms were made in the assumed names as the miners strove to preserve their new identities and the problems caused by this to researchers are obvious.

Pit Boy by kind permission of Scottish Mining Museum

By treating individuals like this however the owners, far from crushing the spirit of the miners, contrived to unite them, as they realised that the only hope they had of standing up to the mine owners and managers was to support each other in the common cause for better conditions and justice. This they did with limited success at individual pits but gradually they were convinced by people like Keir Hardie, Andra and Bob Smillie that their ultimate strength lay in the formation of, first county unions and ultimately national ones. This did not happen overnight and in fact took many long years during which unions were formed under a variety of names and just as quickly disbanded as funds dwindled, unions fragmented and miners became discontented at the seemingly lack of progress. One example of this, as mentioned to me by Andra, was The Blantyre Miners Association which he formed in 1890. It had, he said, about 350 members but only lasted about five or six years. A wealth of information re this and other similar associations can be found in a wonderful book entitled, 'The Scottish Miners, 1874-1939. Volume 2 - Trade Unions and Politics.' written by the aforementioned Alan Campbell.

Pointless Then, Pointless Now

While reading through the notes of my deliberations with Andra, I came across a brief reference to a chat we had one day about some of the side issues which had delayed the unity of the miners at local level. Foremost amongst these, he said, was the resentment many of the Scots miners felt about Irish workers coming to work in the Scottish mines. This prompted me to immediately compare this with the ill feeling felt by some people about the current influx of people from Eastern European countries to the United Kingdom, because they are perceived to be willing to work for low wages and to live in sub standard conditions.

Bearing this in mind it is easy to understand that the recruitment of these Irish immigrants, who were so desperate for jobs that they would accept the low wages offered to them, was a calculated move by the coal owners to force down the already low standard of living in the Scottish coal fields.

Andra explained that the owners principle aim was to 'divide and conquer' and in this they were extremely successful. Because there was, initially, a disinclination to mix, one 'side' was reluctant to support the other in times of wages disputes etc and this led to a lot of friction between them. To people like Andra, who were striving to improve the living standards of the mining communities as a whole, this was a terrible hurdle to overcome and he constantly preached the need for people to live and work together in harmony. Complicating the matter even further was the fact that some of the Irish people brought their religious 'differences' with them, so they were often at odds with each other.

Old Village, Blantyre

Andra himself had renounced all religion at an early age because of the attitude of the churches of all denominations to mining people and the actions of many so called Christians among the ruling classes. He couldn't reconcile their sometimes despicable treatment of fellow human beings with, as he described it to me, their *'holier than thou'* demeanour.

Of the several things he described to me which caused friction between both sides in these early days, the main one seemed to be the annual Orange Walk, which he described as a flash point. About once every ten years or so the parade involving Lanarkshire people of that persuasion took place in the Blantyre area. On this day, he said, most local families stayed indoors because there was always the possibility of trouble. As he described it to me, one side (The Orangemen) wanted to hold a peaceful parade and the other (The Catholics) wanted to make a peaceful protest. That was the theory but, unfortunately, there were elements on both sides of the divide who saw this event as an opportunity to vent their spleen on each other in a violent manner.

Stark evidence of Andra's summary of the situation is to be found in the July 13th, 1894 edition of the now defunct *Hamilton Herald*. Under the heading *'Disturbances At Blantyre'* a lengthy article describes scenes of absolute mayhem in the town on the previous day. I have selected some passages at random which illustrate Andra's observations;

'Orangemen representing, Airdrie, Bellshill, Wishaw, Coatbridge, Armadale, Blantyre, West Lothian and Motherwell, about 1800 in number, met at Greenfield North British Station, thence marched via a circular route round Blantyre to a field between Burnbank and High Blantyre, during the course of which, one of the bands-men had his head cut by one of a number of stones thrown among the processionists. While the contingent were marching along via Burnbank, they were surrounded by several thousands of all classes of people, and stones were pitched every now and again in the direction of the bands and the leaders.'

'At Greenfield Station the crowd must have numbered close on 12,000. The police arrangements up to this point were, however, admirable and there was little chance of any dangerous row taking place without the originators of it being caught.'

'As the procession, headed by two mounted office-bearers, reached Mr Kelly's public house, it was now apparent that a row could hardly be avoided and a stoutly built woman rushed forward and seized one of the horses. This caused a great commotion and stones were hurled from all directions at the men on horseback and the band following immediately behind. The Orangemen now got their swords and halberts in position and retaliated, and men women and children began running helter-skelter in all directions. At length, about a dozen policemen, three or four deep, rushed forward with drawn batons and this had the effect of settling for things down for the time being.'

'Along the route stones were thrown here and there and several persons received slight injuries, Shopkeepers rushed out and closed their doors and windows, and soon there was hardly an open shop to be seen.'

'The last mentioned row is said to have originated owing to a rumour having got abroad that the Orangemen meant to attack the Catholic Chapel.'

'All went well until the field was reached. Here a big fellow, said to be a Catholic, and an Orangeman began to quarrel. The former was pounced upon by Orangemen from all quarters, hit with halberts, kicked, pelted with fists and had to run for his life. For about 400 yards the attack was kept up on him and but for the arrival of a mounted force of police, who beat back his attackers, it is just possible that he might have been killed.'

'Seven arrests for stone throwing were made. There was no damage done to property. It is estimated that the crowd at the finish numbered about 20,000.'

Andra's feelings about such actions (and indeed current resentment re European immigrants), which he saw as counter-productive to the real struggle against the coal owners, could best be summed up in the words of his favourite poet, Robert Burns;

'Then let us pray that come it may,
(As come it will for a' that),
That Sense and Worth o'er a' the earth,
Shall *bear the gree, an a' that.
For a' that, an' a' that,
It's coming yet for a' that,
That Man to Man, the world o'er,
Shall brothers be for a' that.'

*bear the gree - win the victory.

A Different Kind of March

Much as he detested marches with religious connotations, Andra was not averse to joining in if the cause warranted it, and spoke to me several times about 'hunger marches' he had participated in. Confirmation of this was revealed to me in the following article from the Blantyre Gazette, dated 30th March, 1935;

Hunger Marchers In Blantyre

Night Spent In Co-operative Hall

About 400 of the men and a number of the women who took part in the huge demonstration in Glasgow on Sunday against the Employment Assistance Bill, left Blantyre en route to the City shortly after 10 o'clock that morning. The contingent, headed by a few pipers and a drummer, was a very orderly one, and conspicuous at the head of the column was the veteran miners' leader, Andrew McAnulty, who stepped it out gamely alongside District Councillor Beecroft. "Andra" did not march the whole way to Glasgow, but he headed the column until Blantyre was left well behind, when he was persuaded that he had marched far enough. Three hundred of the men from various parts of Lanarkshire had spent the Saturday night in the Co-operative Hall, arriving about 7.30 that evening led by Mr James Beecroft, and escorted to the hall where a hot supper was provided. A fund-raising concert was held afterwards and in the morning each of them received a substantial breakfast and a meat sandwich (to provide sustenance on the march) before setting out for Glasgow.

In both marches described, people from all over Lanarkshire united to demonstrate their support for what they considered to be a worthy cause. One march, which purported to celebrate an event which had taken place 250 years previously yet still divided a community, was led by a rider astride a symbolic white horse. The other, which was trying to send a message to Government about the unfairness of an iniquitous law, was led by a severely handicapped, seventy-five year old on 'shanks's pony.' No prizes for guessing which leader gets my vote!

Local Affairs

Andra and I discussed his activities in the unions on several occasions and also his long career in local politics. By the time he was thirty he was, of course, very active in his capacity as a miners' agent and he said that it had never been his intention to get involved in politics at local council level but, no doubt prompted by his already considerable efforts on their behalf, when he was approached in 1894 (then aged thirty four) by a group of local residents to stand for election to the Blantyre Parochial Board as it was then known (later to become The Blantyre Parish Council), he immediately agreed. He made the decision because he realised that, by so doing, he would have the opportunity to improve the conditions in the village generally on behalf of the mining community. This latter point was quite relevant because the incumbents at that time were, not surprisingly, usually local businessmen who had a vested interest in preserving the status quo in their favour.

Andra McAnulty

Come the election which took place after a meeting of rate payers in The Parochial Chambers, Kirkton, High Blantyre, Andra was duly elected to the board. At a later date he was also elected to The Blantyre School Board. Later still, he was to become Chairman of both Boards and a Justice of the Peace. All of this, in addition to his union activities, meant that his workload must have been considerable to say the least but Andra was no stranger to hard work and, trawling through *The Advertiser*, it was interesting to note the broad spread of his activities, viz.

April, 1917
Blantyre School Board - Monthly Meeting
The representative to The School Board's Conference (Mr. Andrew McAnulty) was given discretionary powers on the important questions which are to be discussed.

June, 1917
Blantyre Parish Council - Monthly Meeting
The Chairman (Mr. Andrew McAnulty) intimated, amidst applause, That a section of miners of the district had agreed to purchase a piano for the local Cottage Hospital.

(Andra had mentioned briefly that he had been a member of the committee which was formed in 1906 to raise funds for the construction of the Cottage Hospital and that, initially, a sum in excess of £4,000 was raised. He also told me that he was subsequently appointed as one of three trustees.)

On reading the above council minute I was prompted to research the history of the Blantyre Cottage Hospital and was rewarded when I discovered the following article in *Stother's Christmas and New Year Annual, 1910/1911;*

A Cottage Hospital Instituted

Blantyre has led the County in the matter of a Cottage Hospital. What has been spoken of for generations in connection with Hamilton, Motherwell, Wishaw, the larger and more wealthy centres, and has been dropped, lifted and dropped again, is now an accomplished fact in Blantyre, the humble home of schemes of loving kindness towards humanity in disadvantageous circumstances.

The movement to establish a Cottage Hospital in Blantyre was started in response to an appeal by local doctors, initiated at a public meeting on the 27th February, 1906, under the chairmanship of Mr. Andrew Millar Bannatyne of Millheugh, who has all along taken an interest in the work. A large and influential committee was formed to carry out the necessary details. The scheme was enthusiastically received, a large sum (£4162) being ultimately subscribed, of which £3,000 was spent on the building. The total subscriptions included large donations by the local coal-masters, Wm. Baird & Co. Ltd., William Dixon, Ltd.; and Merry & Cunninghame Ltd.

Blantyre Cottage Hospital

For more that thirty years the hospital was to serve the community but, in February, 1939, *The Blantyre Gazette* reported that the institution had been wound up and formally handed back to the three trustees - Messrs. A. Millar Bannatyne (solicitor, Glasgow), A.P. Ritchie (Managing Director of Dixons' Collieries, Limited) and Andra McAnulty (veteran miners' leader).

The voluntary committee of local men and women who managed the hospital had had the rather heart-breaking task of endeavouring to make ends meet financially with an ever dwindling annual income. There were no grants or endowments of any kind available and the hospital finances depended entirely on voluntary subscriptions. The closing down of so many collieries in the area in recent times had created a financial loss from which the hospital never recovered, as the miners then working had contributed a voluntary weekly levy towards the upkeep of the institution. The continual drain upon the reserve fund had used up practically all the available cash and the board of management finally decided to close down the hospital. It was provided in the trust deed that, in the event of the hospital closing down, the trustees would utilise the remaining funds for the purpose of assisting sick or injured persons residing within the Parish of Blantyre).

August, 1917
Blantyre Parish Council - Monthly Meeting
Maternity and Child Welfare - At the meeting presided over by Andrew McAnulty, Parish Council Representative to the Middle District Committee etc.
(Having been a parent of twelve children, Andra certainly had first hand knowledge of this particular subject!).

November, 1917
Blantyre Parish Council - Monthly Meeting
A very interesting report on the proceedings at the recent conference in Edinburgh on the Taxation of Land Values was given by Mr. Andrew McAnulty etc.

Cold Feet

Andra's tenure as a local councillor was long and eventful and should no doubt have ended with a 'gold watch' ceremony for services rendered to the community. Being Andra, things were never going to be as simple as that however. As he explained to me, one cold winter's day in December, 1922, while visiting a local school in his capacity as Chairman of the School Board, he noticed several bare-footed, shivering children in the playground. On questioning them he discovered that their parents were unemployed and could not afford to buy them boots or stockings. This induced him to make a quick tour of the other schools in the village to see if similar circumstances prevailed. This revealed that a total of nineteen local schoolchildren were in this disadvantaged situation.

A few days later at the usual Monthly Meeting of The Blantyre Parish Council, Andra (The Chairman) appraised the members of his findings and voiced his fears for the health and safety of the children involved. After a short debate it was unanimously decided that a small grant be made available to provide vouchers for the parents concerned, which could be exchanged at the local Co-op for boots and stockings for their children. The clerk, Mr. A.B. Maxwell, was instructed to make the necessary arrangements for this resolution to be implemented.

So far so good. Unfortunately, Mr. Maxwell took it upon himself to ignore the instruction and communicated the matter to the Board of Health for their opinion. Their opinion proved to be that the decision that had been made was out-with the power of The Blantyre Parish Council and they did not, in any case, consider that the action on health grounds was necessary!

When the clerk intimated this to the council members at their meeting on the 7th January, 1922, Andra and seven others of the eleven man committee immediately left the meeting in protest. On the 14th of January a special meeting of the

Cold Feet (reproduced courtesy of Dunfermline Carnegie Library)

members was convened in the Council chambers which was attended by a Scottish Board of Health Inspector. This gentleman confirmed the previous decision of the Board. At this juncture Andra, on behalf of the others concerned, handed over written confirmation of their resignation from the Council.

The Health Board in its wisdom did not agree with Andra's views that the childrens' health was at risk. Perhaps the decision wasn't made on health grounds alone. Perhaps the real reason was that they were afraid that a precedent would be set and other local Councils might follow the lead given by Blantyre. Perhaps this was the reason that The Health Board's feet were colder than those of the children!

Children of the Neglected

The Communist Party of Great Britain was formed in 1920/21, its aims being *'to draw national public attention to the terrible poverty prevailing in the Scottish coal fields and other areas, and to demand that the Government take steps to alleviate the suffering.'* The Party gradually built up support in the mining unions, eventually totalling approximately 100,000 miners in the United Kingdom. One such eventual convert was Andra McAnulty, who, in 1925, switched from being a long-time supporter of The Independent Labour Party. At the time he was in fact the Chairman of the local Independent Labour Party.

I was aware of Andra's involvement in the Communist movement at this time because he mentioned it to me briefly in our discussions. I say briefly because he told me that I would make my own political judgements as and when I was mature enough to do so and that he had no intention of influencing me one way or the other at my tender age. He himself had taken approximately five years to be 'persuaded' that, when all other attempts to unite the miners of Britain had failed, this movement might just be the catalyst that did just that.

Subsequently, when on a number of occasions as I grew older, I heard the phrase *'poverty breeds communism,'* being so intimately involved with him and having listened so intently to Andra's graphic accounts of poverty amongst the mining people, this immediately made me think that this was indeed the reason Andra and his fellow strugglers for survival were attracted to the ideology of communism.

This thought was reinforced in recent times when I read an article written by Ewen Gilchrist, (the minister of my local church - St. Matthew's, Perth) in our monthly church magazine. Talking about ongoing world events involving terrorists, Ewen says that,

> *'He doesn't know much about terrorism; except that it's often a cousin to fundamentalism. Take any group of people who, for whatever reason, are neglected or oppressed or marginalised year after year. For a while, human nature being what it is, they will stand politely in queues, mutter thanks for whatever hand-outs the U.N. provides. Their leaders and speakers and wise-ones will continue using the tools they have trusted in before...discussion, debate, reasoned argument. Conferences will be held, speeches made, agreements signed... all proof that goodwill can prevail over evil.*

> *But all the time, the children are watching. The children of the neglected, the oppressed, the marginalised. And these children notice, as they grow from bleak childhood in to bleaker adulthood, that despite all this talking, all this posturing, nothing has actually changed. They still live in poverty; they still live in camps, they are still not free to walk where they want to walk, or go where they want to go. And these same children, the children of the oppressed, grow into adults who have all their young lives seen that words are just spitting against the wind...and that is the seed-bed for terrorism and fundamentalism.*

> *So when a firebrand preacher comes into town, holy book in one hand and Kalashnikov weapon in the other, calling people in the name of God/Allah or whoever (in the miners situation, Communism) to rise up and claim what is rightfully theirs...it's a spark to a tinder dry forest. And a great blaze erupts.*

> *And do you know why I know that this is true? Because if it was my life being constantly cheated, neglected, betrayed, forgotten...then I might well be a willing follower of any religious revolutionary who issued a holy call to arms. All the more so if I saw my own children were condemned to that same poverty and hopelessness.*

Poverty, pure and simple, is the breeding ground for revolution. Extreme poverty stirs up extreme responses.'

Bearing in mind the incident involving the schoolchildren with no boots, Ewen's words might well have been written for Andra and his peers. Since birth he/they had lived in abject poverty as their masters flaunted their riches at their expense and sixty five years later things had changed little. Andra's opinion of the situation was that, as the years progressed and young miners returned from the bloody battlefields of WW1, they were less inclined to accept the status quo and were ready and willing to follow any would be leader or cause which promised a better way of life.

At the time, communism, with its dreams of workers being in complete control of their own destiny, seemed to be the ideal vehicle to deliver them from the clutches of the greedy industrial barons of the day and vast numbers of working people climbed aboard. Sadly, communism was to prove to be just an ideological dream (Andra's words) but there can be no doubt that, as Andra described it, it was a catalyst in the eventual consolidation of workers' unions in general and the miners' union in particular.

To me, it is no coincidence that the timing of Andra's and others' affiliation to this movement coincided with a period of great unrest amongst working people. In July of that year (1925), Prime Minister Stanley Baldwin and his Chancellor of the Exchequer, Winston Churchill (who had no love for the miners), announced that the wages of all working people would have to be reduced by between 10% and 15% and one hour extra to be worked each day, to improve the country's export prospects. By this means the coal owners, who would have to reduce their prices, wouldn't of course suffer any reduction in their obscene profit margins. The losers, as ever, would be those that were already living on the wrong side of the poverty line. One can imagine the repercussions if a modern day British Government made such an announcement to all or any group of workers.

Speaking of this incident Andra recalled that, although the miners threat of a national strike, which was supported by The Trades Union Council (TUC), thwarted the plans of the Government on this occasion, it proved to be only a partial success and the situation from then on deteriorated rapidly, culminating in what came to be known as The General Strike of 1926 taking place.

Stonefield, Blantyre

The General Strike 1926

The strike has been well documented in the past but, in the context of Andra's story, a brief resume of events as recorded by reporters at the time is necessary:

Although Stanley Baldwin's Government appeared to back down regarding the wage reduction, in what was seen as a victory for working class solidarity, Baldwin was merely buying time so that the Government could be better prepared for all out confrontation. Accordingly, The Prime Minister announced that the Government would subsidise the miners' wages for nine months while a Royal Commission reviewed the problems of the industry. Not surprisingly, when The Commission published its report nine months later, it damned the coal owners while simultaneously recommending that the subsidy should be withdrawn and miners' wages should be reduced. The exultant coal owners, having once again been looked after by The Establishment, immediately posted notices that all employment on current conditions would terminate on April 30. The British miners, already living a hand to mouth existence, did what any other group of workers then or now would have done in similar circumstances - they said no. On their behalf, the miners' spokesman, Arthur Cook, immediately set out their position, *'Not a minute on the day, not a penny off the pay.'*

On the morning of April 30 the coal owners announced that, as from the next day (1st May), miners who refused to accept a cut in pay of between 10% and 15% and work an extra hour per day would be locked out of the pits.

Next morning , when almost one million miners were indeed locked out of the pits, the TUC declared that a General Strike *'in defence of miners' wages and hours'* which would involve miners, transport workers, dockers, railwaymen iron and steel workers, builders and printers would commence in two days time, if the lock out continued.

With the prospect of over three million people withdrawing their labour, both The Government and the TUC were desperate to reach an agreement which was acceptable to the miners and negotiations were hurriedly arranged. These commenced with some members of the Cabinet demanding 'complete capitulation' by the TUC and, as the day wore on, the TUC negotiators to their eternal shame, were leaning towards accepting the coal owners proposals if the 'correct wording' could be found to sell the idea to the miners. When, at eleven o'clock in the evening, the miners executive joined the meeting and realised what was happening, they rejected what they considered to be a sell out by the TUC, whom they rightly considered should have been taking a firmer stand on their behalf.

Shortly thereafter, while proposals and counter proposals were being put forward, The Prime Minister informed them that all negotiations must cease because, in his opinion, print workers at *The Daily Mail* had already started the strike by refusing to print a leading article condemning the proposed General Strike. Instead of a settlement therefore, the miners and the TUC left the meeting at Downing Street with a letter from the Cabinet demanding *'repudiation of the actions that have already taken place and an immediate unconditional withdrawal of instructions for a general strike.'*

In the event, after nine days only, the TUC, against the wishes of the miners, went to the Government and accepted their proposals, at the same time declaring that the General Strike was over. They did try to obtain a guarantee from the Government that there would be no victimisation of strikers but this was refused. The hapless 'surrender' by the TUC was later described by a member of Baldwin's own Government as *'so humiliating that some instinctive breeding made one unwilling even to look on them.'*

Andra said that the miners were incensed by the capitulation of the TUC and voted unanimously to continue the strike on their own. This, he said, was the beginning of almost nine months of intense suffering by the miners and their families, culminating in them being literally starved back to work, with less pay and longer hours. Many of those miners who were perceived to be leading figures in the strike were refused jobs and remained unemployed for many years thereafter.

During the miserable months of the strike Andra was the rallying point for the miners and their families in Blantyre. It was he who organised the local 'soup kitchens' which were a virtual lifeline during this period. While he and other local leaders took on the responsibility of collecting food or funds from various sources on a daily basis, a team of women including my mother and Andra's other daughters were involved in cooking and serving the food to their hungry 'customers.' My mother told me that, for this purpose, several halls in the village were used and their first task every day at lunch time was to feed the miners children during their school break. On most days, as the name implies, this consisted of a large bowl of soup and a slice of bread. Following this their parents were fed, so in this manner every one involved in the struggle for fair wages was given at least one simple, hot meal every day, without which many of them would have surely died.

When I asked Andra where the ingredients for the meals came from, he told me that in addition to using Union funds (while they lasted) to buy them, his 'team' would visit the local trades people daily, seeking food or small monetary donations from them. Most of the trades people, in particular those selling food, depended on the miners for their livelihood and realised the importance of maintaining the goodwill of their erstwhile customers. No doubt those who supported the miners in their time of need reaped the benefit of their custom when the pits reopened, while those who didn't paid the penalty. Such is human nature in times of severe deprivation.

Auchenraith Silver Band (Andra seated fourth from left in front row)

Apart from this source, Andra told me that other miners went poaching for rabbits and fish in the nearby fields and rivers, usually at the risk of being taken to court if caught. This is borne out by the reports I have seen in the then local papers, of men who were unable to pay the smallest of fines being sentenced to seven days in jail for poaching/snaring rabbits in a farmer's field, or attempting to take fish from a river. Any farmer, then or now, would tell you that rabbits destroy crops and are a nuisance but, despite this, these attempts by desperate people to obtain food for the communal pot were punished in this despicable manner. There was no option of a Community Service Order in those days!

After many months of surviving in this fashion, during which time they also held fund raising concerts etc, the miners realised that they could not keep going any longer. They were now into the month of October and the undernourished people would be unable to easily withstand the rigours of winter. A slow trickle of people back to work became a flood and the strike was over. Once again the coal owners, backed by The Establishment, had ensured that their obscene profit margins would be maintained at the expense of the people who generated them.

Once again, to their eternal shame, they had literally starved the miners back to work on their greedy terms.

Let there be light!

Andra was interested in many things and life around him was never dull. Literally! When we weren't discussing his progress through life, his mind was active in other directions. His interest in electricity was a case in point (I was to discover a possible physiological reason for this later). At that particular time the electricity supply to those homes that had it (many of the older homes in the miners' rows were still dependent on gas mantles as their only form of illumination) was pretty basic, based on the actual requirements of the occupiers. A simple light bulb suspended from the ceiling in each room was the norm and only the most recently built houses (just before the war) boasted one electrical socket sited in the skirting board of the living room. This was deemed adequate because, in those austere days towards and after the end of WW2 literally no one possessed any electrically operated domestic equipment, for the simple reason that little or no such equipment existed and even the items that were available were unaffordable to the average working family.

Barnhill, Blantyre

Younger people today would find it hard to imagine life without the ever increasing array of electric gadgets with which they are surrounded, both in and out of their homes. Almost everything they use in their home is powered by electricity and, when I see them walking around the streets listening to music on their portable players via their headphones, I contrast this with the pleasure that I had listening to music on our old gramaphone, the drive spring of which had to be wound up between records by a handle at the side. On balance, I consider that I probably enjoyed it more because of the effort involved.

Most homes, including ours, had a radio but this was powered by a battery accumulator. I still have vivid memories of this glass 'case' about the size and shape of a milk carton, inside of which were lead plates immersed in acid. This was a device for storing electric energy, a sort of mini car battery in fact. This was connected to the back of the radio until the battery was discharged (usually once or twice a week, depending on how often the radio was played) at which point it required to be taken to Mr. Batters ironmongers shop in Low Blantyre to be recharged. This task usually befell to me and I really hated it! The battery was very heavy and had to be carried by a thin metal handle, in addition to which the acid tended on occasion to splash on to your hands as you walked along. On reaching the shop I would hand the 'dead' battery over to an elderly member of Mr Batters' staff and receive a fully charged one in its place. I cannot recollect how much I paid for this service but I do remember noticing that the assistant's hands bore many small scars as a result the burns that *he* had received from the acid over the years.

My efforts in making sure that the radio always had a fully charged battery were necessary because, in these pre-television days, the radio played an important part in people's lives in the bleak years of World War 2. For instance, a 'must hear' programme for everyone, both at home and in the many factories engaged in production for the war effort, was 'Workers Playtime'. Each day at lunch time the variety show was produced from different factories up and down the country and was a great morale booster for everyone who heard it, either at first hand or on the air waves.

David Livingstone's Birthplace

In its own way it certainly made a great contribution to the war efforts of the British people.

In the evenings, radio serials were extremely popular and audiences around the country listened with bated breath at 6.45 p.m. to the daily adventures of, *'Dick Barton, Special Agent.'* This might be followed by another favourite, *'The Man In Black'* an ongoing mystery series.

Popular as these shows were, the programme which commanded the biggest audience on a daily basis was the Nine O'Clock News. During the war years especially, families, most of whom had relatives or friends in the armed forces, gathered round the radio to hear how the war was progressing. As witnessed by myself in our own house, the chatter in the living room would cease instantly when Big Ben chimed out the appointed hour, as the newsreader began to enunciate details of the campaigns taking place in the various theatres of war.

Now and then, as the individual items were announced, knowing looks and nods would be exchanged between Andra and my father and, immediately the programme ended, an in-depth discussion would take place between them about the particular elements which had caught their interest. Me? As much of it was over my young head, I was merely relieved that the programme was finished so that I could resume whatever I had been doing without being told to hush!

Progressively, the other likely piece of electrical equipment in most homes was a clothes iron. This was a great boon to the housewife but unfortunately it was the common practice in many houses to use the iron in a room which didn't have a proper wall socket. They got round this problem by simply removing the light bulb in the ceiling and connecting the iron to the light fitting. This was an extremely dangerous procedure but people in those days, especially those ones who were using electricity for the first time, were almost totally unaware of this potential hazard. Even if they had been, because of the convenience compared with the previous method of heating an iron either on the gas stove or the open fire, most of them would have carried on regardless of the danger.

Andra, however, was not content just to have a basic light bulb which was switched on and off at the door of his room. If, for instance, he was looking for something in particular on his bookshelf

Glasgow Road, Blantyre

in the corner of the room, he had difficulty locating it due to a combination of poor light and weak eyesight. The amount of daylight afforded by the small window in his room was inadequate and, even with the overhead light bulb switched on, he still had problems identifying a particular book or books.

One day he decided that he had to improve on this situation. Most people would have sought the advice of someone with electrical knowledge but Andra, being Andra, had other ideas. Almost immediately I was dispatched to the library to obtain some books on basic electricity which Andra spent several days reading. Once he was confident that he had sufficient knowledge to do what he wanted to do, it was time for action.

First of all I was sent down to Mr. Batters' ironmonger's shop with a list of the things that Andra required and duly returned with several yards of brown, twisted flex (cable) and various light fittings, screwnails, staples etc. That was to prove to be the least and easiest bit of my involvement however. Although Andra now had the basic knowledge he didn't, of course, have the necessary eyesight or indeed the steadiest of hands to actually do the work himself. This was to be my job, aided and abetted by my older sister Nan, who was 'roped in' to be an extra pair of hands.

Acting on Andra's instructions, we cut the flex into various lengths with, as I recall, his (blunt) tobacco knife and bared the ends which were then inserted into the individual fittings. After doing this we had to stand up on a table and attach light fittings to two corners of the ceiling and lead/staple the flex back to the main light fitting in the centre of the ceiling. Now came the tricky procedure of switching off the electricity supply at the meter and completing the connection. Under Andra's 'expert' tutelage however we confounded ourselves by managing to join the necessary wires together to complete the circuit.

All of this took considerably longer than it has taken me to write about it because we obviously weren't very expert at using screwdrivers and were intermittently hindered by Andra who, being the font of all knowledge, kept telling us that the reason we were having trouble was that we weren't holding our elbows straight enough as we endeavoured to tighten the screws- whatever that meant!

When, despite our uncontrollable elbows, we had completed this part of the job and inserted bulbs in the new fittings, I was given the honour of switching on the power again at the meter before going to the switch at the door and pushing it to the on position. Immediately every corner of the room was illuminated by the combined light of the three bulbs but Andra still wasn't finished. The power was switched off again and we were then instructed to connect another length of flex to each of the two new light fittings. This hung down the wall to about waist height and a torpedo shaped switch was attached to the end. The lights were again switched on at the door and Andra then proceeded to demonstrate to us that each of the lights could now be switched on and off as required, from wherever he happened to be in the room. Miraculously, all this without any of us being electrocuted then or thereafter!

Stonefield, Blantyre. *Barnhill*
Dear R. have sent Box trust you received and

RELIABLE SERIES.

Andra was delighted at the result of his enterprise but his ever active mind saw further opportunities to improve things even more. A few days later I came home from school and found him waiting for me to assist him in his next venture. He produced several sheets of red and green coloured cellophane, which was/is a thin, flexible, transparent material and bade me draw various shapes on them using a pair of compasses. After cutting these shapes out with scissors (fortunately not his tobacco knife on this occasion) he/we somehow threaded wire through these panels until they formed three multicoloured lampshades. These were then attached to the respective light fittings the result of which being, once the lights were switched on, that the coloured shape of the panels of the lampshade were reflected on the ceiling and his room was transformed into something that was unique.

Stonefield, Blantyre

This was, of course, a talking point with Andra's many visitors and, unfortunately for Nan and myself led to him on at least two occasions that we can remember, promising to take us along to *their* houses to install a light in the dark, inside staircases leading up to their houses. Incongruous though it seems now we actually did go to these houses and, in each of them, installed a light fitting at the top of the staircase from which a length of flex was run down the wall to a switch at the bottom of the stair. The occupants were so delighted with the resultant illumination of the staircase that, on each occasion, Nan and I were rewarded with sixpence to buy sweets, a princely sum to children of our age in those days.

Tram in Glasgow Road, Blantyre

When I telephoned my older cousin Mary Morrison in Australia recently, we were discussing Andra's electrical experiments and she recalled her stint as his 'assistant' on another, occasion. This involved amongst other things two projects; the first one was the construction of a 'bed-warmer' which consisted of a box with two light bulb fittings installed inside it and the second was a partially successful attempt to make lights come on when cupboard doors were opened! Both of these seemed a bit incongruous to Mary at the time but future developments would demonstrate what a forward-thinking, fertile imagination Andra possessed.

My earlier reference to a possible physiological reason for Andra's interest in things electrical stem from an article which I recently came upon in the December 17, 1921 issue of the Hamilton Advertiser, which intimated that Andrew McAnulty had been invited to *do the honours* at the inaugural switching on of the street lights in Stonefield, Blantyre.

Intrigued by this revelation, I was prompted to seek further information on the event. Eventually, my research at The National Library, Scotland was rewarded when I discovered a book which had been written in 1933 detailing the history of The Blantyre Co-operative Society. In it, the author revealed that the Society was the driving force behind the installation of electric lighting in the town of Blantyre, by The Clyde Valley Electric Power Company. After interviews with Lanarkshire County Council, the Society was asked to take a plebiscite of the various merchants and others in the town to ask if they were agreeable to having their premises fitted with electric light, should the CVEPC lay a cable along the main thoroughfare. The canvass was a success and future lighting by electricity was assured.

Having had his 'moment of glory' when all the equipment was subsequently installed, was Andra therefore having a quiet smile to himself as he prompted me to switch on *his* new lights? I'll never know!

Author's mother and her niece Mary Morrison

Family Matters

On one of my many visits to Andra's room to record his recollections of his working life, he suddenly produced a group photograph of himself and his family of twelve children and started talking about his family life. Apparently he was normally very reticent about these matters but, on this occasion and others thereafter, he appeared to relish the opportunity to reminisce about his children and what had become of them in later life. My mother was astonished when I appraised her of our discussions because she said that she had never known him to do so with anyone else in the family, young or old. To her it was yet another indication of the bond that had grown between Andra and myself as a result of our frequent interaction.

Andra told me that, until he was twenty one he had never really had a girl friend, but this was to change when he was invited to be best man at a friend's simple wedding ceremony. The bridesmaid on this fateful occasion was a young woman called Mary Crowe, the sister of one of his friends who had been killed in the disaster and whom he had witnessed identifying her brother's body after the disaster. She had been fourteen at that time but was now, in his words, *'a mature young woman of nineteen.'* No doubt in the same way that it still happens when two people come together in a situation like this there was, he told me, a *'spark'* between them. It must have been some spark because, only eight months later, they were married in the church in Blantyre. Little did either of them know as they made their vows on the 15th of July, 1883 that, eventually, they would become the parents of twelve children and experience the highs and lows that come with a family of this size. It was just as well that they also didn't know that some of the lows would be quite distressing.

After all that he had been through, he told me that meeting Mary and getting married had proved to be a turning point in his life. Having 'lost' several members of his family in the preceding years he had, despite all the kindness shown by his landlady Catherine, felt as if he was living in a state of limbo and his marriage to Mary recreated a feeling of stability in his life. He told me that, for the first time since his mother had so tragically died of cancer he was able to envisage a family oriented future in a home of his own, humble though that home might be by today's standards.

Marriage to Mary gave him the motivation to rent a house at Gasworks Row in the village. He explained to me that, by so doing, for the first time in his life he was living in a home that wasn't the property of a coal mine owner. He was also secure in the knowledge that, for this reason, he was immune from threats of eviction from coal owners for the first time in his life. This security allowed him to campaign against the coal owners for better conditions for the miners and their families, free from the fear of being, literally, thrown out on to the street by the owners if he dared to challenge their authoritarian attitude.

This house was to be the first of several in the village occupied by himself and his family during the next fifty years or so. Inevitably as the family grew in size space was at a premium and it became necessary at regular intervals to seek larger premises. At various times during this half century he/they lived at Annsfield Place, Bowie's Building and Pilot Acre in Stonefield Road, School Lane, Hardie Street and Victoria Street.

My mother and other members of the family told me that Andra was very family orientated and was a caring father to them throughout their formative years and beyond. She was one of those born during the family's tenure in the house at 2 School Lane and she often said that, although times were hard for themselves and other working class people, she and her brothers and sisters - Kate, Peter, Joe, Jeannie, Mary, Andrew, Agnes, Nellie, Willie, Charlie and Maggie had an extremely happy childhood. She always qualified this however by reminding me that, by necessity, childhood in those days was of much shorter duration than at present, in that most of them had left school and were in some sort of employment by the time they were fourteen.

As proof of this the 1901 Census at Pilot Acre in Stonefield Road reveals that Kate the eldest, aged 15, was a bottle washer in the local lemonade factory and Peter, aged 13, was a Hutch Drawer in a coal mine. The latter is a clear indication that little had changed in the thirty one years since Andra had gone to work at the age of ten. Notices posted at the pit-head informed anyone who cared to read them that no one under the age of fourteen was permitted by law to work underground but this was totally ignored by all and sundry. According to Andra, if a father took his son along and said he was fourteen no one bothered to check if this was correct. As ever, in most instances it was a matter of needs must. There were many mouths to feed in the average mining household and, in keeping with normal practice in the rest of the mining community, any member of the family who was deemed capable of working was more or less obliged to do so to help the family survive.

McAnulty Family Group (back row, from left to right); Peter, Mary, Andrew, Jeannie, Joe, Agnes (middle row); Lizzie, Andra, Nellie, Mary, Kate (front row); Charlie, Maggie, Willie

In their turn therefore Peter, Joe and Andrew went straight from school at this age to work in the bowels of the earth as this was more or less the only employment available to themselves and others in the village and surrounding area. I asked Andra what young men like themselves did for recreation at the weekends after work and he told me that Peter and Andrew were both prominent local football players, Andrew in particular being a very fast and skilful winger. Football at the weekends or long summers' evenings he said, was the average miner's escape from the harsh realities of the dangerous and taxing work performed by them at the coal face. Matches between local teams were fiercely contested, all the more so if it was between teams from two different coal mines in the village.

These confrontations in particular attracted large crowds of spectators and no quarter was asked or given on the field. Many small bets on the outcome of the match were exchanged and this only added to the tension both on and off the field of play. As many of the matches were played on rough ash/shale (which was obtained from the nearest pit bing) surfaces, cuts and bruises were quite common and accepted as part and parcel of the game.

Some of these pitches were still being used for matches between local teams when I was in my teens and I still have the scars to prove it! Football boots worn by the players in my early days didn't have the stylish shape and man made soles and screw in studs as worn by today's generation. The boots were made entirely of heavy leather as were the studs, which were affixed to the soles of the boots by four nails in each, using a hammer and a cobbler's last or 'de'ils foot' as it was known. During games, especially those played on the hard, ash surfaces, the heads of these nails became exposed and any contact with an opponent's legs etc could cause considerable damage to say the least. On one such occasion after a wild tackle from one of the opposing team I received two, three inch parallel cuts on the inside of my right knee. These were quite deep, in addition to which a considerable amount of ash from the surface of the ground was embedded in the wounds. Although these wounds were cleaned out by my brother-in-law Samuel (using a nail brush!), when they healed I was left with two blue scars, which I still have to this day. As most miners had several similar scars acquired from the many scrapes and scratches they received underground, I always felt, and still do, that I had in some way become a 'blood brother' to my mining ancestors. It was a standing joke amongst the miners that the colour of these scars proved that they were of Royal descent but my imagination was never tempted to stretch that far!

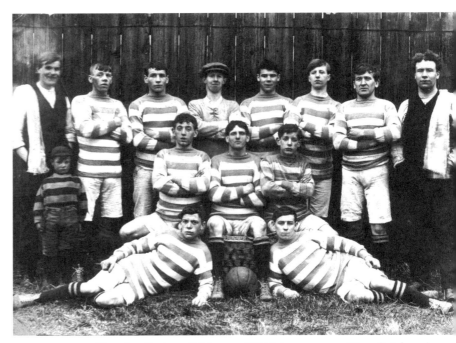

Team from Springwell, Blantyre c1924 (photo courtesy of Betty Swinburne)

Fortunately I received my scars while I was enjoying a game of football and not while I was risking life and limb at the coal face. For this I was truly thankful. Coal mining jobs were plentiful when I left school but, fortuitously and unlike my ancestors, I was privileged to be given the opportunity by my parents to have a decent education and thereafter seek employment away from the coal mining industry. Based on their own knowledge of what a hard, dangerous and unhealthy life mining was, I doubt if they would have let myself or my brother go to work in the mines anyway.

Unlike Peter and Andrew, Andra said that Joe, although he enjoyed watching his brothers playing football, was a more studious type and gave every indication that he would, in different circumstances, have liked to have gone to university. He was a great favourite with the younger members of the family in particular and spent a lot of his spare time with them, especially if they required assistance or encouragement with their school lessons. Andra said that Joe also liked to make playthings for them and remembered vividly the time that he had made them a 'bogie.' This was fashioned by securing a short plank of wood across a set of wheels taken from an old pram to form a makeshift cart. This provided the youngsters with endless hours of fun as they pushed and pulled each other around in the bogie in the streets around the family home. Tragically Joe's life was destined to come to an abrupt and unpleasant end, but more of that later.

Willie, who was born in 1903, was described to me by Andra as a bit of an enigma. He said that Willie had no desire to work in the mines when he left school in 1918 and indeed showed little or no desire to work at anything at all, particularly in the first few years after leaving school. Prompted by Andra he obtained and

Blantyre Bowling Green (J. Cornfield collection)

left a few jobs, most of the time blaming his employers for singling him out for unfair treatment i.e. they probably expected him to work for his money! This penchant for the easy life caused a lot of friction between himself and Andra and, in 1930, Andra told him that he was not prepared to subsidise him with free lodgings any longer. Willie's response to this was to travel down to my parent's home in Penrith, purportedly to live with them until he could obtain employment locally.

This proved to be a bit of a sham and my father (who had himself been forced to move to the area to seek employment after he returned from France at the end of the First World War) said that Willie demonstrated little or no intention of looking for work. Being unemployed appeared to suit him and he seemed quite content to sit around the house all day while my father went out to work to earn money to feed him. This went on for some months until one day my father came home to discover that Willie had obviously spent some considerable time during the course of the day practising his signature on several sheets of note paper! Willie was 'invited' by my father to return to Blantyre forthwith. This appeared to be the making of him because, not long thereafter, he met and subsequently married a local girl called Nan Thompson and this (or her) appeared to give him the incentive to work on a more permanent basis thereafter.

When I asked Andra what type of work the girls in the family did he explained that work opportunities for women in Blantyre were even more limited than they were for men. Some, like the elder daughter Kate, worked in the lemonade factory in High Blantyre owned by the McLean Brothers who's main products were 'Gold Medal' Lemon Squash and 'Superior' Gingerade. The reputation and enjoyment of these soft drinks went far beyond the boundaries of Blantyre and Andra said that, after being bottled by the female employees in the factory, crate loads

McLean Brothers, Logo

of them were loaded on to the back of horse drawn carts and thereafter delivered to their many customers by five teams of carters/salesmen on a daily basis. Like her brothers, Kate too had several scars on her hands and arms but in her case they were caused by the many cuts she suffered from broken bottles in the factory during the bottling process.

Other girls, like my mother and her sister Jeannie, found employment as trainee dressmakers. They were more fortunate than those of their peers who found themselves 'in service' as domestic servants in the houses of the better off people locally and beyond. According to Andra the latter employment in many instances led to the exploitation of many of the young girls involved, depending on the nature of the people they worked for. As with most jobs in these extremely harsh times, the remuneration received was not in direct proportion to the expectations of the employers and these expectancies were considerable to say the least. For their pittance of a wage these very young girls were first required to report for duty very early in the morning and, as in many instances their place of employment was up to three miles distant from their own homes, this distance had to be walked before and after work each and every day. The paths and roads which had to be negotiated by the girls were not, of course, covered in tar-macadam as we know them today and were in most cases full of mud-filled potholes. In that there were also no street lights, the daily excursion to and from work was a hazardous one indeed especially on dark winter mornings and evenings. The time taken to complete this walk, often in cold and wet conditions, added a considerably to the duration of their already long working day but, unlike the situation nowadays, they had little opportunity to escape from it by seeking alternative employment elsewhere.

McLean Brothers, Staff

As my mother explained it to me, based on real life experiences of her friends, once the girls arrived at their place of work after circumnavigating the various pedestrian hazards en route, their first task was usually to clean out the previous days ashes from the several fireplaces in the house and re-light the coal fires. This was a particularly dirty task and involved many trips outside to the rear of the house, first to empty the ashes in to bins and thereafter to carry in enough heavy pails of coal to keep the fires going all day after they were lit. This job completed, there were steps outside front and back doors to be scrubbed and whitened before they moved back inside the house to begin making beds, cleaning, dusting and polishing their way through the various rooms. Each and every one of these tasks was checked assiduously by the mistress of the house to see if they had been done as per her instructions.

As if this wasn't difficult enough they had, in many instances, to survive tests of their honesty by some of the mistresses. One such test, as described to me by my mother, was to place a penny on the floor behind a piece of furniture to see if the girl would either admit to having found it or keep it for herself. If she did neither she would be chastised for not cleaning behind the furniture! Another ploy might be to leave a few oat-cakes on a plate in the kitchen to see if one or more was eaten by the girl. When one remembers that a penny was worth a lot in those days and that the juveniles concerned were often hungry, these were great temptations to place before these youngsters. Although most of them were too honest to appropriate the money, inevitably, one or two did surrender to the delights of an oat-cake and actually lost their employment for so doing.

Lemonade Delivery Men

All work and no play

Reading the notes of my discussions with Andra about the activities and life style of his and others' children between the years 1890 and 1920, made me think of what my generation did in the same village at the time of my deliberations with him in the mid to late 1940's. On reflection, as far as games and activities were concerned, I don't think that much had changed in that fifty years or so. Street games obviously had passed down from one generation to the next and had, I imagine, changed in only minor ways. In comparison, the difference between then and now is remarkable, in that street games are now more or less non existent. .

Being naturally energetic, I didn't, of course, spend all of my spare time in Andra's company, as our in depth talks only took place about twice a week. On most other days, after I came home from school, I would only be with him long enough to read out those items in the newspaper that he was interested in. As soon as I was finished I would immediately be off outside to get involved with my friends in whichever the street games were taking place. Few people had cars in those days and the only danger of being run over was by either one of the horse drawn vehicles owned by the local Co-operative Society, which delivered milk, bread and coal etc to the residents, or that of 'Blin' (blind) Watty Irvine who sold paraffin from the back of his cart. Like others who witnessed it, we used to marvel at the astuteness of Watty's horse as it moved assuredly through the streets from one stopping place to the next; Watty meanwhile walking along holding the side of the cart, confident in the knowledge that the horse knew where they were going. Many of the locals fed the horse titbits at these stopping places and this may have had some influence on its ability to circumnavigate the route!

The games we played were numerous and varied. Inevitably, games of football were in the ascendancy, usually about four or five a side and played in the middle of the road with a small rubber or tennis ball. Great skill was required to retain control of these balls and this is where the expression 'tanner ball players' was invented to describe a player who was good at dribbling the ball round opponents. Jackets or lampposts, or both, served as goal-posts and endless, imaginary cup finals were won and lost on a daily basis. When one considers that this activity was being replicated in streets the length and breadth of the land, it is little wonder that many gifted footballers emerged from this environment to become star players in the senior teams of their generation.

A variation of our football matches took place in the long summer evenings and weekends when games took place a large expanse of nearby waste ground, this time with a proper leather football. Males, young and old, from the immediate area would naturally gather there every evening or weekend and sides would be picked by the two, usually self appointed, captains. A toss of a coin would determine which of them had first pick, the winner then choosing the best player from among the would-be players. The second best player was then chosen by the other captain, this system being repeated until all players had been selected. The number of players on each side could be anything between eight and fourteen, depending on how many had turned up on that particular occasion. the more the merrier seemed to be the thing.

Once again jackets would be put down to serve as goal-posts and basic rules would be agreed as to where the touch lines were etc. There was no referee of course but games were usually played in a good spirit. The most frequent cause of arguments that I can recall was whether or not the ball had gone between the jackets or posts, or was above the height that a proper crossbar would have been. Duration of the games wasn't measured by the clock but by the number of goals scored. Six goals was usually half time and twelve goals time. When one game finished, new sides would be chosen and the whole process would be repeated as often as time permitted, unless of course the bladder inside the leather cover burst, as it did frequently. This usually brought the proceedings to an abrupt end.

Back in the streets, the games played were numerous and often involved both boys and girls. Ones that spring to mind are:

Rounders - A miniature version of baseball in which two sides were picked, one being the batting side and the other the bowling side. Four bases were chalked on the road and battle commenced. Proper bats were unheard of and the batting side had to improvise with whatever was available - usually a piece of wood from a garden fence. On occasion an old tennis racquet would be used but not very often.

Hide and Seek was also a favourite but I'm sure that I don't have to describe that to anyone.

Tig (tag) - In the same category as hide and seek.

Kick the Can and Run - A variation of hide and seek in which a circular *'den'* was chalked on the road, in the middle of which a tin can was placed. After people went to hide, as each one was found they had to go and stand in the middle of the circle until, either everyone else had been 'caught' and made to stand in the circle or someone managed to run from their hiding place without being caught and kick the can out of the circle. This allowed those in the den to run off and hide again. Traditionally, the person who kicked the can away shouted out *'Nurkie, Nurkie'* as he/she did so but none of us had a clue why. It was just one of those things that was passed down from one generation of children to the next as we grew up.

Moshie - This was a game played with marbles, or bools as we called them. Three small holes in a straight line, at approximately three foot intervals, would be scooped out of the ground, with a fourth off at an angle a further few feet away. One had to negotiate this course by 'plunking' their bools in and out of the holes in to reach the fourth one in less shots than their opponent(s) to win.

Beds - This was our version of Hopscotsch. Although this was traditionally a girls game, often we boys would take part. Rectangles would be chalked on the pavement in a formation and numbered one to ten. Players had to hop on one foot and push a small 'peever' from one to ten and back again with the side of this foot, without letting the 'peever' land on one of the chalk lines. The 'peever' was usually an empty shoe polish tin which had been filled with gravel or dirt to make it heavier.

Girs and Cleeks - The gir was a round metal hoop, made by the local blacksmith, which was pushed along with a piece of wire called a cleek. The cleek was about two feet long and one end was bent into a small 'u' shape, which assisted whoever was pushing the gir to control it. The wire to make the cleek was usually 'acquired' from one of the old fences which ran alongside the nearby railway line.

Peerie - This was our name for a wooden spinning top, which was made to spin by hitting the peerie with a small whip made from a short stick and a piece of string. Again this was traditionally a girl's activity but we boys frequently got involved. We often decorated the peerie with coloured chalks to create patterns as the peerie revolved.

Apart from the horse-drawn vehicles, the only other interruptions that I can recall were when some of the local worthies made their appearance in our midst. One regular was a man called John Graham. John was a Christian and an extremely religious man and appeared to have dedicated his life to preaching God's message in the streets of Blantyre at every opportunity. Andra told me that John had been doing this for at least forty years that he could remember. When he appeared in our particular street, he stood in the middle of the road for about ten minutes and told anyone who was listening that they were sinners etc. This obviously included us, as we normally stopped whatever activity we were involved in at the time and squatted down on the adjacent pavement to wait patiently for him to finish his declamation. Passers by, who like ourselves knew John so well, rarely paused to listen to him but he carried on regardless, being content to project his message towards us and in the general direction of the houses on either side of him. Despite the fact that he came across to us as being extremely eccentric, we would never have dreamed of mocking him and, if we had, our parents would have made sure that it didn't happen again!

Another frequent 'visitor' to our streets that I remember was a man called Willie Tonner. Willie liked a drink and his means of earning money to buy it was to go round the streets of the village busking. His chosen method of entertaining the public at large was to play the mouth organ, stamping his foot in time to the music as he did so. I use the word music in its loosest term because it was sometimes difficult to tell which tune he was playing. As with John Graham, we used to squat down to watch and listen to Willie until he moved on to his next venue.

Pech Brae, Blantyre

In decent weather, if we weren't involved in the various games or activities described above, everyone would walk the mile or so to a deep pool in the nearby River Calder or 'Cawther' as it was known. This was reached by walking down a very steep brae (hill) which was/ is called the Peth Brae. Climbing back up the brae on the way home it was easy to work out why the locals called it the 'Pech Brae, 'pech' being an old Scottish word for pant (as in breathing heavily when exerting oneself).

The pool had been formed in bygone days by locals piling rocks across the river to create a dam of sorts. The gently sloping, grassy banks on both sides of the river formed a natural amphitheatre, which easily accommodated the many people who congregated there on these occasions to swim or sunbathe, or both.

This being a time when people were content with the simple things in life, whole families spent many happy hours at this venue. An old blanket would be spread on the grass and that would be the family's base for the duration of their visit. When not in the pool, the children played endless games along the river banks, their parents secure in the knowledge that other parents would be keeping an eye on them also to prevent them coming to any harm.

Unlike today, thirsty/hungry children did not have access to cans of juice, potato crisps etc. Instead they quenched their thirst by drinking from bottles of tap water brought from home and, if they were lucky, gratefully ate slices of bread and jam to appease their hunger.

By the time everyone got home in the evening, adults and children alike were tired but happy. A great day had been had by all at little or no expense.

Tossing and Turning

One place that we youngsters weren't welcome at certain times was on a particular part of the banks of the much larger River Clyde, which flows through the bottom end of the village and forms a boundary between Blantyre and Bothwell. The reason that we weren't welcome ' doon the braes' was because this was where the local 'Tossing School' activities took place, usually on Saturday and Sunday afternoons.

In those days, to obtain maximum coal supplies for the war effort, miners and others worked till lunch time on a Saturday. On reaching the surface at the end of their shift the miners collected their wages at the pit head office and most of them then went home. Be that as it may, a dedicated minority (those of a gambling persuasion), made their way to the secluded spot on the river bank, their hard earned wages in their pockets. There, after posting lookouts to alert them if the police were seen approaching the venue (this of course was an illegal activity), they formed a large circle round a ringmaster or 'babber' as he was called and the proceedings were set in motion.

The 'babber' would call one of the players forward into the circle and hand him a thin, flat piece of wood about four inches long by one and a half inches wide. Two pennies were then placed on the wood, 'tails' side uppermost, and the player would then send these spinning into the air, allowing them to land on the flattened earth at his feet. Immediately before he did this, bets were struck amongst the crowd as to whether the coins would land showing either a pair of 'tails' or a pair of 'heads'. The player himself usually had a few supporters who placed bets on his behalf. If the coins landed showing one 'head' and one 'tail' they were tossed up again until a pair was achieved.

LIVINGSTONE'S BIRTHPLACE, BLANTYRE. (BEFORE IT WAS RESTORED).

David Livingstone's Birthplace Before Restoration

I have refrained from calling this a game because it was taken very seriously by all concerned, in that money was involved. Occasionally there were disputes about the authenticity of individual tosses and this is where the 'babber' became involved. He was usually one of the local 'hard men' with a reputation of being able to handle himself in a fight, and he was the sole arbitrator in all such disputes. For his trouble in controlling events he received a remuneration from each person who was elected to toss the coins, so this was a highly prized position. His reputation was usually enough to dissuade potential trouble makers but from time to time an impromptu fight would take place to settle an individual issue. The 'babber' had to be seen to be able to control the proceedings by winning these fights convincingly, because any failure to stamp his authority on the session would mean that his position would become untenable.

In addition to the 'Tossing School' there were, in the near vicinity, several small groups playing cards for money. Pontoon was the usual game and each hand would be keenly contested.

As in all forms of gambling, there were winners and losers and those who took part in the tossing schools and the card games were no exception to the rule. For this reason, a good number of the participants would trudge home to their wives and families at the end of the day having lost their entire wages, causing great distress to one and all.

At this time, as it still is today generally in our society, addiction to gambling was a problem for certain people and the mining communities had more than their share of addicts. For some it was a weakness for taking part in the tossing schools or the cards, or both. For others it was a daily wager on horse racing. For many, unfortunately, it was a liking for all three.

Unlike modern times, those who wished to place a bet on the horses, didn't have access to the many bookmakers shop which we have in our midst today and this provided another spectacle for we bystanders. Legally, betting was only allowed on the actual race courses so, on selected street corners in both High and Low Blantyre and always in close proximity to a public telephone box, the 'street bookies' (illegal) would take up their stance each racing day. Individuals (men and women alike) could then be observed approaching them to put on their betting lines. In addition to this, most factories, collieries etc would have an employee who was a designated 'bookie's runner' and his job was to collect the bets from his co-workers and pass them on to one of the illegal bookmakers, often via the public telephone.

The bookmaker or one of his runners would use the telephone to pass (lay off) some of their bets to the course bookmakers, and also to ascertain the winners of individual races. Their activities were well known to the local police and now and then what amounted to a token 'raid' was made on an individual bookie and his runner(s). Local rumour had it that these bookies were tipped off in advance about the raids and paying a fine periodically was an acceptable price to pay for their activities. The police, some of whom it was alleged had surreptitious means of using the services of the bookies, were of course also seen to be doing their duty!

Glasgow Road, Blantyre

Other Pursuits

In the autumn and winter months of course our activities after school were curtailed, as it was dark shortly after we returned from school. Because of war regulations there were, of course, no street lights to illuminate our play area so playing outside was more or less ruled out. Instead, as we didn't have access to the many electronic games which seem to have taken over our present generation of childrens' lives, we had to content ourselves with simple indoor games like Snakes and Ladders, Ludo and/or card games like Old Maid.

At weekends in the autumn, when the time was right, we used to go searching for chestnut trees in the nearby fields and lanes. When we found one, we had great fun throwing sticks up into the branches to dislodge the green shells which held the chestnuts. When they fell to the ground, each of us prised as many chestnuts from the shells as we could and we then took them home to someone's garden shed, where we duly bored holes through each chestnut with a nail and threaded it on to a piece of string. Thereafter, we had endless contests as we tried to break a 'chessie' held up by an opponent on its piece of string with one of our own.

Numerous ploys were used to make one's chestnuts harder to break, the most common of these being to either heat them in a hot oven or soak them in vinegar for a while - or both. Although we convinced ourselves that these stratagems worked, I'm quite sure that it made little or no difference to the durability of any individual chestnut, as they all ended up broken anyway.

When winter arrived we were delighted if we were 'blessed' with a period of icy weather because this allowed us to make slides on the pavements. In particularly cold spells, I can recollect an almost continuous slide all the way from where we lived in High Blantyre to Low

Broadway Cinema Glasgow Road, Blantyre

Blantyre. Adults, of course, didn't always appreciate our slides and, when the surface got too slippery for some, they would bring out ashes from their coal fires and throw them on the slide in front of their particular house, much to our dismay. Our leather footwear was appropriate for making a good contact with the icy surface and the fact that so many youngsters in modern times wear trainers on their feet is probably the reason why we rarely see children sliding nowadays.

When we weren't involved in any of the activities described we relied on the cinema to entertain us. Blantyre had two cinemas to vie for our custom, The Picture House and The Broadway. Although I've given The Picture House its Sunday name, it was affectionately known to all and sundry as 'The Doocot'. As a youth I always understood that it acquired this nickname because the corrugated materials used in its construction and its shape gave it a 'pigeon loft' appearance, or that it was because people were crammed into it like pigeons in their lofts. Not so. While researching the reason, I unearthed an article in the Hamilton Advertiser about the cinema and its long serving manager, Jack Brown. When asked how it came by the nickname, Jack said that he deliberately turned up the heating on winter evenings so that it was just a *'cosy, warm wee place'.* Jack also spoke of the cinema's association with Blantyre, dating back to the 1920's, including its services to the community during the General Strike of 1920, when management dispensed free soup and meals to the hard pressed strikers. Ending his interview (given after he retired), Jack said that he had never found a town that was so welcoming as Blantyre. The people were so honestly warm and open and he and his family would always have very happy memories of the thirty years they had spent in the town.

In contrast to The Picture House, The Broadway, being of more modern construction, was more upmarket and altogether more comfortable. It also had a balcony which was favoured by courting couples.

Blantyre Picture House (J. Cornfield collection)

Probably because it was an escape from the harsh realities of life in the war years, cinemas were extremely popular and Blantyre's two were no different to the rest. Every evening, without exception, queues of people could be witnessed outside both cinemas, as they waited to see the latest epics involving their favourite film stars. Admission to the front rows of 'The Doocot' was three-pence and six-pence for the seats at the rear. Prices for The Broadway were six-pence, nine-pence and one shilling and six-pence (about 8p) for the balcony.

Although this seems relatively cheap nowadays, raising funds for admission required a little ingenuity and a lot of effort from my half dozen or so friends and myself. For some, maybe once a week for the Saturday matinee showing, it was simply a matter of using our meagre pocket money or asking our parents for it, but this also presented problems. Not everyone, including me, received pocket money on a regular basis and those that did received little in any case. Many parents simply couldn't afford it. Our answer to this was to pool the money that we had amongst us to find out the shortfall for our combined admission: having established this we then went foraging for empty lemonade and beer bottles, each of which could have the monetary deposit, which had been charged at the time of purchase, redeemed by the appropriate shop or pub.

Sometimes obtaining the empties was easier than others as, based on previous experience, we methodically knocked on the doors of neighbours who had handed over bottles to us in the past. On other occasions we had to cast our net further until we had reached our target. I suppose in some respects we were the forerunner of today's bottle banks!

Once we had sufficient bottles we then had the task of trying to get the relevant shopkeepers or bar staff to compensate us for our efforts. In the main they would only accept bottles whose labels matched the brands sold by them in their particular outlet, so we had to ultimately learn how to match bottles to outlets to improve our chances of success. Each pub normally had a side door which led in to a tiny room separate from the main bar. Customers (us) had then to ring a bell at the small counter to attract the attention of one of the staff so that we could try and negotiate our trade in. This separation from the main bar was important because it prevented any contact between ourselves and the men drinking in the pub. I say men because it was almost unheard of in those days for a so called decent female to enter a pub. If and when we were successful in disposing of all of our bottles our little band of budding entrepreneurs would make immediate haste to either The Doocot or The Broadway.

Whilst we obtained our quota of empty bottles the hard way, we knew at least two enterprising (if that's the word) youths who would regularly climb over the wall at the rear of a particular pub in Glasgow Road, Blantyre and remove empty bottles from the crates that were outside of the back door of the pub awaiting collection by the delivery men. They would then take them round to the side door of the same pub and trade them in for cash!

As was common in those days, films were shown twice nightly and each film was shown for two nights only. Unlike today, audiences would, in addition to the main film, see a 'B' film or 'wee' picture as we called it. This was shown first followed by the newsreels and possibly a cartoon. After a short interval for the sale of ice cream, the main or 'big' picture was shown.

Because the first showing commenced at or just before 6 p.m. which was too early for many working people, it was a common occurrence for patrons to enter the cinema half way through one of the films, view it from there to the end of the performance, and then sit through the second performance until it had reached the point where they started watching. The theory was that they would then leave but many, for various reasons, would remain to the end of the film again. This of course caused problems for the people who were still waiting outside in the queues to get in. On a nightly basis, cinema staff were always trying to 'encourage' those whom they thought had seen the full programme to leave. The staff didn't always get this right and these instances gave rise to the well known cry of *Burn The Doocot* which was yelled by disgruntled youths if they considered that they had been ejected unfairly.

At the risk of repeating something mentioned earlier in my story, in comparison the present day there is no doubt in my mind that, when we then settled back in our seats to watch the latest adventure epic in these very basic cinemas, we really appreciated it. Any similarity between this and the present day set-up of multi-cinema complexes is, in my mind, merely coincidental. We were just pleased to get in to the cinema and watch the films: based on the experience of taking my godchildren to a film of their choice, children observed nowadays need at least fifteen minutes to select a bag of sweets from the pick and mix selection, a box of popcorn and a carton of cola before they will even contemplate entering the auditorium to view the film. Once inside, their attention is divided between the consumption of said goodies and actually watching the film. In some cases repeat visits, during the performance, to the aforesaid sales area to top up their supplies of goodies seem almost mandatory. Adults accompanying said children, especially ones of my generation, literally watch and wonder, i.e. try and watch the film and wonder at what is going on around them.

Reading over the last two chapters, I realise that, although these were austere times or, perhaps because of it, young people of my generation had a happier and healthier lifestyle than our counterparts today. Lots of natural activity and frugal meals ensured that overweight children were almost non existent. In the main, our games and activities cost our parents nothing and there was literally no threat to our security while we were outside the family home. Happy days.

Family Losses

While discussing the family life with my mother one day, she told me that Andra had 'lost' four of her five brothers and two of her sisters over the years in various circumstances. She didn't elaborate, perhaps sensing that the explanation would be more in context if it came from Andra himself. This reticence on her part merely whetted my appetite to learn more and I resolved to seek the answers from Andra himself when I next had a chat with him. This was my intention of course but, being somewhat naive, I thought it would only be a matter of asking him and the answers would be immediately forthcoming. Oh the innocence of youth!

When I first broached the topic with Andra he adroitly changed the subject, using the skills that he had honed in countless debates over the years. Despite being thwarted in my first attempt to elicit the details of Andra's 'losses' I was determined to persuade him to tell me about them, as my involvement and interest in his life had by this time extended far beyond the original brief. Accordingly I made another attempt on a future occasion but, yet again, I was gently rebuffed. I discussed my frustration with my mother and she advised me that, if and when Andra felt the need to talk about these sensitive matters, he would do so. I can recall that her use of the word sensitive made me realise that it would be prudent to wait for Andra to take the initiative, if indeed he ever did.

Our regular discussions on general matters continued for a few weeks without either of us broaching the matter but eventually my patience was rewarded. On entering his room on this particular occasion I immediately noticed the photograph of the family group propped against the clock on the mantle-piece. I said nothing and, after a few seconds of silence between us, a knowing look appeared on his face. He confessed that, apart from the disaster at Dixon's Pit, he had never found it easy to discuss the sadness he felt about some of the events that had occurred in the personal life of himself and his family. He had given my request a great deal of thought and had concluded that it was unfair to expect me to be privy to selected parts of his life only. Accordingly, he was going to give me a brief insight into the various family related events in chronological order as they occurred in his life. I never knew what inspired him to do so on this occasion but always suspected that, behind the scenes so to speak, my mother may have acted as the catalyst between us.

GLASGOW ROAD, BLANTYRE

Glasgow Road, Blantyre

Heartbreaks by the Number

The first and by far the worst of these events occurred in the family home at 17 School Lane, High Blantyre, on the twenty second of March, 1914 when his wife Mary (51) tragically died after a short illness. Cause of death as recorded on her death certificate was due to a cerebral embolism. Such was the suddenness of her death that the family were in a state of complete shock for a long time thereafter. She had always been a loving, hard working wife and mother and the family were absolutely distraught. Apart from her domestic duties she had, for many years, been secretary to the headmaster of the local school and, for this reason allied to the fact that she was the wife of such a well known personage in the community, was known and respected by almost everyone in the Blantyre district. My mother, who was only thirteen years of age at the time, recalled that there was a massive crowd of people of all ages at her funeral.

As was the custom then and no doubt still is in similar circumstances Mary, the eldest daughter still living at home, immediately gave up her job and undertook responsibility for looking after the family. This was absolutely necessary as, apart from my mother, Joe (22) Andrew (18) Agnes (15) Nellie (12) Wull (11) Charlie (10) and Maggie (8) were still living in the family home. In many ways the transition was a simple one in that Mary was very mature for her age and had always been of great assistance to her mother with housework etc. She was also much loved by her brothers and sisters and she quickly assumed her mother's mantle. Andra related that he had suffered badly from acute depression in the immediate aftermath of the bereavement (this was later confirmed by my mother) and he said that, unable to cope as he was for a considerable time, he and the rest of the family would have been in dire straits indeed if it hadn't of been for Mary.

Maggie McAnulty

Under Mary's careful guidance the family gradually got back to some sort of normality, except that is for the youngest member Maggie. Despite Mary's finest efforts to take her mother's place in as many ways as possible, Maggie was inconsolable and simply lost interest in everything and every one. Probably as a consequence of this, it took a great deal of persuasion on Mary's part to induce her to eat even the tiniest meal. Her brother Charlie who was normally very close to her tried every subterfuge that he could think of to bring her out of her misery but even he had to admit failure. As my mother succinctly described it, quite clearly Maggie was suffering from a broken heart.

This state of affairs prevailed for several months and several medicines and tonics prescribed by the doctor were tried. Each and every one in their turn failed either to lift her depression or improve her appetite. Gradually she became so weak that she was confined to bed but after several weeks of this her condition became so bad that she was removed to the Victoria Hospital in Glasgow. Doctors at the hospital diagnosed her as suffering from tuberculous meningitis, which they said, had found little or no resistance when it attacked her weakened body. Notwithstanding the administrations of the caring staff and the literally round the clock bedside attendance of the family, about two weeks later Maggie slept peacefully away on the nineteenth of December, 1914. It was almost exactly nine months since the death of her beloved mother.

This must have been another shattering blow to Andra and the family, coming so soon after the loss of Mary, and I could clearly see the painful memories of both events imprinted on his features as he described them to me. He had obviously found it very difficult to talk to me about these sad circumstances but, to conceal this in his own inimitable manner, Andra concluded our session by asking me to go to the shop for tobacco for him. Having done so only the previous day I knew that he didn't actually need it but I appreciated that he/we had spoken enough for one day.

Casualty of the Great War

On the next occasion that we discussed personal family matters Andra spoke of another sad episode in his life.

The First World War affected the lives of millions of people all over the world but it was in the close confines of Andra's room that I was destined to learn at first hand how it had affected yet another member of my own family. I was already aware that my father had been involved in the campaign as a member of the Highland Light Infantry and that he had suffered badly from mustard gas inhalation while in the trenches at Paschendale, but knew little or no details of this. Like many of his peers, he never spoke of his experiences in those horrific battlefields, not even to my mother. One of the few facts that we knew was that he was in a trench in France on the day of his seventeenth birthday. Being just a few years short of this age myself I found it extremely difficult to comprehend this. Having researched these battles many years after his death, it is one of my greatest regrets that I did not appreciate fully in his lifetime the terrible experiences endured by himself and the others involved. No wonder he and many others didn't want to discuss them after they returned from the killing fields. They had no desire to be reminded of the horrors they had witnessed there.

Andra explained that Joe, then twenty three years old, had been amongst the first to volunteer when Field Marshall Kitchener called for men to sign up for his 'new army.' He had of course been working as a miner and Andra said that he and many of his fellow miners saw this as a way to not only fight and defeat the Germans but as a means of escaping the day to day drudgery of the mines. At first he joined the 10th Gordon Highlanders but some months later he transferred his allegiance to the 2nd. Camerons. Andra told me that the reason for this was that he wanted to 'look after' his younger brother Andrew who, although only eighteen years of age, was already serving with the 2nd. Camerons in France and who had only recently escaped certain death due to the courage of a brave comrade. Apparently, during an advance on the enemy, he had been knocked unconscious when a shell landed near him and was dragged to the 'safety' of a nearby trench by another soldier. This incident, Andra told me, was revealed in a subsequent letter to him to reassure him of Andrew's well-being - written at Andrew's behest by the soldier who had saved him.

Joe McAnulty

After the briefest period of training, in June 1915 Joe went to France with the regiment and was immediately linked up with his brother. For the next eighteen months or so Joe and Andrew fought alongside each other in the trenches, each looking out for the other, but at the beginning of 1917 Joe wrote home to Andra and advised him that he had been transferred to the 181st Tunnelling Company of the Royal Engineers. His skills as an ex miner were required to assist in the dangerous task of tunnelling under the German lines for the purposes of laying mines. The detonation of these huge mines under the enemy lines, as we now know, was to be the preliminary to the infamous Battle of the Somme. This task completed, on the 5th of March, 1917 he and the other ex-miners involved reverted to being cannon fodder again and took part in one of the many ill fated full frontal attacks on the enemy lines in the battle. During this attack Joe received a gunshot wound in the chest.

Andra was advised by a telegram from the War Office that Joe had been wounded and had been removed to the military hospital at Etaples, France. Shortly thereafter he received a letter from Joe to say that he was recovering well and didn't want them to worry. The family were elated at this news, especially as during the next few weeks, he wrote another letter in similar vein. However, just when they were looking forward to him being sent home to convalesce, Andra received another telegram, this time to advise him that Joe had died on the 5th of April, 1917. Joe's demise, like many of his comrades, had occurred because the wounds became infected, ultimately causing death by blood poisoning. In modern times these infections, which were almost inevitable in the makeshift surroundings of the field hospitals, would have been rapidly countered by use of antibiotics but the discovery of penicillin and their like was long in the future.

Andra looked strained as he went on to tell me that the extreme sadness caused by this tragic occurrence was compounded when, several days later, the postman delivered a letter for young Charlie (10) which had been written by Joe the day before he died. At this point in his narrative Andra directed me to get and read the aforementioned letter, from one of the drawers in his desk. The contents revealed that, even the day before he died, Joe himself seems to have been assured by the medical staff that he was going to recover from his wounds. His letter to Charlie, based on their optimism, was obviously intended to reassure his younger brother that all was well. He concluded on a happy note by telling Charlie that he would, as Charlie had asked him to in a letter, build him a 'hen cavey' (which was local parlance for a hen shed/run) when he came home. Sadly, the hen cavey was destined never to be built.

Nestled in the drawer beside the letter were the only other visible mementos of Joe: a large service revolver in a brown leather holster lay side by side with two bayonets in their scabbards. Apparently it was then the normal procedure to return these things to the next of kin with their other meagre possessions. To an impressionable youngster like me these were fascinating items and, on a few occasions thereafter, Andra was prevailed upon by me to let me take them out and admire them. This displeased my father greatly when he found out about it and the weapons quickly disappeared from the drawer. I learned later that he had persuaded Andra to let him drop them into the nearby River Clyde from the viaduct bridge which spanned the water between Blantyre and Bothwell.

Typically, Andra, despite his grief, reacted to Joe's death by initiating a fund raising campaign to allow the people of Blantyre to donate a military ambulance to the war effort. He said that the public responded in their usual generous manner and the target was achieved in a few short weeks.

As part of my lengthy research into events described to me by Andra, I recently made the long journey to the cemetery in Etaples, France where Joe was laid to rest. Situated near the Port of Boulogne, Etaples was a small, quiet town until WW1. Because of its proximity to the port, where constant shiploads of troops were disgorged, a large military base camp, including a complex of hospitals, was established there. This was/is the largest camp ever built abroad by Great Britain and up to seventy thousand troops a month were processed through this camp before being sent on their way, by train, to the front line. The trains did not return from the front lines empty however. A history of the camp, written by renowned war historians Douglas Gill and Julian Putkowski, reveals that more than forty thousand sick and wounded soldiers were treated at Etaples in the course of any one month. When one considers these vast numbers it is little wonder that the staff were constantly over-stretched.

Etaples Military Cemetery, France

In view of the nature of Joe's end, it was interesting to read the following passage in this extremely well researched and written book:

The chief concern of medical services, in respect of patients who had survived the initial treatment and the journey to the base, related to the complications which were likely to set in. Of such complications, sepsis was the most frequently encountered. Given the prevalence of sepsis, and given the fact that bacteriology was in its infancy and that antibiotics were of course unknown, the hospital staffs had recourse to careful monitoring, to elaborate means of draining - and to very little else.

Perhaps as many as 70 per cent of the men struck in the chest died in the field and, of those who survived to reach a casualty clearing station, 24% died after an operation and a further 13% without.

The cemetery itself was an inevitable extension to the camp and hospital. Situated in what is now an extremely quiet area, it contains 10,769 Commonwealth burials of WW1 and the graves are beautifully maintained by the local people. As I stood at Joe's graveside, I was acutely aware that I was the first person from his family who had done so since that fateful day in 1917 and will probably be the last. It was a poignant moment for me. My mother had often expressed her regret at being unable to visit the grave and pay her respects to her dear brother, but family members in earlier times did not have the resources to make what would have been a long and complicated journey for them. As I added some small plants of Scottish heather to the existing display and scattered some pebbles taken from Andra's grave in High Blantyre, which I know she would have done if she'd had the opportunity, I hoped I had fulfilled her wishes. I know Andra would have been pleased.

Not long after completing this part of my family history, I was greatly but pleasantly surprised to receive the following poem (written by Andra) from Wilma Bolton, Hamilton. Wilma had discovered the poem in the *Hamilton Advertiser* during her own research into the lives of local miners and kindly passed it on to me. When I read it, I was stunned when I realised that it was highly probable that the soldier referred to was the one who had saved Andrew's life in the incident described to me by Andra;

TO MR AND MRS FRANK KANE, 3 Burnblea Street, Hamilton,
Whose son George Frederick Kane was Killed in Action on 24th September 1915:

I am now in receipt of your beautiful card
To memorise dear Fred,
But it seems to me to be awfully hard
To think that he is dead.

Now the card itself shows quite good taste.
And fills the artist's eye,
But the printed verse has not quite graced
The soul I ranked so high.

This stereotyped verse that is always on tap
Is a libel imposed on the dead
It's insultingly vague and leaves such a gap
When applied to a lad like Fred.

I have not had the pleasure of meeting your son
(A privilege on which I was set)
But I knew him so well for the good he had done
That I feel to be so much in his debt.

Since first I received his brusque human note
(From somewhere in Kitcheners camp)
I have treasured and praised every line that he wrote
For they fired me like Liberty's lamp.

Now the risks Fred took on behalf of my son,
Are the things that the world cannot know;
But for deeds of less merit big honours were won,
Whilst my gallant young hero laid low.

Let we who are left now cherish with pride
The love and the light that he shed.
And rejoice in the thought that we still have a guide
In the single-souled life that he led.

Andrew McAnulty
High Blantyre

On checking the War Graves Commission's web site for details of Fred's death, I discovered that his parents would not even of had the comfort of knowing when and where their son had been buried. Like many thousands of other brave soldiers, Fred's body was never recovered from the battlefield. All that remains to remind the world of his bravery is his name carved in stone at The Loos Memorial, his parents memories - and Andra's poem.

Information: The Loos Memorial forms the side and back of Dud Corner Cemetery, and commemorates over 20,000 officers and men who have no known grave, who fell in the area from the River Lys to the old southern boundary of the First Army, east and west of Grenay. Loos-en-Gohelle is a village 5 kilometres north-west of Lens, and Dud Corner Cemetery is located about 1 kilometre west of the village, to the north-east of the N43 the main Lens to Bethune road. Historical Information: Dud Corner Cemetery stands almost on the site of a German strong point, the Lens

Blantyre's Gift (J. Cornfield collection)

Road Redoubt, captured by the 15th (Scottish) Division on the first day of the battle. The name "Dud Corner" is believed to be due to the large number of unexploded enemy shells found in the neighbourhood after the Armistice. On either side of the cemetery is a wall 15 feet high, to which are fixed tablets on which are carved the names of those commemorated. At the back are four small circular courts, open to the sky, in which the lines of tablets are continued, and between these courts are three semicircular walls or apses, two of which carry tablets, while on the centre apse is erected the Cross of Sacrifice.

Pastures New

The next privations described to me by Andra, although not as shocking to me as his description of the loss of Joe, had obviously been very distressing to Andra when they occurred and this was evident as he described them to me during the course of our next few get-togethers.

Peter, his eldest son who like his father and brothers was also a miner, had met and married a local girl called Alice Heron, who lived with her family at 27 Calder Street, Blantyre. He and Alice set up home 184 Main Street, High Blantyre and were eventually blessed with a son named John, who was born in 1914. As Andra recalled, John, like so many infants of that era, was not a healthy child in the first few years of his life and Peter and Alice were quite concerned about his survival on one or two occasions. However by 1922, when John was eight years old, he seemed to have overcome his earlier health problems and this encouraged Peter to make a momentous decision.

Peter McAnulty

Alice's father John Heron was also a miner who, like all others of his ilk, was always struggling to survive on the meagre wages paid by the local coal mine owners. Inspired by the example of many of his colleagues, he had decided to emigrate to America to seek a better standard of living. Coal Mines in New Bedford, Massachusets, U.S.A. had inserted recruitment notices in the local newspapers offering assisted passages (payable by instalments from their wages) to miners and their families and a number of miners had already taken advantage of this offer. When one considers the deprivations the miners and their families had suffered, this was hardly surprising. As far as they were concerned nothing could be any worse than their present circumstances.

John Heron encouraged Peter and Alice to come with himself, wife Mary, daughter Margaret and sons James and Thomas, so that the two families would be able to mutually support each other in the new venture. Peter was keen on the idea but Andra said that, when he came to discuss it with him, he had tried very hard to dissuade him from the idea but to no avail. He had pointed out to Peter some of the obvious drawbacks and several that weren't so obvious, such as being stranded in America without the money to return home if things didn't work out. Going to this far off corner of the world Andra told him, also meant that they would probably never see each other again.

Hard though it was to leave the family behind, Peter decided to go and so it was, on the 19th of September, 1922 Peter and the others went to Glasgow and boarded The Algeria, a passenger ship owned by the Anchor Line, and set sail for New York en route to Massachusets and what they hoped was a new life. Andra recollected standing on the quay side watching the ship and its 535 passengers disappear from sight as it moved down the River Clyde on the first stage of its long journey. He told me that he was not afraid to admit that he shed a few tears as Peter's figure on the deck diminished as the distance between them increased, until finally he and the ship vanished round a bend in the river. He told me that, as he watched them depart, he instinctively knew that it was unlikely that he would ever see Peter again.

As Andra had feared, Peter's weekly letters home quickly revealed that the venture was proving to be an ill fated one. The mining community they had moved to was primitive to say the least and the living conditions were even more sparse than the ones that they had left behind. Working conditions in the mines weren't any better than at home and men, who had migrated to America from all corners of the globe, were hired and fired at the owners' whim. This intermingling of races also created many problems as the various cultures involved strove to learn to live and work beside each other.

Irrespective of these integration problems, the workers had no option but to survive as best they could. They didn't have the option to seek other employment because they had contracted to work for their employers at least until they had repaid the cost of their passage from home. In Peter's case there was the added complication that his son John's health, which had been aggravated by the dreadful bouts of seasickness he and they had suffered during the voyage across the Atlantic Ocean, was again causing anxiety. Andra said that it took Peter a little while to clear off his debt to his employers and that , during this period of time, letters from him became less frequent. He considered that Peter was either not wanting to worry him by constantly referring to the difficulties he was encountering, or was having guilt pangs about not heeding Andra's advice before he left home. Whatever the reason, it was a stressful time for Andra as he awaited the infrequent letters, which of course took a long time to come from America anyway.

Not long after Peter wrote in one of his letters that he had cleared his liability to the mine owners, Andra received another letter from him informing him that young John had died suddenly, citing pneumonia as the cause. Peter also indicated in this letter that, prompted by young John's death, he and Alice were going to move elsewhere to make a fresh start, hopefully finding employment away from the cursed mining industry. Andra was of course devastated at the loss of his grandson but was pleased that Peter was making a positive move to escape the clutches of the mine owners.

After a period of time with no further news from the couple, eventually a letter did arrive with an American postmark. Andra did not recognise the handwriting but when he opened the envelope he realised why. The letter had been written by Alice and, much to his surprise and consternation, she wanted to know if Andra could give her any information about Peter's whereabouts!

Apparently Peter had been very depressed for some time before John's death and his son's demise had affected him very badly. Discussions with Alice's father John Heron resulted in an arrangement being reached whereby Alice would stay with her family while Peter went on ahead to New York to both secure employment and find them somewhere to stay. Peter duly left and they had one message from him saying that he had arrived in New York, was staying in a hostel, and was going out the next day to look for a job. That had proved to be the one and only contact they had had from him. Sadly, from that day onwards, Alice never heard from Peter again. This was entirely out of character and she immediately feared the worst.

Andra said that, as soon as he received the dreadful tidings, he called a meeting of the other members of the family to discuss the situation. Several suggestions were put forward but Andra said that it didn't take long to persuade them to give him their blessing to go to America at the first possible opportunity to try and trace their brother. Accordingly, within a week he had withdrawn his life savings from the bank and this, added to by donations from family members and friends, allowed him to book himself a second class passage to New York on The Columbia, which was another of the Anchor Line's ships.

Thus it was, accompanied by my mother and father who were there to see him off, on the eighth of January, 1923, he found himself standing on the quay side at Broomielaw, Glasgow, one of 1,303 passengers (295 first class, 218 second class and 740 third class) waiting to embark on the ship. To her surprise my mother recognised a young man, Alexander Hall, who was standing nearby, as the fiancé of Margaret Heron (Peter's sister-in-law). It transpired that Alexander was emigrating to be with Margaret and was in fact going to the same address as Andra. My parents were delighted that Andra was going to have the company and assistance of this much younger man on what was known to be a fairly hazardous journey. Likewise, Alexander's parents, who were there to see him on his way, were equally happy that Andra would be able to provide counsel and support for their son should it be required.

Andra said little about the voyage other than to say that the boat seemed to be vastly overcrowded in proportion to its size and that the food provided was often revolting. Several people actually died during the voyage but he was unaware as to the cause of any individual death.

Despite these tribulations, Andra and Alexander duly arrived at the family home at 309 Maxfield Street, New Bedford, Massachusets. Two days after he arrived, although still fairly exhausted by his voyage, Andra, accompanied by Alice, began his search for his son. During the next few weeks he tried every means possible to either trace Peter or to find out what fate had befallen him. On contacting the police authorities in New York, although they were very sympathetic, he was advised that there was a constant turnover of the population of New York, as people arrived from the various ports around the world seeking a new life. This made it impossible for them to check the many thousands of lodging houses etc where these people lived, as they waited to move on to other areas or searched for work in New York itself. They told him that most of the arrivals had little or no money and crime was rife. Many of the victims of the more serious crimes had little or no means of identification on them when discovered, making it extremely difficult for the authorities to inform the next of kin. All of these unfortunate people were interred in unmarked graves. Andra said that, although they didn't put it into words, the inference was that Peter could have been the innocent victim of such a crime.

Andra confessed to me that, approximately one month after he arrived, he had to admit to himself that he had explored every avenue available to him without even a glimmer of success. In addition Alice and the other members of her family were concerned for his mental and physical well-being. Weeks of trailing around New York in his fruitless quest, often without stopping to eat or drink, had brought him to the point of complete exhaustion and he told me that he felt every one of his sixty two years. The family prevailed on him to return home and this he duly did.

Stonefield Road, Blantyre

When I asked Andra if he considered that some terrible fate had befallen Peter he said that, although like most people in his situation he still (twenty five years later) awaited each and every postal delivery with keen expectation, he was a realist by nature and didn't expect to hear from Peter now. Knowing his son as well as he did, he knew that Peter would not have knowingly lost contact with his family if he was alive and well. His sadness at not knowing what had become of Peter was felt by my mother and all of her brothers and sisters. He had been their oldest brother and was always there for them in a time of need when they were younger.

As a post script to this sad episode in Andra's life; I have made efforts in recent times via the internet etc to try and unravel the riddle. There are many sources now available that Andra's generation did not have access to death certificates etc but, despite this, the result is identical. Peter's disappearance from the face of the earth was, and still is, a complete mystery.

Domestic Upheaval

On checking the notes of our discussions I was reminded that, around about this point in Andra's narrative, there was a short break in the regular get-togethers between us as we all made preparations to move to a new address in the village. Since arriving in Blantyre from London my parents had been waiting for the opportunity to move to a house of their own and, when the chance arose, they grasped it. Although it had not been in their original plan to take Andra with us, growing concerns about his health motivated them to persuade him to come with us. It was quite a wrench for Andra to leave the house that he had lived in for so long but he obviously realised that it was in his best interests to do so.

No more would the front door of 55 Victoria Street be pushed open by one of the many people who visited Andra for all sorts of reasons, followed by a shout of, '*Are you in Andra, it's only so and so.*' This had been a long established practice and Andra told me that no door, in any house that he had ever lived in, had ever been locked. This was easy to believe because, although there was a lock on the door of 55, no matching key was to be found anywhere in the house.

The reasons people had to visit him were diverse, some social of course but the preponderance of callers were seeking help and advice from him on a variety of subjects. His lifetime's work in campaigning for social justice, allied to the vast experience gained in his time in local politics and as a Justice of the Peace, meant that he was well qualified to offer guidance to working class people who had little or no knowledge of such matters. No matter what he was doing when they called or, latterly, how well he was feeling, he afforded each and every person who called the same warm, bright welcome. His legion of contacts was innumerable and, if he was unable to help people who called, he would direct them

Tram in Stonefield, Blantyre

to the person or local office bearer who would be most likely to assist them with their particular problem. On these occasions his parting words were usually, '*Just tell them Andra McAnulty sent you.*' From personal experience I know that this phrase opened up most folks hearts and minds to even the humblest caller seeking their help.

Many who called were, of course, drawn from the ranks of those close friends who had worked alongside him over the years in local government, trade union and political fields. These included two who were serving Members of Parliament but who still found time in their busy schedules to come and pay their respects to the old fellow. They were no doubt well aware that if it hadn't of been for the strenuous efforts in earlier times of Andra and his likes, working class people like them would have had no chance of being elected to represent the interests of the common man.

For a youngster like me there were occasional perks to be had as a result of these visits, in the shape of the odd sixpence (2p) or two, the most memorable being a half-crown (12p) given to me by William Gallacher, one of the M.P's.

The Grass Seemed Greener

Once we had all settled in to our new surroundings our talks eventually assumed their normal pattern. To a youth of fifteen Andra's disclosures were spellbinding and I was eagerly compliant when he next chose to talk about the events surrounding the unfortunate reasons for the departure of another three members of his immediate family and the ultimate premature death of one of them.

Following the death of Joe at The Battle of the Somme, his brother Andrew had been transferred to another arena of conflict known as The Salonika Expedition (Greece). The Greek government had called on the Allies for assistance after becoming embroiled in hostilities when their neighbours Serbia had been attacked by Bulgaria. This involvement of the Allies had been going on since late 1915 but the timing of Andrew's arrival in September 1918 coincided with a full frontal attack on the Bulgarians which, after two weeks, resulted in unconditional surrender of the Bulgarians. This short but nevertheless bloody action was to prove to be Andrew's last combative action of the war and he returned to Blantyre and civilian life at the end of the year.

Andra said that the four years that he had been away from home had changed Andrew in many ways. This of course was not surprising considering his experiences in the trenches during this lengthy, dangerous period. Gone was the carefree youth who had set off to fight for his country. In his place was a mature man who proved to be a much more serious, broody type of individual. The death of his brother Joe, who had fought shoulder to shoulder with him in the trenches for so long, had clearly left its mark on him and Andrew said to his father, not once but many times, that he felt guilty that he and not Joe had returned from the war unscathed.

Understanding the reasons for the change in Andrew, his brothers and sisters did their best to integrate him into family life once more. He started work again in the coal mines and started playing football again for one of the local teams and, to the family's delight, soon discovered that there was more in life than work and football. This revelation occurred when he met and started going out with a nineteen year old Blantyre girl called Margaret Thomas who worked in the local Dye Works. After a courtship of about ten months they were married in The Manse of the local Established Church Of Scotland, on the fifth of December, 1919.

The Cross, High Blantyre

Andra recalled that they set up home in a house at The Cross, High Blantyre and, almost exactly one year later, their first child Mary was born, followed two years later by their second child Peggy. All seemed well but, on the 1st of February, 1924 Margaret, who was seven months pregnant, was rushed to the maternity hospital at Bellshill where she suffered a miscarriage. Complications set in and four days later she died. Her recently viewed death certificate indicates that cause of death was a miscarriage, leading to pneumonia and cardiac failure. Sadly miscarriages were an all too common occurrence among working class women, living and working in such poor conditions as they did.

Andra told me that, following the death of his wife, Andrew reverted to being the broody person who had returned from the war and generally seemed to go off the rails a bit and only the shortage of money prevented him from drinking more than was good for either himself or his family. Fortunately, immediately following their mother's death, the youngsters Mary and Peggy had been taken into Andra's home to be looked after by his daughter Mary and this proved to be a major factor in the events which thereafter unfolded.

Andrew McAnulty, Junior

This situation prevailed for another two years or so until what became known as The General Strike of 1926 occurred. During this strike, in which almost the entire industrial working population of the United Kingdom took part for a short period and the miners for many months thereafter, the United Kingdom was almost brought to a standstill as working people took desperate measures to improve their lot. The deprivations suffered during this long strike prompted many people to consider accepting assisted passages to other lands where job prospects seemed better. To Andra's consternation, two of those tempted to seek a more worthwhile life in the coal mines in far off New Zealand were Andrew and Charlie.

Andrew had never really settled down following the death of Margaret and the strike was the last straw. Although he was aware of the outcome of his brother Peter's ill fated American enterprise he considered that he could and would be successful where his older brother had failed. He made the point to Charlie and Andra that the many New Zealand troops he had met at Salonika had all spoken of what a great, if developing country they lived in. Twenty two year old Charlie had been extremely impressed by Andrew's declamation and was really keen on the idea also. Despite Andra's best efforts, nothing that he could say or do would dissuade them from their concept. Andra said that, on reflection in later years, he thought that what Andrew and Charlie probably didn't realise was that many of the men Andrew had met in the trenches lived and worked in rural communities. Few if any of them would have first hand experience of living and working in a mining environment in their homeland. If they had, he doubted if they would have inspired Andrew to consider going to work in them.

Mary McAnulty

Andrew's only problem was that he would not be able to go if he did not have someone to care for his children Mary and Peggy, who were now six and four years old respectively. Fate was to intervene however. When his sister Mary learned of Andrew's plans to take the children to the other side of the world she was thunderstruck. Since Andrew's wife had died she had been a mother figure to the children and couldn't contemplate life without them. She was now thirty years old and all of her brothers and sisters except Charlie had, by this time, married and left the family home. A great bond had developed between her and the children and, although she realised the effect it would have on Andra, she informed Andrew that, for the childrens' sake, she was willing to accompany him and the children across the world.

Andra intimated to me that, although he had been stunned when Andrew first appraised him of his plans, he understood and ultimately accepted the reasons behind his son's decision but said that he couldn't understand Mary's determination to go with them. What I didn't know at the time, but later learned from my mother, was that Mary had confided in her as to the deciding factor in her decision.

Apparently, since about twelve months previously a fellow member of the local council, who was frequently in their home 'talking shop' with Andra had, without Andra's knowledge, been paying a lot of attention to Mary and was hinting at marriage. When Andra discovered this he was less than pleased, knowing that the gentleman in question had a drinking problem and was, in his opinion, not a fit partner for his beloved daughter Mary. Unlike today, a father's approval (especially one like Andra) was essential in these matters and he made it quite clear that he would not condone any kind of relationship between them. It is hard to believe, living as we do in today's permissive society, but Mary acceded to her father's wishes and broke off all relations with her suitor. My mother said that, while this decision had pleased Andra, Mary, because of her age and the fact that she had sacrificed her own life looking after the family, considered that this had been her last chance of establishing a family of her own. From circumstances like these the seeds of discontent are often sown.

As he sorrowfully explained to me, Mary's loss to him, apart from the personal sorrow it inflicted, was twofold. First of all he was losing an excellent housekeeper and faithful companion who took great pride in making sure that he led as comfortable a life as possible at home. By now in his sixty-sixth year, he would thereafter become dependent on his other daughters (by now married) to care for his daily needs, which wasn't quite the same thing at all.

Equally as painful to him was the loss of Mary as physical and spiritual support to him when he ventured forth to attend the meetings of the many organisations in which he was involved. She it was who, in the main, assisted him to board and alight from buses, trams etc and also to clamber on and off platforms when he spoke at the various functions he attended. At many of these meetings, particularly the ones which took place during the mining strikes, it was she who stood up and made sure that the miners' wives and families points of view were aired.

He said that, apart from his admittedly selfish needs, her loss to the community was just as great. On many occasions she spoke out on behalf of the working people in the town and had always been an able assistant to Andra during the many strikes, when he organised soup kitchens for the families of the striking miners. As he described it, he organised the kitchens and the donations of food and she took charge of serving and distributing it.

In addition to this, when and if she heard of someone who was either ill or living in extremely poor circumstances or, what was often the case, both, she would immediately go and offer whatever help

Blantyre Railway Station (J. Cornfield collection)

was necessary depending on the situation. Friends and strangers alike benefited from her kindness on a regular basis and many people were nursed back to health due to her faithful ministrations.

Morning Departure

Despite his misgivings, on the appointed day Andra had arranged transport to take Andrew, Charlie, Mary and the two children to the railway station at Low Blantyre, from where they were to commence their long and arduous journey to far off New Zealand. He accompanied them to the station and there they were astonished to find that, as well as my mother and father and all the other members of the immediate family, approximately 400 local people who had preceded them were patiently waiting for them so that they could say a personal farewell to Mary in particular. Such was the esteem in which she was held by the villagers. According to Andra, the station officials were all but overwhelmed by the number of people who descended upon the relatively small station, causing them to send frantic messages down the line to warn relevant train drivers to approach the platform with caution. So dense was the crowd that many of them had to be asked to cross over to the platform at the other side of the line for safety reasons.

After much delay and countless embraces from all and sundry, the party waved their final farewells as the train slowly pulled out of the station. Andra said that, because all of this was so overwhelming, it wasn't until he returned home to a quiet, empty house that the full implications of what had happened struck him. By far the worst of these, he said, being that he knew that, although he knew it was Mary's intention to eventually return home when the children were older, it was unlikely that he would ever see any of them again.

Author's mother and father

126

Out of the Frying Pan

Andra had again been quite emotional when he described Mary's departure to me but, far from being put off of appraising me of the sequence of sad events in his life, this seemed to galvanise him into telling me about what had befallen Andrew, Charlie, Mary and the children after they reached New Zealand. It was as if he wanted to ensure that he had told me it all in case anything should happen to him. As I grew older I often wondered if he perhaps had a premonition about his mortality.

After what can only have been a hazardous journey the emigrants reached New Zealand and initially took up residence in Southland, which is the lower part of the South Island. It was in this area that Andrew and Charlie had their first experience of what it was like to work for New Zealand mine owners as opposed to their Scottish counterparts. As indicated in Charlie's initial letters to my mother it was not a pleasant baptism. According to her it was like rereading the first letters received from Peter when he went to America. Descriptions of working and living conditions were horribly familiar and the fact that his premonitions had proved to be right brought little comfort to Andra when he heard the depressing details.

After a short time in Southland the group, in an act of sheer desperation, moved to Dobson, a very small mining village on the West Coast of the island. Here Andrew and Charlie went to work in the Denniston Mines and the family took up residence in one of four settlements with a total population of 1,500 people approximately. Conditions generally were little better there but the brothers had little option but to buckle down and get on with it.

In late 1927 Andrew met and eventually married Annie Glen Bell, a widow with two children. Annie was a Scottish lady from Hamilton, Lanarkshire and her husband, a miner, had been killed in an accident in the local Cadzow Pit. She and six or seven of her brothers and sisters had recently arrived from Scotland. {An interesting aside to this story, as told to me recently by Andrew and Annie's daughter (also called Annie), was that another of their sisters wasn't allowed to emigrate as she had lost a leg as a result of an accident when she was a child. The New Zealand authorities in their wisdom considered that she would be a burden on the country!}

Andrew duly set up home with Annie and her sons William and George from her previous marriage, his own children Mary and Peggy and their own daughter Annie. His sister Mary and brother Charlie lived in the vicinity and, not long afterwards, Mary and Peggy went to stay with them 'for a while.' I'm not sure of the reasons for this, but family legend has it that there was some sort of disagreement amongst the various people involved as to the best interests of Mary and Peggy and this was considered the best option. In the event, the girls never returned to live with Andrew.

Andrew and Annie's daughter Annie (Burns) recently told me that, although Mary was only about 5ft tall, she was 'an awesome person' and had worked like a slave to bring up the girls. Annie said the girls adored Mary and so did she. Until Annie left school she spent her six weeks' Christmas holidays with her Aunt Mary and the girls. This allowed her to witness at first hand how hard Mary had to work to make ends meet. Mary 'took in' washing and young Annie helped her to turn the mangle to press the sheets and towels. At the local bank the teller lived on the premises and Mary, in addition to keeping the place clean, also did the man's washing and ironing. Annie tells a lovely story about going with Mary to the bank to help her with polishing the brass fittings. When she commented to her aunt that it was fun her reply was, "No hen, it's hard work when you have to do it all the time." Her abiding memory of Mary was that, *she was a feisty, little, hard working, loving person.*

Andrew remained in Dobson for another six years. During this time he and Annie had two sons, Andy and Charlie and because he was determined that none of the boys in the family would ever work in a coal mine, the family moved to Christchurch where Andrew did general labouring work until he secured employment as Sexton of the Sydeham Cemetery in Christchurch.

Despite all the upheavals in his life Andrew had retained his love for football but found that, at this time in New Zealand, football was only played by immigrants, and that situation was to prevail for many years. He tried for a long time to get football played in local secondary schools but was always shown the door. During the late 1940's and early 1950's his house, adjacent to the cemetery, was the place where young male Scottish immigrants who were interested in football congregated. This was when Andrew and others were founder members of The Thistle Football Club which became part of the Canterbury Football Association in 1951. Ultimately, Andrew became President of the Association and was also sole selector of representative teams for a period of three years. His daughter Annie Burns recalls that during

Andrew McAnulty And Daughter Annie

this period he never once selected either George or Andy, although they were always in representative teams both before and after his term of office. Hearing this, one must presume that he was bending over backwards not to show favouritism, because George actually went on eventually to play for the New Zealand national team.

In late 1963 the jinx on the male members of Andra's family continued as Andrew had a serious accident on his motor scooter. He never really recovered from his injuries and died in 1965 at the age of sixty nine.

Annie told me that her father would have been delighted when New Zealand qualified for the World Cup Football Tournament in 1982. Although they didn't win any games the two goals they scored against Scotland in the competition were enough to ensure that Scotland were eliminated from the tournament on goal average. How Andrew would have relished that!

Charlie was their Darling

Heading into 1930's, the New Zealand economy was descending in to what became known as The Great Depression. Charlie was one of the early victims of the recession and quickly found himself on the unemployed list. For almost two years he strove unsuccessfully to obtain regular employment but was unable to do so. Like many others in his position this inevitably led to many hours spent on the local beaches in the summer months, where swimming and surfing were the perfect antidotes to the depressing, poverty stricken circumstances they found themselves in. To a man, they were all convinced that things could only get better once the recession passed. Charlie shared their optimism but, alas, in his case the suffering was soon to be over, though not in the way that he imagined.

Clues as to the reality of conditions in New Zealand at the time and his state of mind are to be found in a letter which he wrote my mother on the 18th August, 1932. His opening remarks read:

'We received your welcome letter a few days ago, pleased to see you are all well. We are just about holding our own down under in the slave state of New Zealand, land of low wages, no work and poverty. Since being paid off from the mine I have been active in the unemployment movement, being partly responsible for the formation of a district council - being elected chairman of that body at its inception.

Conditions for working people have been hard, generating protests and demonstrations, resulting in wholesale imprisonment of leaders as the authorities try to intimidate the weak and the wavering. Anyone, and this includes me, who speaks out about these matters is considered to be a crank or a malcontent.

The employers are, as usual, organised on the old craft basis, their leadership failing to develop with the development of Capitalism. I can't see myself getting work here and our economic position is bad enough now but, judging by events, it is going to get a whole lot worse on its way to bedrock.

I think that I am here for keeps but I applaud Geordie's (author's father) efforts to try and save for our fare home. However, I realise that it will be almost impossible for him to do so, given the circumstances at home. Meanwhile we will wait and hope.'

Charlie McAnulty

Amongst the personal comments at the end of his letter, he jokes with my mother about having let his hair grow longer that previously and says that his waves are the *'talk of the town'*. Not long enough as things turned out!

No one who reads the full contents of his letter could doubt the suffering that Charlie and the others like him were enduring. Here we have many thousands of hard working, honest men and their families who had travelled half way round the world, lured by the promise of full employment and a better way of life. The reality of course was the complete opposite. There was little or no work, more poverty than they had left at home and little prospect of being able to return to their homeland.

His letter also indicates to me that Charlie was heavily involved in the workers' struggle for jobs and better conditions, as was befitting a son of Andra. Like others in the family he had, over his formative years, watched and admired his father's efforts on behalf of the working people and he could have had no better teacher. Indirectly, through Charlie and latterly his sister Mary, Andra's ideals had thus been transposed to another continent to be implemented in the world wide movement of working people for fairness and equality.

Andra resumed his story about the new Zealand episode after I had read this letter, which he had asked my mother to let me see. He told me that, approximately five months after this letter arrived, he had been sitting at his table replying to another of Charlie's letters which he had received about a fortnight previously. While doing so he had a visit from the owner of the local *Blantyre Gazette*, John Clifford by name. John had been contacted by a Glasgow newspaper who had received a cable from New Zealand (Reuter), intimating that a young man named Charles McAnulty, said to have been born in Blantyre, Scotland, had been drowned at Greymouth, West Coast, Dobson, New Zealand. John had been asked by the Glasgow newspaper to trace the family of the deceased and his local knowledge had directed him to Andra's house.

After reading the cable Andra had confirmed to John Clifford that his son Charlie had been living in that township and said he felt sure that, although he had had no other word, the victim of the tragedy was his son. In his own words to me he:

> 'was stunned at the news and the manner in which I had received it. It was days before I could take in that, first my brother and father in the mines and now the third of my five sons had been taken from me in tragic circumstances'.

It was a sad Andra I left sitting in his room that day I can tell you.

{Ironically, as I have already indicated, his son Andrew died as a result of injuries received in an accident; his remaining son Wull survived until his mid sixties but he too was to have a premature end, being knocked down and killed by a car when out walking. Thus it was that all five of his sons died in less than normal circumstances, albeit that two of them occurred after Andra's death}.

My recent efforts to amplify my knowledge of the circumstances of Charlie's untimely end by drowning were rewarded, when the combined wisdom and efforts of my newly found cousin Annie (Andrew's daughter) and her daughters Irene and Jean unearthed the appropriate newspaper cuttings from the *Grey River Argus* (Greystone) newspaper and forwarded them to me.

Apparently, on the 25th January, 1932 the Blaketown Surf Club, which had been closed for six years, was revived by some former members. The club's lifebelt and safety reel were severely tested and the lifeline was found to be in a weakened condition after such a period lying idle. It was temporarily fixed up for immediate use - if necessary - and practice. It broke after a couple of practices, which reduced its length somewhat, and it was decided that a new, longer reel was required.

Only two days later Charlie and his close friend Jack Nordstrom had been with a party of thirty other surfers on the local Blakestone Beach when the tragedy occurred. There had been a calm sea all day and the waves were coming shoreward without a roll, quickly breaking and the cresty billows were free of any great force; but there was a heavy suction apparent on a stretch just to the north of where the crowd of surfers were disporting.

Charlie and Jack, neither of whom could swim very well, had waded out backwards until the surf was up to their armpits, as they and others had done countless times before. On this occasion however, an undertow suddenly carried them off their feet and beyond their depth.

The first indications that they were in trouble were witnessed by two men, William Smith and Ivan Curin who were bathing nearby. Smith immediately made for shore to have the rescue reel manned and Curin went in the direction of the two who were in trouble. As he neared them he saw that McAnulty was trying to pull Nordstrom towards the shore but appeared to be in a near exhausted state, eventually losing his grip. Curin managed to get close enough to McAnulty to grasp him by the hair of his head, but later said Charlie had struggled so much that, after bringing him about a half a dozen yards towards the shore, he was forced to leave go his grip for his own safety and come ashore.

Simultaneously two strong swimmers from the group on shore swam out approximately 250 yards with the safety reel, this being the extent of its limit, but they were still approximately fifty yards from the desperate struggle Charlie was making for his life in the heavy swell. Reluctantly, drained by their own efforts, they had to leave Charlie to the mercy of the sea and signal to those on shore to pull them in while they still had the strength to hold on to the reel. Praying no doubt that it didn't break again!

The next day, the 26th of January, The Grey River Argus reported that the Surf Club had wired to Wellington for a 1200-foot lifeline, the present one being deemed to be unsuitable. The newspaper also contained a report of a public meeting that had been called to protest against the treatment given to the unemployed, which had been held in the Greymouth Town Hall the previous evening. The Mayor of Greymouth, Mr J.W. Greenslade presided. Before the meeting started, the chairman referred to the deaths of Charlie and Jack, two very prominent members (chairman and secretary respectively) of the local Unemployed Workers Union (shades of Andra). As one who came in close contact with both of the deceased during the course of his duties, he (the Mayor) had always found them to be fine, courteous, sincere types of men, and the areas' unemployed and the town generally deplored their loss. As a mark of respect and sympathy all present then stood in silence for two minutes.

Sadly, several later editions of the paper featured some gruesome reports, in the aftermath of the tragedy which had befallen the two close friends;

3 February - A human hand with a portion of forearm was found off nearby Cobden Beach and was identified as Jack Nordstrom's.

6th February - A portion of a the body of either Jack or Charlie was found at Utopia Beach, three miles north of the scene of the accident. It comprised of a left foot and a portion of shin.

13th February - Jack's body was found on North Beach about half a mile from the scene. It was badly decomposed but identified by the swimming suit. An arm and a leg was missing.

This edition also reported that a Benefit Dance had been held in the Town Hall by the Greymouth United Workers' Movement in aid of the dependants of the mens' families.

The attendance was the largest seen at a town hall dance in many years and net proceedings were £35, which was to be shared equally by the two families concerned (in Charlie's case, his sister Mary and the two girls Mary and Peggy).

14th February - Funeral of Jack Nordstrom.

18th February - What was probably a portion of Charlie's body, a left foot was found on Cobden Beach (Jack's left foot was still intact).

The fact that the Tasman Sea had claimed another two victims was not surprising, in that it appeared to have been a fairly frequent occurrence on what is known as the Gold-Coast. Searching on a surfing website for information regarding the Blaketown Beach, I noted the following graphic description;

> *'the turbulent Tasman Sea continuously assaults the South Island, West Coast with three metre steam-roller waves lined up to the horizon. Ironically, surfers on 'The Coast' often have to wait for swells to drop before they can safely get amongst the waves. Blaketown Beach is listed as being in the world's top 30 surfing venues'.*

In such conditions no doubt there are still accidents at this location but today's sophisticated rescue equipment and procedures on such beaches prevent many of these from becoming fatal. Sadly, Charlie and Jack's would be rescuers did not have the benefit of these aids and this, allied to the fact that neither were strong swimmers, meant that the two friends were literally out of their depth.

When I read the grisly extracts from the newspaper regarding the obvious involvement of sharks in the tragedy, I drew comfort from the fact that neither Andra or my mother knew the ghastly details of Charlie's death. The loss of a son and brother from drowning, and the fact that, as far as they were aware, his body was never recovered, must have been hard enough to bear but their suffering would have been tenfold had they been appraised of the macabre circumstances.

New Zealand 'Clan' Of The McAnulty Family (back row, from left to right); Robert McKendry, Tommy Heptinstall, Denny McKendry; Peggy McHendry (nee McAnulty), Dinny McHendry, Sue-Ellen McHendry, Annie McAnulty, Bruce McHendry, Mary Heptinstall (nee McAnulty), Annie Burns (front row from left to right) Peggy Heptinstall, Irene Burns, Jean Burns

Ambition Realised

At this juncture our discussions were interrupted for a while by what was described to me by Andra as the greatest event in his long and colourful life. Coming from Andra, that was some statement. The occasion, on January 6th 1947, was a red letter day in the lives of British coal miners in general and Andra in particular. This was the day when he was rewarded for literally seventy years of mental and physical effort to have the coal mines taken out of the hands of the greedy owners. This was the day that the coal mines in Great Britain were Nationalised.

When the decision was announced by the Government, Andra was in a state of elated bliss. He was so excited, my mother was afraid that he would have a heart attack. When she said this to him, in typical Andra fashion he told her that he wouldn't care because he would be dying a happy man! While I was as pleased as everyone else in the family at the time, it was only in later years that I was able to appreciate fully the reason for his elation. Here was an eighty six years old man who, literally since the day his father had been killed in 1877, had ceaselessly striven to make the general public aware that the unfeeling owners of the mines did not deserve to have control of this industry which was vital to the economy of the country. In addition, during the war years the miners had worked tirelessly to provide the energy to keep the British factories etc going and were continuing to do so in the difficult post war years. Andra felt that the nation in general and the miners in particular would be better served and more fairly, if they were in public ownership.

How proud my family and I were therefore, as we joined what seemed to be the whole population of Blantyre to watch this great old man unfurl the National Coal Board flag. Union leaders, representatives of the local colliery managements and others interested in the mining industry made appropriate speeches to mark the occasion, all of them mentioning the role played by Andra in bringing about the change and, when it came his turn to speak, the ovation given to Andra by the large audience seemed to go on for an eternity. The warmth of this reception clearly affected Andra but, once he regained his composure, he was quick to remind everyone that so many others who were no longer with us had literally given their lives to the cause also.

Unfurling The Flag

Despite this statement from him, by their applause and shouts of acknowledgement, the people of Blantyre who were present left him in no doubt that, as far as they were concerned, *he* was the man who had been at the forefront of the struggle on behalf of *their* community.

This feeling of euphoria almost caused a disaster. As Andra was being assisted from the temporary platform that had been erected for the occasion, so many people wanted to either pat him on the back or shake his hand that he was in great danger of being knocked over. Only the intervention of several burly miners prevented this calamity, as they quickly formed a protective cordon around his slight figure.

Following what had been a weekend of celebration in the village there was a meeting in the Broadway Cinema on the Sunday evening. This well attended meeting was also addressed by Andra who told the assembly that,

> 'from now on, the miners must put their best foot forward and prove to those who were against Nationalisation that such a step would bring prestige to the miners and the industry generally. Production was the keynote for this country as, the greater their export of coal, the greater would be their buying power which they could never otherwise express.'

Similar ceremonies were taking place all round the country and it is interesting but sad to note that, in Lanarkshire alone at that time, 20,000 miners were employed. Today unfortunately there are none.

The culmination of the miners' celebration of this momentous occasion was A Scottish Miners' Gala Demonstration in the King's Park, Edinburgh on Monday 5th of May, 1947, where the principal speaker was Emanuel (Manny) Shinwell, Minister of Fuel. Included in the vast crowd which attended were nine busloads of Blantyre miners. The contingent from Blantyre included representatives from each of the local collieries.

The *Edinburgh Evening News* reported that the platform party included six 'Pioneers of the Coal Industry', the eldest of which was Andra McAnulty, and that they were accorded a great ovation by the crowd. Accompanying the article was a photograph of Andra shaking hands with Manny Shinwell. I was delighted when I read the caption underneath the photograph, *'Andra McAnulty (3rd from left) at the 1947 Gala.* (Manny Shinwell was 4th from the left but wasn't named!)

Andra told me that he had shared many a platform with Manny earlier in their careers but neither of them could remember an occasion that had given them so much pleasure.

Andra and Manny Shinwell

Final Blow

During another discussion with Andra after the euphoria of the Nationalisation of the pits, I took the opportunity to clarify some of the things he had told me about his daughter Mary's departure to New Zealand. Amazingly, about two weeks after we discussed this in general and Mary's service to the local community in particular there was a dramatic postscript to this part of Andra's narrative. On returning from school one day I was met at the front door by my tearful mother, who told me that Andra had just received a cable from New Zealand advising him that Mary had died after a short illness. Andra was distraught and for almost a week thereafter I did not go near his room, fearing that the bereavement would have opened old wounds which would preclude him from discussing family matters.

The opportunity to do so however, occurred when the next edition of the *Blantyre Gazette* (2nd April, 1949) was delivered, which included an article on Mary's death. Later that day Andra came through to our part of the house and asked if I would come and read it to him. Settling in my usual chair in his room I read out the following to him;

LOCAL WOMAN'S DEATH IN NEW ZEALAND
Daughter of Andra McAnulty.

Mr. Andrew McAnulty, veteran miners' leader and champion of the working class in Blantyre for over half a century, was the recipient of sad news at his home in 55 Victoria Street, Blantyre, recently when he was informed by cable that one of his daughters, Mary, had died in New Zealand.

Mary, who was 55 years of age, was the third daughter of Mr. McAnulty and was unmarried. Like others of Mr. McAnulty's family she was well known in this district and, like her father over thirty years ago, played a prominent part in the fight to obtain better conditions for the miners and working class people generally.

She was one who carried out many acts of kindness on behalf of the less fortunate people in the locality and as such was well respected and held in very high esteem. The extent of her popularity was fully manifest when she left for New Zealand 21 years ago, when people from all over Blantyre gathered at the local station to see her off on the first part of her journey to her new home across the water.

During her long stay in New Zealand, Miss McAnulty had been engaged in mainly hospital work, carrying on the example she had set in Blantyre of trying to bring comfort to those people less fortunate than herself. A few weeks before her death she apparently developed an inward complaint which brought about her untimely end. (The inward complaint was in fact bowel cancer. Her niece Annie says that Mary had an operation but the stress was just too much for her and she died shortly afterwards.)

As I finished reading I could see that, although he was hurting he was proud that Mary's dedication to people less fortunate than herself, in whatever community she found herself in, had been recognised and placed in the public domain via the newspaper article. Indeed, many people who thereafter visited him to offer their condolences told him in my presence that, in him, she had had the best teacher in human relations that it was possible to have. If Andra were alive today I'm sure he would have been even more proud if I'd been able to read him an article from a New Zealand publication entitled *Seaman's Journal*, which was issued in July, 1999. The article, (which was sent to me recently by Bridget Hendry, a young relative in N.Z.) concerned the death of Mary (Bridget's grandmother), the youngest of the two children looked after by Mary, both at home and into their adult life in New Zealand.

Young Mary had married Tommy Hepinstall, who was described as legendary activist and, ultimately, life member of the Seafarers Union. Mary, who was my full cousin, was obviously more than just a chip off the old (Andra) block, as the essence of the article indicates:

"A Champion Of The Seafarers Fraternity"

The other day we said our goodbyes to Mary. To know Mary was to know the everyday struggle of the ordinary folk, on the sea, in the factory or down the mine.

For her, the solution wasn't just a few crumbs from the rich man's table, although that wasn't left out of her calculations either.

She was a relentless advocate for wage slaves to grab for themselves a piece of the action, to throw of the political chains that bind them to any kind of exploitation and poverty, and to share the world's production in a truly socialist way.

Mary was an unpretentious feminine personality, always interesting to listen to, able to analyse a situation and people, and a confident champion of the working classes.

More than once, if she thought noses weren't pointing in the right direction, a straight word or two from Mary pulled a trade union official's head out of the clouds.

Way back in the 1960's Mary, and other women, to their everlasting courage and New Zealand's integrity, flung themselves under the then racist sprigs of the N.Z. Rugby Union on Athletic Park. They were protesting the non-selection of Maori players in an All Black team to tour Vorster's apartheid South Africa. Mary and those wonderful women made world headlines when, in full view of the world's media, they displayed their banners in the centre circle of the pitch prior to an International match. By so doing, they carved themselves forever an historical place of honour in our not so honourable history. This in turn has led to a renaissance in our Maori partners standing tall on equality, opportunity and redress under the Treaty of Waitangi.

There can be no doubt that this was the turning point in public opinion against those in New Zealand and beyond prepared to appease and support apartheid.

As Nelson Mandela visits the capitals of the world, a free man, he would have been proud to know Mary as a soldier in his cause and acknowledge the part they undoubtedly played in his subsequent release.

Mary and Tom were just two working class folk who had exceptional ability and courage to stand up for other working class people. They had contempt for 'socialist pretenders' and those who climb on the backs of workers for privelege and gain. Mary believed we all pass this way but once, so it isn't much good mucking around just being an observer - she was a participant in life every step of the way! And she proudly struck a blow for the working plug at every opportunity.

Mary gave a lot of herself but asked for very little, unless it was for a few bob for someone else. True friends, and she had many, a smile and a song, would probably say it all. Oh yes - and a rose, she would like that.

We salute you Mary Hepinstall.

When I read this I quickly realised that here was another prime example of Andra's philosophical approach to life being passed on through the generations of his family in a positive fashion. His daughter Mary, who had literally reared her niece from childhood had, unquestionably, been a great influence in moulding Andra's grandchild in his/her image. The Maori people, who were after all the indigenous inhabitants of New Zealand, wouldn't know it; but they had a lot to thank Andra for in their struggle for basic human rights.

Mary's last memory of Blantyre

The Final Battle

Shortly after Andra and I discussed his daughter Mary's untimely end, he had an accident in the house one day while I was at school. Unsteady on his feet at the best of times, as he was entering the bathroom he stumbled and fell to the floor, striking his shoulder on the wash hand basin on the way down. As she assisted Andra to his room to lie down on top of the bed, my mother realised that he was badly hurt and at her behest a neighbour hurried to the family doctor's house seeking his urgent help. When Doctor Jope arrived he quickly diagnosed that Andra had broken his left shoulder blade and strapped his arm across his chest, that being the only treatment possible for such an injury.

When I came home from school and entered Andra's room his already diminutive figure seemed even smaller as he lay in his bed, propped up against his pillows. Displaying all the awkwardness of youth, I was at a loss for words and, as if he was aware of my discomfort and concern, he endeavoured to assure me that he would soon be back on his feet. Whether he believed this himself or not I will never know but alas it wasn't to be.

As the days and weeks passed he gradually lost his appetite and it was as if all of the privations he had endured in the long and eventful eighty nine years of his life were slowly exacting the ultimate penalty from his now frail body. The latest in the equation being the grief he was suffering regarding his beloved daughter Mary, the news of who's death had been conveyed to him just six months previously. This had really floored him and, since her death, there had been a perceptible dimming of the spark that burned inside him.

Word of his illness soon spread in the community and many people from all walks of life called to inquire after his well being. Eventually my mother had to become increasingly selective in her choice of those who were actually allowed access to Andra's room, due to his failing energy levels. Only close members of the family and those who had featured strongly in his various activities were granted a few minutes with Andra but, in the fullness of time, even these short visits had to be denied.

Throughout this period the only constant visitor, apart from my mother and father of course, was me. Although in a weakened state, Andra still wanted me to read newspapers to him and this I did as and when he was able. He particularly enjoyed hearing the contents of the *Blantyre Gazette* and keeping up with what was happening in the village. It was perhaps appropriate that, after reading this to him, our last short conversation took place about seven days before he died.

As usual at the beginning of our dialogue, he asked me how I was doing at school and reiterated the necessity of a good education. As he had done so often before, he reminded me that sacrifices made by people like himself would have been in vain if people of my generation did not take advantage of the opportunities they now had. He also said that he was glad that he had passed on a lot of his experiences to me and he hoped that some day, when I was a bit older, I would understand the things we had talked about a bit more fully. Andra was such a discerning individual that it is entirely possible that he envisioned that I would someday delve deeper into the events he had so graphically described to me. It is also conceivable that he hoped that he had planted the seed inside me which would, one day, grow into a story about the sacrifices that himself and others had made on our behalf. Whether this was his intention or not there is no doubt that, once I had made my first tentative effort to expand on the details he had passed on to me, I was inspired by situations and events that were revealed during my research to collate and record his story.

Leaving him that afternoon, I was totally unaware that I would never see him again. During the course of our relationship I had become very attached to him and sensed that the feeling was mutual. Others who knew him intimately have since told me that he could be a bit cantankerous on occasion and did not suffer fools gladly. I have no reason to disbelieve these observations by people who's opinions I respect but, reflecting on my own in-depth knowledge of his life I recognise that, without these characteristics, he would not have achieved a fraction of the successes he had in public life. Neither could he have failed to be mentally scarred by the many personal tragedies in his life.

Almost immediately after our last get-together Andra contracted pneumonia and my mother continued to nurse him faithfully night and day until, a few days later on the 12th of November, 1949, the old campaigner slept peacefully away. The indefatigable Andra, like all mortals, had finally met an opponent who wouldn't ultimately be denied. When confronted with this sad news on my return from school I was terribly upset. This was the first occasion in my short life that I had to deal with the loss of someone close to me and, once undertakers etc started appearing at the house, it needed little persuasion by my aunt Nellie to encourage me to go home and stay with her family overnight.

My return home the next day coincided with the delivery of a telegram (which I still have) from William Gallacher M.P. to my mother, offering his deepest sympathy and advising her that he would be 'with her tomorrow.'

Another letter I have, which arrived the next day from one Harry Pollitt, paid a glowing tribute to Andra:
> *'He was a fighter and leader in many struggles, particularly on behalf of the Scottish miners, always at his post in good or stormy weather. His home was a centre of hospitality for his working class colleagues at all times. His talents were many and varied. His voice and pen, in speech and poetry, were at all times at the service of our movement.*
>
> *All of his life he fought against the squalor, misery and insecurity that characterised the Lanarkshire mining community in which he grew up.*
>
> *His name is associated with Keir Hardie and Bob Smillie as pioneers who faced stupendous odds and suffered persecution and privations to build the trade unions in the coalfield. His name is forever linked with John McLean as a pioneer for the age of socialism.*
>
> *The advances won by the mining population gladdened his heart and are a fitting testimony to the work of our veterans, of whom Andra stood out as an indomitable fighter.'*

I have at least a dozen other letters in similar vein which arrived between then and his funeral on the 15th of November. What made the date of his burial doubly memorable for me was the fact that it was also my 16th birthday.

The Last Farewell to Blantyre's Champion

Andra's coffin was uplifted from our home on that cold winter's morning and I joined the many family members and several hundred mourners as they walked slowly behind the funeral hearse on its mile and a half journey to High Blantyre Cemetery. As we proceeded through the streets of Blantyre on our way to the cemetery I was amazed, but latterly not surprised, at the way ordinary people in the village came to the pavements in front of their houses and stood shivering, heads bowed in respect, as we passed by. Andra's efforts on behalf of the people of Blantyre were common knowledge and the below freezing temperature didn't deter them from paying their respects.

In the fullness of time we arrived at the cemetery, where there was quite a delay in the proceedings due to the enormous crowds of people who were endeavouring to gather round the graveside. Eventually, when the assembly had settled as best they could in the circumstances, my father, brother Bob and myself, cousins Jim and Tom Gibson, Andrew and Tom McKinlay and my Uncle Wull were called forward to grasp the cords and gently lower Andra to his last resting place.

Performing this act in front of so many people was a very moving experience for a young man of my age. On the one hand I was extremely upset at losing my beloved grandfather but on the other I was so proud that this large gathering of people had felt the need to come along and honour Andra's achievements with their presence.

As a hush descended over the assembled crowds, William Gallacher, the Member of Parliament for Fife, stepped forward to the graveside and paid this personal tribute to Andra:

> *'We are gathered here today to take a last farewell of a great son of the working class. He had a long life, a life of toil and strife, a life of great service to his fellow men and to the great cause of the working class emancipation.*
>
> *He was a dear comrade but he was also my friend over many long years and, with his family which was always dear to him, I grieve his passing.*
>
> *Andrew McAnulty was born away back in 1860, when the period known as the Hungry Forties was still haunting the minds and lives of the people. It is not easy for us now to realise the conditions that prevailed in 1860, for all workers but particularly to the miners.*
>
> *Living in isolated communities, their hard life, their appalling housing and the tragic accident rate that was a daily occurrence, went past unnoticed in the towns and cities. Only when disaster, involving heavy loss of life struck, was the conscience of the nation moved. Only then was the miner remembered.*
>
> *Very early in his life Andra experienced such a disaster. The Blantyre Pit Disaster was the worst that Scotland had known. Seventeen years of age as he was then, he carried for the rest of his life the scars of that terrible and terrifying event, as he carried the memory of his father and brother who were victims of the disaster.*
>
> *He also carried in his heart a desire to change and improve the lives of his own people, the miners. Thus it is not to be wondered at that he became one of the pioneers of mining trade unionism in Lanarkshire, as a part of the organisation growing throughout the country. This later became the Federation of Great Britain, later still the National Union of Mineworkers.*

I wonder if any of those who occupy ministerial positions in the Labour Government of today realise the part that Andra McAnulty and those associated with him played in making it possible for them to come into existence, for it was they who were pioneers in securing Parliamentary representation for working people in the first instance.

My mind goes back many years to the days when, here in Lanarkshire, I as a young activist first came into contact with Andra McAnulty, James Robertson, Alex. Hunter, Willie Small, Bob Smillie, Ned Hawke, Joe Sullivan, Paul McKenna and many others who, in their different ways, made their contribution to the rise of the Labour movement. They were great days, when the street corner or the end of the miners' row was our meeting place. Our hearts were in the movement and there was no one more heavily committed than Andra McAnulty.

Although I remember his associates, even more I remember his family. Devoted to their father and, like him, devoted to the cause of working people. They have reason to be proud of him and the service he gave and should take comfort that he was always happy in the knowledge that they were with him in what he sought to do.

Who that knew the family will ever forget that ever open door, the warm generous hospitality that was freely extended to visitors. I remember with true gratitude the dear friendship the McAnulty family gave to me. Above all, as I stand here today taking a last farewell of the father, I remember his beloved daughter Mary. A great and good person here, she was also a great and good activist far away on the other side of the world, where the latter part of her life was spent. Though she was so far away, we kept in touch with each other until her untimely end.

Andra, like so many others, worked without thought of reward but it was a great joy to him to be awarded a Diploma as a pioneer of The Lanarkshire Mineworkers Union, in the building and leadership of which he played a worthy part. Later on he was awarded a pension from the Scottish Miners Union in recognition of his life's work for the movement.

From personal knowledge I can tell you that, one of the great joys of Andra's eventful life was to be involved in the creation of Blantyre Miners Welfare, which was opened in the 1920's. Inspired by another great miners' champion the late Willie Small, then Secretary of the Lanarkshire Miners' Union, Andra and others of his ilk threw their weight behind the effort to raise funds for this great project. Andra's main contribution was to organise several fund-raising concerts by The Auchenraith Silver Band, of which he was a Founder Member and President.

Money was not the thing that mattered to Andra, but recognition from those who came after him, of the long years of service so selflessly given. What more could a man desire from life, than that those for whom he had laboured would say of him, "You have blazed a trail that we will follow. From the dark valley of oppression and poverty you have led us forward and upward. We have not yet reached our ultimate goal but, because of the service you gave, we know that one day we will."

That's what the miners can say about Andra McAnulty, as here in the surroundings where his long and valiant life was lived, we lay him quietly to rest.

Sleep peacefully old friend, your work goes forward. The service you gave will never be forgotten. You were the last of the old leaders, who's like will never be seen again.'

The original copy of this glowing tribute to my beloved grandfather, typed on Houses of Parliament notepaper and given to my mother by Willie Gallacher immediately after the funeral, is one of my most treasured possessions.

A Tribute from the Blantyre Gazette

Andra's deeds had graced the pages of the Blantyre Gazette since it was founded and it was fitting that the final tribute to him was recorded in the next issue of the Gazette, dated 19 November, 1949:

Death of Andra McAnulty

Champion of the working class and one who spent a lifetime fighting for better conditions for the mining industry, Mr Andrew McAnulty, died on Saturday night at the home of a married daughter, Mrs George Paterson, at 105 Parkville Drive, Springwells, Blantyre, Lanarkshure.

So far as the working class is concerned Andra's career provided a colourful chapter. For years he was the champion of those whose circumstances were such that they always seemed to be struggling with adversity, and the good work which he achieved in this direction would be impossible to relate. Twenty or thirty years back it was a common thing for people in need or contesting a trade union matter to seek advice from the old 'war horse' who at an early age made it his policy to champion the cause of working people.

In Dixon's Explosion

Mr McAnulty was not a native of Blantyre. He was born in Craigneuk, Wishaw on 24th November, 1860 but came to Blantyre when he was about fifteen years old. He had started work in the pit when he was a ten years old boy and was employed at Dixon's Colliery when the disastrous explosion occurred on the morning of 22nd October, 1877, causing the death of 216 men and boys. His father Peter was killed in the explosion and he himself only avoided being involved because, at the time he was off work recovering from serious burns as well as the loss of sight in one eye and the loss of several toes in his right foot - sustained in a fire damp explosion on the 22nd August in the same pit. His brother Joseph was killed in this explosion and another brother, William, escaped with minor injuries.

While still in his 'teens' Mr. McAnulty began to show a very lively interest in the trade union movement and became one of the pioneers of the old Lanarkshire Miners' Union. He was a contemporary of other such miners' stalwarts as Keir Hardie, Bob Smillie, Duncan Graham, Willie Small and Joe Sullivan and was elected as first president of the Union in 1920.

In 1942 the Lanarkshire Miners' Union recognised his work on behalf of the miners in the County by presenting him with a pioneers' diploma. The diploma, which hangs on a wall in the house where he died, contains a picture of himself and those mentioned above, together with John Robertson, Jimmy Tonner and James Murdoch. 'Andra' was the last survivor of this illustrious group of laymen who between them gave years of service for the benefit of the men in the pits.

When the pits were Nationalised in January, 1947, Mr McAnulty was called upon to unfurl the N.C.B. flag at Dixon's Colliery. He had by then reached the age of eighty six but took the greatest pride in carrying out this ceremony, which he described on that occasion as one of the greatest events in his lifetime. Andra had worked for years to see the coal pits pass from private enterprise to the control of the State and was happy that another historic milestone had been reached in the mining industry.

A Unique Tribute

A month later, Mr McAnulty was paid a unique tribute by The National Union of Mineworkers (Scottish Area) when they agreed to pay him a pension of £2 weekly during the remainder of his lifetime, as a tangible token of appreciation for his work on behalf of the miners during a period of seventy years. It is interesting to recall the terms of the letter which the Blantyre veteran received at that time from the general secretary of the union, William Pearson:

It read :

> *Dear Andrew,*
> *My Executive Committee had your position under discussion and I have been asked to convey their gratitude for the splendid work you have done on behalf of the miners and to express or best thanks for the part you played in bringing about the nationalisation of the industry. We trust that you will be long spared to come amongst us and you will always be welcome within our movement. I am sure that it will be very pleasing for you to know that in a questionnaire which we sent out recently to almost 200 young miners, in connection with a mining college, almost everyone gave the name of Andrew McAnulty as being one of the old pioneers of the movement. You will see therefore that you have not been forgotten, and I want you to accept this gift from the Executive Committee in the spirit in which it has been made.*
>
> *Yours sincerely,*
>
> *William Pearson,*
> *General Secretary.*

At one time Mr McAnulty took a keen interest in parochial affairs and was, for a period, Chairman of the old Parish Council in Blantyre, of which he was a member for over thirty years. He also served the community for many years as a Justice of the Peace and was one of three trustees of the local Cottage Hospital. Great achievements all, considering that he left school at ten years of age.

He had already reached what many people look on as the veteran stage when the great miners' strike of 1921 swept the country, bringing untold misery and hardship, but he was the leading figure at that time in organising soup kitchens from which the miners' children and others whose fathers were unemployed were supplied with meals at local schools.

The Funeral

The funeral of the veteran took place from his daughter's home to High Blantyre Cemetery on Tuesday. About 200 people walked in the funeral procession, prominent amongst whom were Mr William Gallacher, M.P. for West Fife; representatives from the Communist Party in Blantyre and from the District Headquarters in Motherwell; officials of the National Coal Board and the National Union of Mineworkers and representatives of the local pit union branches. Amongst others present were Provost Alex. Hunter, Hamilton, a lifelong friend of the deceased, County Councillors Jas. Beecroft and Edward Daly and people from many walks of life who had known 'Andra' and respected him in his lifetime. The coffin was lowered to its last resting place by his son and grandsons and, at the graveside, a glowing tribute was paid to Mr McAnulty by another of his great friends and associates, Mr William Gallacher M.P.

William Gallacher M.P.

A Personal Tribute

When, as a schoolboy, I started my journey through Andra's life and times, it was because I had been asked to talk to the most unforgettable character I had ever met. For someone of my then tender years that was quite a narrow field of choice but, fifty odd years later I can say without fear of contradiction that, none of the innumerable personalities I have encountered in all walks of life during my lifetime since then, come even close to impressing me as much as Andra did. The stern exterior which his adversaries in the coal industry saw was in complete contrast to the father and grandfather that we the family knew. Having researched his life I'm quite sure that many of his opponents must have thought that, like the souvenirs I see in the gift shops of mining museums etc, he was chiselled out of a chunk of coal which had come from the pit bottom.

I do not and have never professed to be an author but I hope that, in my own modest way, by putting all the personal knowledge I have of Andra and his life and times on paper, reinforced by things I have researched based on this knowledge, I have in some small way ensured that the service he gave will not be forgotten. He and his like deserve to be remembered.

Miners are of little significance in our modern society and their image was somewhat tarnished in their badly led struggle against Thatcherism in the eighties. Despite this, we should never forget that,
without coal, the industrial revolution which took place in this country in the times covered by this narrative wouldn't have been possible. The sacrifices made by the miners throughout these historical times and their dangerous drudgery in the bowels of the earth on our behalf should never be forgotten.

Coal Carving

The following excerpt is from a poem, "Colliers Every Wan" written by Jim Cornfield of Blantyre Mining Heritage Society;

'The horn on the pithead blew long and forlorn,
Tae signal bad news, on that fateful morn,
Folk came runnin' fae aw' o'er the toon,
Every wan tae a man, volunteered tae go doon.
Nae thought o' danger, nor religion too,
They aw' worked thegither wi' a common view.
The fellowship o' man was born on that day,
In Blantir Toon, how I wished it wid stay,
Two hundred an' fifteen colliers lay dead,
Killed in pursuit o' their daily bread.

Following the tradition of their fathers

145

The following two poems, unearthed in her own research of the Blantyre Disaster, were kindly passed to me by Wilma Bolton, Hamilton for inclusion in this book;

The Blantyre Explosion - An Appeal

In the mirk of an autumn morning,
When most of us lay asleep,
Along the road to their daily work
In a coal-pit dark and deep,
Two hundred colliers were wending their way—
A harvest for Death to reap!

And from many a home that Monday
There sallied out three or four,
In sooth from some of the cottages
Came forth, alas! Even more,
Who never again- never again
Passed under the cottage door!

The looks of some many a winter
Had dabbled with a touch of rime,
Some of them were in the flush of youth,
And some were in manhood's prime,
And some were but little laddies yet,
And barely beyond school-time.

For the season was hard and bitter,
And sore was the collier's need—
The price of food was never so high,
And many the mouths to feed;
And bairns must work to support the house,
Though the mother's heart should bleed!

Two of the pits are together linked,
The fatal pits Two and Three,
And by six around their yawning mouths
The colliers all ready be
To descend below, but they never dream
Their last glimpse of the sky they see.

Or even the cage its living freight
Of the doomed bore underground,
In both of the pits had the firemen gone
Upon their usual round;
One speaks in life, and one spoke in death,
Not a trace of fire was found.

And the men began their daily darg
With never a touch of fear,
If they thought of the fire-damp and choke-damp,
Twas to dream "there's safety here"
But after they wrought two fleeting hours,
Grim death crept horribly near.

It was a quarter to nine by the clock
When up the Three Shaft there came
A roar as the loudest of thunder,
And the hissing sound of flame;
And dust and smoke and a wrenched out limb,
A ghastly horror proclaim.

And the sound was heard in the village,
And women with faces white,
Half crazed with dread and with scarcely more,
Than the garments of the night,
Rushed to the spot—it was pitiful
To see their dazed looks of fright.

But as sad a sight as the women
Was the bairnies, who alone,
Went crying all through the village streets
For their mothers making moan,
Their mothers, who by the pits of death
Were waiting rigid as stone.

And the news of the great disaster
With swiftness of lightening spread,
And hundreds of eager colliers soon
Were watching at each pit-head,
Proud to risk their lives for the living—
Ay, willing to die for the dead!

They toiled the whole of the weary day,
The whole of the livelong night;
And at intervals through the drenching rain,
The moon poured its fitful light:
And crowds of men, in hope to give help;
Sat by the braziers bright.

But hope was fading and dying fast
Or ever the morning came;
They could not get in despite their toil,
Through the interlacing frame.
The explosion reared, barring the pit,
Choked with gas after the flame.

Yet Tuesday morning saw four brought out—
Who have died, alas! Since then—
And after that it was surely known
All hope was utterly vain;
But still they worked, with the hungry cry,
"Give us back our dead again".

They watched and they toiled and they waited;
We think of them all the more
That their hearts grew sickened and angry
When forbidden to explore.
From risk to themselves, for the sacred dead,
When all hope of life was o'er.

And a kindlier thought for the colliers
Has thrilled all over the land:
We have dwelt on their steadfast courage,
And have seen how, hand on hand,
They have toiled, as brothers for brothers,
A proud and resolute band.

God knows that it is a fearful thing
To behold a loved one die—
To see the life of a darling child
Ebb into eternity;
Or watch by a husband's bed of pain,
And wait the death-agony.

But, oh! Can you picture to yourselves?
How terrible is the blow,
When a husband and three stalwart sons
Are in one fell swoop laid low!
Pray God, that never a woman here
Such a crushing grief may know.

And both sires and sons of many homes
In these pits lie stark and cold;
Lads scarce more than bairns, and youth's fresh strength,
And men cast in iron mould.
Oh, the grief of a thousand lifetimes
In a single moment rolled!

Oh, ye husbands with your happy wives
Oh, ye mothers with children dear!
You can give more than a passing sigh
And the tribute of a tear;
You can shed a ray of comfort still
On the homes so changed and drear.

And the nation's notes of sympathy
Are heard ringing in the air;
Be it ours the charge of the orphan—
Be it ours the widow's care,
Give what ye can ye rich, and ye poor,
It is not a time to spare.

The above poem from the pen of Mr Sheriff Spens was delivered by the learned author at a Reading in Hamilton on behalf of the sufferers at Blantyre. We publish this poem at the earnest Solicitations of a large number of subscribers, and by permission of the author.

Ref. Hamilton Advertiser
1/12/1877. Page 1.

The Explosion At No. 3 Pit (reproduced courtesy of The Scots Magazine)

Blantyre Disaster 22ⁿᵈ October 1877

What means that muffled sound we hear!
The trembling women cry in fear,
What means that smoke from Number Three.
We fear some dire catastrophe.

The pit has blasted. Oh my God!
The women rush along the road
With frantic looks, dishevelled hair,
They wail aloud in their despair.

But soon our clergymen are there,
To soothe them with the voice of prayer,
The only thing to give relief
In this dire spasm of their grief.

At the pit-head such is the shock
That men roll breathless 'midst the smoke,
And welter there they know not why,
But feel almost as they would die.

Confusion seizes everyone;
They know not what should first be done,
For Doctor's rush by road and rail,
But ah! Their skill's of no avail.

Eight of those gallant men are there,
But soon they look in blank despair;
For ah' too direful's been the blast,
For in it human life to last.

At Number Two some volunteers,
Whatever were their hopes and fears
All gallantly their services gave,
To try their comrades' life to save.

They reach the bottom of the shaft,
Through sulphuric smoke the breezes waft,
They call aloud —soon footsteps hear—
A tottering comrade staggers near.

With scorched looks and wailing cry—
"Oh save me, comrades! Else I die."
Others are reached in the same plight,
Alas! It is an awful sight.

But, ah! The numbers are but few
That the explorers can rescue;
Out of two hundred and thirty three
Not more than eighteen are set free.

At Number Three a gallant band
In kettle with bell-wire in hand,
Hard, hard with brawny muscles toiled,
Though their best efforts are foiled.

For in that pit by fury driven,
As if by thunder bolts from heaven.
Great beams and pit trucks choke the shaft
The very sides of which are raft.

THE BLANTYRE PIT DISASTER

Andy Paterson lived in Blantyre and worked in Hector Powe's for many years. He also has happy memories of playing football with High Blantyre Hearts. His book includes the true story of The Blantyre Pit Disaster as told to him by his grandfather Andra McAnulty, who was a great champion of the Blantyre mining community. It also describes the harsh living and working conditions (including 99 photographs and etchings) endured by the Blantyre and other mining families as they struggled to survive under the oppressive regime of the mine owners.

Andy will be at The Miners' Welfare **TODAY** (30th April) from **12 noon** to **4p.m.** to meet as many old friends as he can and to sign copies of his book, which costs **£10** only.

or contact Andy at;

01821 642592

rowantree@aol.com

www.blantyrepast.com

A Blast from the Past

by ANDREW PATERSON

But still the gallant work goes on,
Rally after rally go down,
At last they hear some voices near;
It is their entombed comrades dear.

Who have survived the awful blast,
And still it's hoped that life may last
Till they receive the proffered aid,
Which sciences and art has made.

By the next day a charred form
Which has withstood the fire-damp storm,
Is reached and brought to heaven's own light—
Alas! He's in a fearful plight.

A second and a third are found—
The living all that's underground—
No other voice is heard, nor wail,
No other now to tell the tale.

Widows and orphans wander near,
And try to find their fathers dear,
In cold abstraction there they lie
Most difficult to identify.

And to and fro the hearses ply
Wending their way to the cemetery;
The numbness increases, so great's the yield,
It minds one of the battle field.

And soldier like in battle-field.
As duty's post their lift did yield;
And there they lie as lie the brave,
Side by side in long one grave.

A hundred widows now do mourn,
The husbands from their homes torn;
The strike of death the ruthless blast
Has them on the cold world cast.

And shall it be while pitying heaven,
The charity of love has given,
To shine in that effulgent ray,
The orphan's help, the widow's way

E.D. Blantyre.
Ref. Hamilton Advertiser

Many of the orphans attended Auchenraith School

The Blantyre Disaster, 22 October, 1877

The following list of men were noted by the Hamilton Advertiser as having escaped from No 2 Pit (including those who were working at the top of the shaft);

OWEN BRANNIGAN	THOMAS BLACK	HUGH BROWN
EDWARD DOCHERTY	WILLIAM DUNCAN	TOM FERGUSON (DRIVER)
ANDREW FOREST	TOM GALLACHER	ROBERT HERON
JOHN HILL	WILLIAM HILL	JOHN JEFFREY
WILLIAM KIRKLAND	JOHN LITTLE (FOREMAN)	THOMAS MARTIN
ALEX McCALL	MICHAEL McCOUSKER	PATRICK McCOUSKER
TOM McCDONALD	DUNCAN McMILLAN	SAM NEILSON
JOHN NELSON	JOHN PICKERING	JOHN SHARP
GEORGE WATSON	GEORGE WATT	WILLIAM WELSH (SENIOR)
WILLIAM WELSH (JUNIOR)	ALEXANDER WOODS	

List of the know victims of the Blantyre Disaster, 22 October, 1877
(from list given to me by Andra)

JAMES ALLAN	22	S	AUCHINRAITH, BLANTYRE
PETER ANDERSON	15	S	HUNTHILL, BLANTYRE
THOMAS BAXTER	12	S	PRIESTFIELD TERRACE, BLANTYRE
WILLIAM BLACK	38	M	38 PRIESTFIELD TERR, BLANTYRE
JAMES BOLTON	17	S	4 HALL STREET, BLANTYRE
THOMAS BOLTON	15	S	48HALL STREET, BLANTYRE
THOMAS BOLTON	16	S	AUCHINRAITH, BLANTYRE
WILLIAM BOLTON	13	S	AUCHINRAITH, BLANTYRE
SIMON BOYLE	15	S	8 HALL STREET, BLANTYRE
WILLIAM BOYLE	49	M	8 HALL STREET, BLANTYRE
OWEN BRANNAGHAN	19	S	19 STONEFIELD, BLANTYRE
MICHAEL BRANNAN	26	S	20 DIXON STREET, BLANTYRE
JAMES BRODIE	25	M	CAUSEYSTANES, BLANTYRE
JAMES BROWN	43	M	11 McALPINE'S LAND, BLANTYRE
JOHN BROWN	18	S	11 McALPINE'S LAND, BLANTYRE
JAMES BROWN	14	S	11 McALPINE'S LAND, BLANTYRE
JOHN BURNS	33	M	McALPINE'S LAND, BLANTYRE
PETER BURNS	13	S	McALPINE'S LAND, BLANTYRE
THOMAS BURNS	24	M	McALPINES LAND, BLANTYRE
PATRICK BURNS	34	M	LARKFIELD, BLANTYRE
ANDREW BURT	24	S	10 DIXON STREET, BLANTYRE
MICHAEL CAIRNS	29	M	46 DIXON STREET, BLANTYRE
ANDREW BURT	33	M	DIXON'S ROWS, BLANTYRE
WILLIAM CAMPBELL	35	W	KIRKTON, BLANTYRE
WILLIAM CAMPBELL	14	S	KIRKTON, BLANTYRE
PETER CARLIN	15	M	2 HALL STREET, BLANTYRE
PETER CARMICHAEL	16	S	AUCHINRAITH, BLANTYRE
JOHN CAVANAGH	17	S	5 CALDER STREET, BLANTYRE
JAMES CAVANAGH	18	S	5 CALDER STREET, BLANTYRE

JOHN CAVANAGH	19	S	19 MILLER ST, BLANTYRE
JAMES CLARK	20	S	PILOT ACRE, BLANTYRE
TURNBULL CLEGHORN	21	S	HART'S LAND, BLANTYRE
JAMES CLYDE	22	M	44 DIXON STREET, BLANTYRE
WILLIAM CLYDE	23	S	44 DIXON STREET, BLANTYRE
JAMES CLYDE	38	S	44 DIXON STREET, BLANTYRE
JOHN CONAGHAN	14	S	5 CARFIN STREET, BLANTYRE
JOHN CONLAN	12	S	57 CALDER STREET, BLANTYRE
FRANCIS COSGROVE	27	S	15 CARFIN STREET, BLANTYRE
JAMES COSGROVE	28	S	15 CARFIN STREET, BLANTYRE
JOHN COX	29	M	54 HALL STREET, BLANTYRE
ANDREW COX	30	S	54 HALL STREET, BLANTYRE
CHARLES COYLE	31	S	LARKFIELD, BLANTYRE
JOHN CRAWFORD	24	M	STONEFIELD, BLANTYRE
CHARLES DIVERS	27	M	49 CALDER STREET, BLANTYRE
THOMAS DOBBIE	27	M	DIXON'S ROWS, BLANTYRE
JOHN DOBBIE	25	S	DIXON'S ROWS, BLANTYRE
JOHN DOLAN	19	S	DIXON'S ROWS, BLANTYRE
PATRICK DOLAN	22	S	17 DIXON STREET, BLANTYRE
WILLIAM DUNSTAN	24	S	PILOT ACRE, BLANTYRE
ROBERT EADIE	50	S	KIRKTON, BLANTYRE
WILLIAM FRICKLETON	23	W	BURNBANK, HAMILTON
CHARLES GAINOR	23	S	STONEFIELD, BLANTYRE
SAMUEL GARDINER	21	S	NEWTON, CAMBUSLANG
MATTHEW GEMMEL	31	S	BURNBANK, HAMILTON
JOHN GEMMEL	22	S	BURNBANK, HAMILTON
WILLIAM GEMMEL	19	S	BURNBANK, HAMILTON
JOSEPH GILMOUR	35	M	CLYDESDALE STREET, WISHAW
JOSEPH GILMOUR	13	S	CLYDESDALE ST, WISHAW
BENJAMIN GOLD	24	M	AUCHINRAITH, BLANTYRE
ANDREW GOLD	22	S	AUCHINRAITH, BLANTYRE
JAMES GOLD	33	M	AUCHINRAITH, BLANTYRE
JOHN GOLD	28	M	LARKFIELD, BLANTYRE
THOMAS GRACIE	57	M	KIRKTON, BLANTYRE
WILLIAM GRAHAM	13	S	57 HALL STREET, BLANTYRE
ROBERT HALLIDAY	39	M	34 HALL STREET, BLANTYRE
THOMAS HALLIDAY	19	S	35 HALL STREET, BLANTYRE
MATHEW HALLIDAY	48	M	STONEFIELD, BLANTYRE
THOMAS HALLIDAY	22	S	STONEFELD, BLANTYRE
JOHN HAMILTON	31	M	BURNBANK, HAMILTON
WILLIAM HANLON	23	S	31 CALDER STREET, BLANTYRE
JOHN HASTIE	11	S	11 MILLER STREET, BLANTYRE
THOMAS HENDRY	21	S	LARKFIELD, BLANTYRE
JAMES HENDRY	19	S	LARKFIELD, BLANTYRE
ROBERT HENDRY	15	S	LARKFIELD, BLANTYRE
JOHN HENDRY	14	S	LARKFIELD, BLANTYRE
JAMES IRVINE	36	M	BURNBANK, HAMILTON
JAMES KELLY	33	M	18 HALL STREET, BLANTYRE
JOHN KELLY	23	S	DIXON'S ROWS, BLANTYRE
PATRICK KELLY	27	M	7 HALL STREET, BLANTYRE

JAMES KELLY	16	S	43 CALDER STREET, BLANTYRE
JAMES KEMP	22	S	MERRY'S ROWS, BLANTYRE
JOHN KENNY	55	M	50 HALL STREET, BLANTYRE
ROBT. ORR KIRKLAND	20	S	4 PRIESTFIELD TERRACE, BLANTYRE
NICOL KYLE	35	M	KIRKTON, BLANTYRE
ARCHIBALD LANG	25	M	KIRKLAND, BLANTYRE
JAMES LANG	55	M	PILOT ACRE
HUGH LARKIN	24	M	9 GOVAN STREET, BLANTYRE
JAMES LAUDER	20	S	TOWNHILL, HAMILTON
GEORGE LAUDER	16	S	TOWNHILL, HAMILTON
JAMES LIDDEL	41	M	HALL STREET, BLANTYRE
JOHN LIDDEL	12	S	HALL STREET, BLANTYRE
THOMAS LUCAS	24	S	PILOT ACRE, BLANTYRE
PETER MACKIE	31	S	DIXON'S ROWS, BLANTYRE
JAMES MARSHALL	20	S	14 CALDER STREET, BLANTYRE
DAVID MARTIN	28	M	DIXON'S ROWS, BLANTYRE
HUGH MARTIN	51	M	BACK PRIESTFIELD, BLANTYRE
THOMAS MEECHAN	39	S	FLEMINGTON, CAMBUSLANG
ALEXANDER MILLER	18	S	BLANTYRE
JOSEPH MILLER	27	M	DIXON'S ROWS, BLANTYRE
WILLIAM MILLER	23	M	8 GOVAN STREET, BLANTYRE
JOHN MOIR	36	M	BARNHILL, BLANTYRE
EDWARD MOIR	16	S	BARNHILL, BLANTYRE
HUGH MORGAN	37	M	5 CALDER STREET, BLANTYRE
ANDREW MORRISON	48	M	DIXON'S ROWS, BLANTYRE
WILLIAM MUIR	21	S	BURNBANK, HAMILTON
THOMAS MURDOCH	17	S	DIXON STREET, BLANTYRE
FRANCIS MURPHY	25	M	LARKFIELD, BLANTYRE
JAMES MURPHY	20	S	8 CARFIN STREET, BLANTYRE
GEORGE MURPHY	13	S	8 CARFIN STREET, BLANTYRE
BERNARD MURRAY	21	S	LARKFIELD, BLANTYRE
JAMES MURRAY	50	M	3 CALDER STREET, BLANTYRE
ROBERT McADAMS	28	M	53 HALL STREET, BLANTYRE
PETER McANULTY	54	W	57 HALL STREET, BLANTYRE
EDWARD McCALLUM	14	S	21 HALL STREET, BLANTYRE
PATRICK McCUE	19	S	21 DIXON STREET, BLANTYRE
JOHN McCULLOCH	44	M	AUCHINRAITH, BLANTYRE
JOHN McCULLOCH	16	S	AUCHINRAITH, BLANTYRE
THOMAS McCULLOCH	25	M	HART'S LAND, BLANTYRE
HENRY McCUSKER	30	M	26 CALDER STREET, BLANTYRE
JAMES McCUSKER	28	M	DIXON STREET, BLANTYRE
THOMAS McDONALD	29	S	1 GARDINER PLACE, BLANTYRE
JAMES McFADYEN	21	M	DIXON'S ROWS, BLANTYRE
JOHN McFADYEN	23	S	2 CARFIN STREET, BLANTYRE
JOHN McFARLANE	31	M	LARKFIELD, BLANTYRE
JAMES McGARRY	35	M	62 HALL STREET, BLANTYRE
ABRAHAM McGHEE	18	S	LARKFIELD, BLANTYRE
JOHN McGHEE	16	S	LARKFIELD, BLANTYRE
WILLIAM McGHEE	14	S	LARKFIELD, BLANTYRE
JAMES McGOWN	24	M	GARDINER'S PLACE, BLANTYRE

GILBERT McINTYRE	47	M	KIRKTON, BLANTYRE
WILLIAM McKAY	48	M	11 MILLER STREET, BLANTYRE
JOHN McKELVIE	19	S	BURNBANK, HAMILTON
JOHN McKILLOP	14	S	BURNBANK, HAMILTON
ARCHIBALD McKILLOP	12	S	BURNBANK, HAMILTON
JAMES McKINNON	32	M	BURNBANK, HAMILTON
EDWARD McLACHLAN	15	S	1 JACKSON PLACE, BLANTYRE
MOSES McLACHLAN	23	M	COMMERCIAL PLACE, BLANTYRE
WILLIAM McLACHLAN	13	S	2 JACKSON PLACE, BLANTYRE
EDWARD McLAUGHLAN	18	S	17 MILLER STREET, BLANTYRE
JOHN McLAUGHLAN	23	M	18 MILLER STREET, BLANTYRE
THOMAS McMEECHAN	45	M	28 CALDER STREET, BLANTYRE
JAMES McMILLAN	30	M	LARKFIELD, BLANTYRE
ROBERT McNAUGHT	26	M	DIXON'S ROWS, BLANTYRE
BERNARD McTAVIE	56	M	BACK PRIESTFIELD, BLANTYRE
GEORGE NISBET	27	M	LARKFIELD, BLANTYRE
JOHN O'BRIAN	24	M	10 CALDER STREET, BLANTYRE
PETER O'BRIAN	21	S	10 CALDER STREET, BLANTYRE
JOHN O'DONNELL	26	M	LARKFIELD, BLANTYRE
JOHN O'DONNEL	23	S	14 MILLER STREET, BLANTYRE
ROBERT OVENS	21	S	12 HALL STREET, BLANTYRE
JOHN PARK	34	S	KIRKTON, BLANTYRE
WILLIAM PRIMROSE	17	S	BLANTYRE WORKS, BLANTYRE
JAMES RAE	35	S	
THOMAS RAMSAY	25	W	PILOT ACRE, BLANTYRE
JOHN REEVIE	59	M	DIXON'S ROWS
ALEXANDER REEVIE	19	S	DIXON'S ROWS, BLANTYRE
WILIAM REID	27	M	BURNBANK, HAMILTON
JAMES REID	13	S	BURNBANK, HAMILTON
GEORGE RENWICK	48	M	BLANTYRE
WILLIAM RICHARDSON	17	S	KIRKTON, BLANTYRE
THOMAS ROBERTS	20	S	60 HALL STREET, BLANTYRE
MOSES ROBERTS	17	S	60 HALL STREET, BLANTYRE
SAMUEL ROBERTS	14	S	60 HALL STREET, BLANTYRE
WILLIAM ROBERTS	24	M	LARKFIELD, BLANTYRE
RICHARD ROSS	30	S	AUCHINRAITH, BLANTYRE
JOHN RUSSELL	20	S	KIRKTON, BLANTYRE
GEORGE SAWERS	24	M	KIRKTON, BLANTYRE
GEORGE SEMPLE	32	M	AUCHINRAITH, BLANTYRE
WILLIAM SHARP	63	M	48 CALDER STREET, BLANTYRE
JAMES SHARP	40	S	48 CALDER STREET, BLANTYRE
JAMES SIMPSON	24	S	LARKFIELD, BLANTYRE
ROBERT SIMPSON	60	W	BURNBANK, HAMILTON
PATRICK SMITH	40	M	LARKFIELD, BLANTYRE
EDWARD SMITH	22	S	LARKFIELD, BLANTYRE
JAMES SMITH	35	M	DIXON'S ROWS, BLANTYRE
JAMES SNEDDON	39	M	AUCHINRAITH, BLANTYRE
JOHN SNEDDON	19	S	AUCHINRAITH, BLANTYRE
JAMES SNEDDON	16	S	AUCHINRAITH, BLANTYRE
GEORGE SPEIRS	16	S	BARNHILL, BLANTYRE

JOHN SPEIRS	15	S	BARNHILL, BLANTYRE
JOHN SPEIRS	13	S	9 MILLER STREET, BLANTYRE
WILLIAM SPEIRS	28	M	KIRKTON, BLANTYRE
JOHN STARK	29	M	ANNSFIELD PLACE, BLANTYRE
JAMES STEELE	36	M	FLEMINGTON, CAMBUSLANG
ROBERT STEELE	13	S	FLEMINGTON, CAMBUSLANG
ALEXANDER STEVENSON	42	M	15 GOVAN STREET, BLANTYRE
JOHN STEVENSON	19	S	15 GOVAN STREET, BLANTYRE
WILLIAM STEVENSON	14	S	15 GOVAN STREET, BLANTYRE
JAMES STEWART	19	S	34 HALL STREET, BLANTYRE
ROBERT STEWART	17	S	34 HALL STREET, BLANTYRE
MALCOLM STEWART	15	S	52 CALDER STREET, BLANTYRE
JOHN THOMSON	17	S	LARKFIELD, BLANTYRE
GEORGE TODD	43	M	KIRKTON, BLANTYRE
HUGH TONNER	48	M	13 CALDER STREET, BLANTYRE
CHARLES TONNER	15	S	13 CALDER STREET, BLANTYRE
JOHN TRAYNOR	15	S	PILOT ACRE, BLANTYRE
JAMES VALLELY	22	M	4 GOVAN STREET, BLANTYRE
NEIL WARD	57	W	CROFTFOOT
ROBERT WARDROPE	37	M	DIXON'S ROWS, BLANTYRE
ALEXANDER WATT	28	M	DIXON'S ROWS, BLANTYRE
FRANCIS WELSH	23	S	HART'S LAND, BLANTYRE
JOHN WELSH	22	S	HART'S LAND, BLANTYRE
JAMES WELSH	15	S	HART'S LAND, BLANTYRE
ANDREW WHITE	37	M	LARKFIELD, BLANTYRE
THOMAS WHITE	13	S	LARKFIELD, BLANTYRE
ROBERT WHITE	16	S	AUCHINRAITH, BLANTYRE
HUGH WILSON	36	M	55 CALDER STREET, BLANTYRE
JAMES WILSON	17	S	55 CALDER STREET, BLANTYRE
WILLIAM WILSON	17	S	55 CALDER STREET, BLANTYRE
THOMAS WILSON	45	M	LARKFIELD, BLANTYRE
JAMES WILSON	17	S	LARKFIELD, BLANTYRE
THOMAS WILSON	21	S	GREENFIELD, BURNBANK, HAMILTON
WILLIAM WOOD	51	M	SPRINGFIELD TERRACE, BLANTYRE
JAMES WRIGHT	49	M	3 PRIESTFIELD TERRACE, BLANTYRE
JOHN McEWAN WRIGHT	17	S	3 PRIESTFIELD TERRACE, BLANTYRE

The following Lanarkshire mines, as listed by Andra, were still being worked on the day the coal mines were Nationalised (January 1, 1947).

Ardenrigg
Auchlochan
Baton
Blackrigg
Blantyre
Bothwell Castle - Nos. 1,2,3,4.
Calderhead
Cardowan
Coatspark
Gartshore - Nos. 3,9,11,12.
Glen Mine
Hamilton Palace
Kennox
Lochend
Overton
Stane
Thankerton

Ashgill
Bankhead
Bedlay
Blackstone
Blantyreferme - Nos, 1,2,3.
Branchal
Canderrigg
Castlehill
Douglas
Gateside - Nos. 1,2.
Glentaggart
Headless Cross
Kingshill Nos. 1,2,3.
Mossrigg
Quarter
Swinstie
West Auchengeich

Auchengeich
Bardykes
Benhar
Blairmuckhill
Boglea
Broomside
Canderside
Chapel
Douglas Castle
Gillhead
Greenrigg
Hillhouserigg
Knowehead
Northfield
Skellyton
Southfield
Woodside